Timpson's Travels in East Anglia

Also by John Timpson

The Lighter Side of *Today*
John Timpson's Early Morning Book
Timpson's England
Norwich: A Fine City
Timpson's Towns

Autobiography
Today and Yesterday

Fiction
Paper Trail

Timpson's Travels in East Anglia

JOHN TIMPSON

HEINEMANN : LONDON

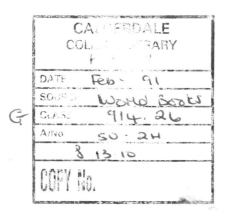
William Heinemann Ltd
Michelin House, 81 Fulham Road, London sw3 6rb

LONDON   MELBOURNE   AUCKLAND

First published 1990
Text © John Timpson 1990
Photographs © C.J. Nicholas 1990

A CIP catalogue record for this book
is held by the British Library
ISBN 0 434 78084 7

Produced by Mandarin Offset
Printed and bound in Hong Kong

Contents

Acknowledgements

Helmingham Hall and Helmingham Model Cottages photographed by kind permission of The Lord Tollemache.

Royal Hospital School photographed by kind permission of Royal Hospital School, Holbrook.

The Tattingstone Wonder photographed by kind permission.

Sheringham Park, Blickling Hall, Oxburgh Hall and Melford Hall photographed by kind permission of the National Trust.

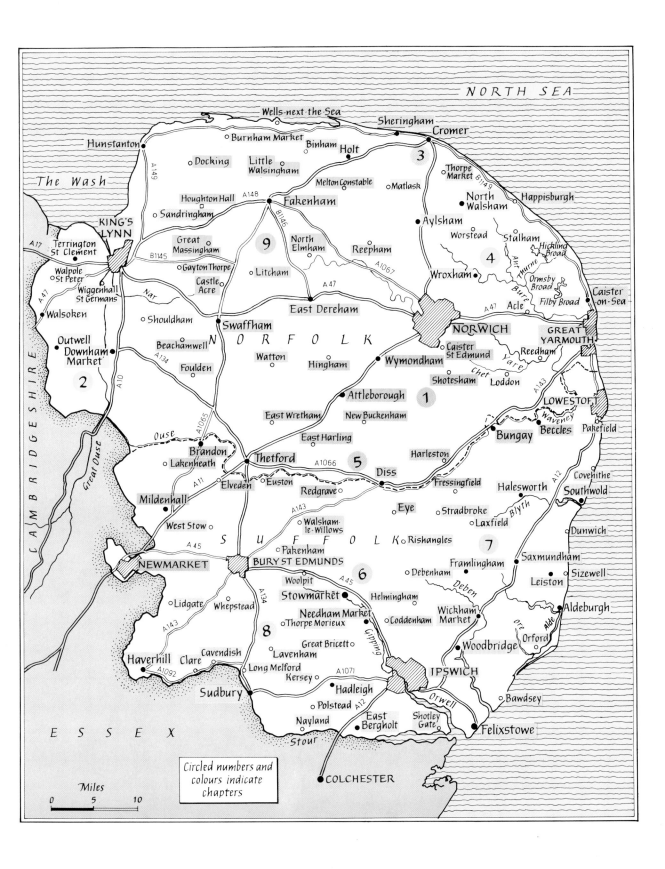

NORTH SEA

The Wash

Wells-next-the-Sea

Sheringham
Cromer
③

Hunstanton

Docking
Binham
Holt

Little Walsingham
Thorpe Market
B1149

Melton Constable
Matlask
North Walsham
Happisburgh

A149

Houghton Hall
A148
Fakenham

Sandringham
B1146

KING'S LYNN

Terrington St Clement
A17

Great Massingham
North Elmham
Reepham
Aylsham
Worstead
Stalham
Hickling Broad

⑨

Gayton Thorpe
Litcham
A1067
Wroxham
Ormsby Broad
④

Walpole St Peter
Wiggenhall St Germans
B1145
Castle Acre
Ant
Thurne
Bure

A47

Walsoken
Nar
East Dereham
Filby Broad
Caister-on-Sea

Shouldham
Swaffham
NORFOLK
Acle
A47

Beachamwell
A134
Watton
Hingham
Wymondham
Caister St Edmund
NORWICH
GREAT YARMOUTH

Outwell Downham Market
A10
Foulden
Reedham

②
Shotesham
Chet
Loddon
Yare
LOWESTOFT

A1065
Attleborough
①
Waveney
Beccles
Pakefield

East Wretham
New Buckenham
Bungay

Ouse
East Harling
Harleston

Brandon
Lakenheath
Thetford
A1066
⑤
Diss
Fressingfield
Halesworth
Covehithe
Southwold
A12

A11
Elveden
Euston
Redgrave
Eye
Stradbroke
Laxfield
Blyth

Mildenhall
A143
Walsham-le-Willows
Rishangles
⑦
Dunwich

West Stow
Pakenham
Framlingham
Saxmundham

NEWMARKET
A45
SUFFOLK
⑥
Debenham
Leiston
Sizewell

Woolpit
A45
Stowmarket
Helmingham
Wickham Market
Aldeburgh

Lidgate
Whepstead
BURY ST EDMUNDS
Needham Market
Coddenham
Deben
Ore
Alde

A34
Thorpe Morieux
Great Bricett
Woodbridge
Orford

⑧
Lavenham
Gipping
IPSWICH

Haverhill
Clare
Cavendish
Long Melford
Kersey
A1071
Hadleigh
Orwell
Bawdsey

A1092
Sudbury
Polstead
A12
Shotley Gate
Felixstowe

ESSEX
Nayland
East Bergholt

Stour

CAMBRIDGESHIRE

Great Ouse

Circled numbers and colours indicate chapters

Miles
0   5   10

COLCHESTER

Foreword

I hope my East Anglian friends will not regard this book as an impertinence. I have lived in Norfolk for only twelve years, with a long gap in the middle while I was working for the BBC. But for my wife Pat and myself, although we both grew up in the London suburbs and spent so many years back in that area, Norfolk has always been our first love. Returning to it was just like returning home.

The area I became most familiar with in the nineteen-fifties was the farming hinterland between Dereham and Fakenham, in the heart of Norfolk, a rolling landscape of beet and barley, of winding lanes and tiny villages, of woods and parkland and hidden streams; and over it all that vast Norfolk sky. We are back in 'High Norfolk' again, and even in the nineteen-nineties little has changed. The only traffic hold-ups are caused by the sugar beet trailers, the only railways are either privately operated or converted into rural walks, the only tourists are those who have got here by mistake.

However, since our return I have been able to explore the rest of the county, overcoming the natural reluctance of anyone in West Norfolk to venture east of Norwich. I have also had the chance to learn more about Suffolk, a county which I once regarded as a place I passed through on the way home. I did not realise then what I was missing. I do now, and I hope I have made restitution.

I have not attempted to delve too deeply into the beginnings of East Anglia. I leave it to the experts to explain, for instance, how Norfolk's ubiquitous flints, its principal building material for many centuries, actually started life as sponges on the bed of a Cretaceous sea. (If you are eyeing your bath sponge apprehensively, I gather the process takes about 135 million years.) Similarly I still like to think of the Queen of the Iceni as Boadicea, heroic champion of the innocent against the bloodthirsty Romans, though the experts say she was just as bloodthirsty as they were, and her name was really Boudicca. I suspect we are both wrong and the Iceni, being early Norfolkmen, actually called her Boudiful . . .

My only qualification in fact for writing about East Anglia is that I am an Angliaphile, one of those many thousands of 'incomers' who came here on holiday or to take up a job, and found there was something about this little-known corner of Britain which is very special indeed. Even though its furthest point is only a hundred miles from the outer suburbs of Greater London it has an atmosphere, an isolation, an independence all its own. There are those who say that parts of Essex and Cambridge and Lincolnshire should be included in East Anglia too. They are probably the same people who cheerfully abolished Huntingdonshire, the Soke of Peterborough and the Isle of Ely. Historically East Anglia is just Norfolk and Suffolk, and everyone in Norfolk and Suffolk is very happy to keep it that way.

That does not mean the two counties are as one. They differ greatly in many ways, and within each county there are differences too. Noël Coward, famous for his 'Very flat, Norfolk' could hardly have penetrated much further than the Fens.

I have tried to follow these divisions, not concentrating too greatly on the larger towns and cities, which have been well documented already, but more on the unexpected discoveries to be made out in the rural areas, particularly alongside the main roads where one can leave the traffic behind and boldly go where no coach party has gone before.

For a start, therefore, I have explored the villages on either side of the notorious A11, from its spasmodic entry into Suffolk – in and out and in again – to its ultimate destination, Norwich. Then a reconnaissance of the fens and marshlands of West Norfolk which once cut off East Anglia from the Midlands and the North, but now allow safe if slow access through the network of sea walls and dykes. There is the surprisingly hilly area along the Norfolk coast, then the villages in Broadland which all those holiday craft miss as they chug along the waterways.

The Waveney and the Little Ouse, forming the boundary between Norfolk and Suffolk, offer a remarkable range of riverside scenery. Then there is the A45 in Suffolk between Newmarket and Felixstowe, the only really fast road in East Anglia, so fast that travellers hurtle past some of East Anglia's pleasantest countryside seeing nothing but a green blur. The Suffolk coastline, with its estuaries and rivers, provides quite a change from Norfolk's unbroken curve, and the thatch and colour-wash of the Suffolk farming villages are also a contrast to the pantiles and flints of High Norfolk – which is where I return in the final chapter, to my own remote corner, and it seemed appropriate to approach it around the edges and finish up in the centre.

Thus the chapters fell almost lyrically into place:

Up and down the city road,
In and out of the sea walls,
That's the way the coast road goes,
Putt-putt go the diesels.
Verging on the border-line,
No real need to hurtle,
Rivers and sand,
The hinterland,
An ever-decreasing circle.

I said earlier I hoped East Anglians would not think me impertinent.
I hope also they will not regard me as an enemy in their midst, writing
about my own enjoyment of East Anglia and thus perhaps encouraging
more 'incomers' to invade it. The argument is never likely to end
between the 'progressives' who want to improve the infrastructure,
expand industry, build more homes and attract more tourists, and
the 'drawbridge brigade', so called because they just want to pull
it up behind them. As usual we shall probably have to settle for
a compromise.

The influx is already under way, for better or worse, and even
in the remoter rural areas the villages are going to expand. I hope
I can encourage those who have come, and those who may think
of doing so, to appreciate these areas for what they are: 'not just
as pleasure centres for the newly affluent,' as another Angliaphile,
David Kennett, once wrote, 'not just as retirement havens for the
work-weary, not merely as dormitories for the more highly placed
of twentieth-century society'. These are living, working communities
who have been here for many centuries, and it should be counted a
privilege to join them.

It is a privilege too to be able to stroll through these lanes or on
to the saltmarshes or along the river valleys, with the quietness all
around and that huge open sky above. Even in the winter, when the
fields are bleak and the wind is bitter, somehow the world seems a
gentler, a calmer, a more civilised place.

By all means come and share all this; but do help us to
keep it that way.

John Timpson
Wellingham
Norfolk
1990

I Up and Down the City Road
Alongside the A11 from Newmarket to Norwich

The only motorway that attempts to approach East Anglia is the
M11. Just beyond Cambridge it wisely gives up the idea, and peters
out. Norwich-bound traffic is diverted much earlier on to the notorious
A11, once misread by a BBC newsreader as 'the All' – which is not
entirely inappropriate, since if you wish to drive direct from London
to Norwich it is All, or nothing at all.

Its only sizeable stretch of dual carriageway is the Newmarket
bypass, which cuts across the little knob of Suffolk that juts into
Cambridgeshire and effectively takes you in and out of East Anglia
before you even notice it. I was always bewildered, having driven
several miles beyond Newmarket, to find a sign welcoming me to
Suffolk, when I thought I was already in it.

This eccentric feature of the county border has not escaped
the notice of the Boundary Commission. In 1989 they suggested
it would be much more logical to chop off the projecting knob
and put Newmarket in Cambridgeshire. Suffolk was appalled at the
prospect of losing its famous racing town. The county council was
appalled at the prospect of losing all those community charges. The
local MP was appalled at the prospect of disrupted public services.
But Cambridgeshire County Council, having joined in the initial
protest, decided that every prospect pleased it, and voted in favour.
The argument continues.

Meanwhile Newmarket remains in East Anglia, and so does
Exning, on the other side of the bypass, which is the extreme tip
of West Suffolk. It is now little more than a commuter suburb for
Newmarket, but if there had not been an outbreak of plague in the
thirteenth century the situation might have been reversed. Exning was
a thriving market town until the plague hit it and a new market was
established three miles away. The Newmarket flourished, the old one
declined, and when they found that Newmarket Heath was ideal for
horse-racing it was the final blow. Exit Exning.

13

Up and Down the City Road

That happened much earlier than you might think. The Stuarts are given the credit for making Newmarket fashionable, but there was royalty racing on the Heath long before that. When Richard II was still Prince of Wales he raced there against the Earl of Arundel. One hopes for the Earl's sake Richard won; in those days the royals were bad losers.

Present-day successors to the mounts ridden by Richard II and the Earl of Arundel when they raced against each other on New-market Heath. It has been the home of the Sport of Kings – and one or two Queens – ever since.

The first real influx of the horsey set came after the defeat of the Spanish Armada. Horses from the sunken Spanish ships were washed ashore in Galloway. They were appropriated by the gentry and brought to the Heath for exercise. The odd wager led to full-scale racing, and the royals joined in. James I enjoyed it, Charles I loved it. When Parliament passed the Declaration which led to the Civil War, they had to send a man to Newmarket to deliver it.

Not all the riders who frequented the Heath were there for the races. It was a happy hunting ground for highwaymen – who included, unexpectedly, a local freelance clergyman. The Revd William Cratfield was forced to leave his parish at Wortham, near Diss, because he upset his parishioners by ignoring his clerical duties. Instead of disappearing into obscurity or going into show business, like his much later colleague at Stiffkey, Mr Cratfield swapped his dog-collar for a black mask and hit the road. For nine years racegoers lost their money before they had even placed a bet, thanks to this rascally rector. He was eventually hanged in Newgate Prison, and the bookies took the money instead.

When I first drove to Norfolk there were still hold-ups, but only because of the congestion in Newmarket's single main street. On race days the queues extended for miles out of town. The bypass solved all that, but it meant that travellers not only missed Newmarket but drove straight through the Devil's Dyke without even seeing it. The Devil is credited with more dykes in Britain than Queen Elizabeth had beds, but this one is quite dramatic, an earthwork seven miles long, eighteen feet high and twelve feet thick. It was a line of defence across the Icknield Way, a chalk ridge which runs from Wiltshire to Norfolk and provided a convenient route through the forests and fens of East Anglia for anyone who felt like invading it. The A11 often follows the Icknield Way between Newmarket and Thetford; the Roman chariots probably got along it a lot faster.

The Devil had as many dykes in Britain as Queen Elizabeth had beds, but Devil's Dyke at Newmarket is one of the biggest, once a line of defence across the Icknield Way, now a free grandstand for the races.

The first scattering of buildings along that stretch give quite the wrong impression of what you are getting into. The dreary collection of fast-food diners, petrol stations and transport cafés used to sport the sign 'Red Lodge (Freckenham)' but the Red Lodge is now painted cream and Freckenham is actually a pleasant village a mile off the main road. Similarly Barton Mills would appear to the motorist to be just a very large roundabout and a pub, but there is an attractive village tucked away beyond The Bull. And Mildenhall, a name which most people associate with Americans and aeroplanes, still has its sixteenth-century market cross from its days as a prosperous river port, and among the shoppers around it you can still detect an occasional English accent; on rare occasions even a Suffolk one.

The church has a famous carved roof full of angels, but for the connoisseur of eccentric saints the reredos has a painting of St Elegius, patron saint of blacksmiths. Legend has it that if a horse became fractious and refused to be shod, Elegius removed the horse's leg, fitted the shoe, and then – here's the tricky bit – put the leg back on the horse. Not even James Herriot thought of that.

Once I get that Barton Mills roundabout behind me I feel I am really in East Anglia, whether I am on the quieter of the main roads heading for my home in West Norfolk, or continuing on the

The tallest landmark on the A11, the 100-foot Elveden war memorial sited where three parishes meet.

A11 to Thetford. They both pass through great areas of heath and forest, and you begin to get an idea of the vast spaces and empty countryside which are so different from the counties to the south. I cannot suggest a diversion because there aren't any until you reach Thetford. On the way you come to a hundred-foot war memorial at the junction of three parishes, Elveden, Eriswell and Icklingham, and you know you have arrived at the Elveden estate, owned by the Earl of Iveagh, head of Ireland's biggest brewery. It is a demonstration of how Guinness can be extremely good for you, let alone your heirs and successors.

Agriculturists always go on about Coke of Holkham and Turnip Townshend of Raynham and how they transformed the face of rural Norfolk, as indeed they did, but Lord Albemarle and those who followed him did much the same at Elveden. He acquired 'a barren, windswept, rabbit-infested estate' of four thousand acres and put it under cultivation. Then it passed to the exiled Maharajah Duleep Singh of Lahore, known to the locals – in the days before the Race Relations Act – as the Black Prince. He turned the house into an oriental palace. He also enlarged the village church – a rather nice gesture from an Indian prince – and did much good work among the villagers.

But this was peanuts compared with his successor the Earl of Iveagh, who used the Guinness millions to double the size of the house, build a water tower the height of Big Ben, rebuild the village, lay six miles of estate roads, give the church a new bell tower, and extend the estate to twenty-three thousand acres. In the fifties he had the largest arable farm in England.

You get no idea of all this investment from the A11. You can't even climb the monument to take a look, because the steps up to the balcony have been blocked up. But you can inspect the latest and most improbable development at Elveden, which was introduced not by an Indian maharajah nor a Guinness millionaire but by a Dutch company called Center Parcs – though there is a link (albeit a tenuous one) with Lord Iveagh as the company was later bought by a brewery.

The Elveden Forest Holiday Village must be the most unexpected all-year-round holiday facility in East Anglia. I remember a nightmare six weeks in that same area in the winter of 1947, in an Army hut awaiting embarkation to foreign parts. It was the coldest winter of the decade but the Army thought it was summer and ran out of fuel. We broke up the spare beds to burn in the boiler, and when we ran out of beds we started burning the rafters from the roof. I have never been quite so cold. I vowed then that if I survived I would never return to East Anglia. Certainly I never believed that in this Siberian wasteland people would be relaxing in subtropical conditions, winter and summer.

I was wrong on both counts. The holiday village was built with a swiftness rare in East Anglia, completed in seventy weeks at a cost of seventy million pounds. It opened in the summer of 1989 with amenities for three thousand guests, including three thousand bikes, the only transport allowed. Even with frost and snow all around, the residents feel no chill; they live like human cucumbers under an enormous glass roof.

In its own way this is quite as spectacular a transformation of the Norfolk countryside as Lord Albemarle's transformed heathland, the Maharajah's transformed mansion and Lord Iveagh's transformed estate. Perhaps there are enterprising elves in Elveden who lure these transformation artists from India and Ireland and the Netherlands. If only they could attract one to transform the A11 into a dual carriageway . . .

This congested and often lethal road continues into Norfolk, and here at last there is a reprieve. The Thetford bypass opened in 1989, only single carriageway at first but it should be dual by the end of 1990. However the respite doesn't last for long, and if you have a day to spare instead of an hour to get to Norwich, you can escape from the traffic and make your way there through the lanes and villages a few miles to the east of the main road. Similarly you can return a few miles to the west of it, all the way back to Thetford. As for Thetford itself, it is more accessible and a lot more attractive if approached along the river and I shall leave it until a later chapter on the Waveney and the Little Ouse.

A corner of Thetford Forest in autumn, the largest stretch of lowland wood in Britain. It covers 50,000 acres.

Both those rivers are quite well known outside East Anglia, if only because they form the boundary between Norfolk and Suffolk, but there is a third river in this area which meanders through the villages east of the A11 and offers a much more peaceful route through South Norfolk. It is the river from which Thetford takes its name, though I am not sure why, since the Thet is just a small tributary of the Ouse and much less important to ford. Perhaps the early settlers decided that the more logical name of the town would look rather odd on their postcards home. 'Having wonderful time at Ouseford. Wish you were here,' somehow sounds unconvincing.

Once you have found the River Thet you can head for the backwoods. All right, if you insist: 'Ready, get Thet, go!' There is no route alongside it but you can pick it up by following the signs to Kilverstone Wildlife Park. By all means linger in the park if you wish, but the real Norfolk lies beyond, on the road to Brettenham, where at last you will find that Norfolk's tree population is not limited entirely to Scotch pines. Here are natural woodlands which originated several centuries before the Forestry Commission took over. There are oaks and birches and beeches – and there are also modest hills. You have left behind the Scandinavian forest and re-entered the English countryside.

A row of elegant new stables, looking as luxurious as the living quarters beside them, add to that Englishness, and the picture is complete when you reach Brettenham, take the lane down to the river, and come upon your first Norfolk stately home.

I am still astonished by the profusion of grand houses in Norfolk. The churches get most of the publicity and the praise – every Norfolk enthusiast can tell you that there are 650 medieval churches, each one with its particular treasure, and indeed I shall be mentioning a good many of them, not so much their fine roofs or ancient fonts or splendid tombs but the rarer curiosities they contain. I wonder, though, if anyone has counted all the great manor houses which are tucked away on private estates, generally well out of sight of passing tourists.

The famous ones are very famous – Blickling and Holkham and the like. But nearly every village in Norfolk once had its Big House, and a remarkable number of them still survive, sometimes occupied by the same family for many generations. Often the only hint of their existence is an impressive gatehouse at the roadside and a gravelled drive disappearing into the parkland beyond. No notices here proclaiming opening times or admission charges or the way to the coach park. These are still the private homes of the Norfolk gentry, and sometimes there is a 'Private' notice on the gate, but it is hardly necessary because few tourists know of their existence and the locals would not dream of intruding anyway.

Brettenham has just such a Big House, though technically it is in the hamlet of Shadwell, just across the Thet, and its land stretches away to the Suffolk border. Shadwell Court is less than 150 years old but the Buxtons who built it have been around for four or five centuries. They made sure the architect did not stint himself; there is a central tower with a turret on one corner and the roofscape goes on from there: Dutch gables, decorated chimneys, battlements, the lot. I only know this from photographs – you get only a brief glimpse of all this grandeur from the main gate.

The next village upriver is Bridgham, which has nothing to match Shadwell. There is not a battlement in sight, not even on the church. But inside the church there are two fonts, and the story of the spare font leads us away from the river to the tiny village of Roudham, which lies only a mile or so from the A11. In fact its principal feature – one could say its only feature – is visible from the main road and the railway that runs beside it. From that distance it looks like a green oil-tanker, a high bridge at one end, a smaller prow at the other and a low hull in between. But the 'bridge' is the remains of the tower of this ruined church, the 'prow' is the east wall and the 'hull' is the chancel and nave. All of it is completely overgrown with vegetation.

St Andrew's has been in this state for a couple of centuries. It is said that a workman knocked out the ashes of his pipe on the thatched roof. The church was burned down and never restored. Its fitments were removed and the font found its way to Bridgham.

The road from Roudham to East Harling takes you past another rare sight in Norfolk – a station which still has trains. Not many, admittedly, perhaps two or three each way in the course of a day. Nevertheless Harling Road is one of the very few branch line stations which still functions, and has thus attracted a handful of light industries to add to the area's prosperity, if not its charm.

East Harling itself may strike visitors from the big cities as little more than a village, too, but it regards itself as a small town and by Norfolk standards it is. The population has doubled since the war to about two thousand. It has been the focal point of this corner of South Norfolk for many centuries, since the days when Sir Robert Harling was one of the dear friends who followed Henry V once more into the breach. I always feel a little sad for West Harling, a few miles away, which is actually a larger parish but somehow failed to keep up. Its Big House was demolished in the nineteen-thirties, its church is closed and the village has faded away. But it does retain one fragrant memory of better days, a memorial to a former Rector who rejoiced in the name of Ralph Fuloflove. I know of no name more suitable for a parson – nor one more difficult to live up to.

The Big Houses are still functioning at Kenninghall and Quidenham, further up the river, which is now confusingly called the Wittle. Kenninghall Place is one of the few Norfolk properties actually owned by the Duke of Norfolk, and Quidenham Hall was the family seat of the Albemarles – the same family that was at Elveden, but it was not unusual for the gentry to have a second home, or a third, or a fourth . . . In this case the family has cut

19

back, and Quidenham has become a Carmelite priory. It is believed
that Queen Boadicea of the Iceni, who was maltreated by the Romans
and wreaked a spectacular revenge (remember those chariot wheels?),
had a palace at Kenninghall and is buried at Quidenham. It is one of
those theories that are difficult to prove or disprove, but if it appears
in print often enough it may convince future historians so here we go
again.

There are a couple of Quidenham curiosities which I can confirm.
The church steeple, rare anyway in a county which is not strong on
steeples, is even rarer because it has wooden tiles. This is a source of
great delight for wooden tile enthusiasts, including woodpeckers. They
made their home in the steeple and pecked away with such enthusiasm
that in 1989 a wood-tiler – almost as rare as a wooden steeple – had to
be called in to repair the damage. The weathervane was taken down for
regilding at the same time, and revealed the second curious feature of
this church. It had been holed by a bullet. Even at that height it was
not safe from the vandals . . .

In this part of South Norfolk every signpost seems to have a
fixation about Banham Zoo. Even my road atlas blots out Banham
with a large blue elephant. One gets the impression that the village is
occupied solely by multicoloured mammals. There are, however, quite
a lot of people in Banham and the pleasant village green is surrounded,
not by cages but by some attractive old shops and houses. Among them
is the Old Bakery, easily spotted thanks to the big oven door which has

Don't call for bread at the
Old Bakery in Banham, it's
a private house now. But
the original oven door is
still set in the wall.

been preserved in its outside wall. There is not much else to see in Banham except the wooden effigy of a knight in the church, which is nearly as rare as Quidenham's wooden steeple. Do your duty and give it a look – then feel free to visit the zoo.

By now we have run out of Thet or even Wittle, but we can cut across to another river which takes us all the way to Norwich. Unfortunately the Tas also takes us into more populous areas as the main roads from Thetford, Bury St Edmunds and Ipswich converge on the city and the space between them diminishes. This is still open country but there is an air of busyness about it which you also find in the rural areas of the Home Counties. This, too, on a much smaller scale, is commuterland. There is still much worth seeing, but do not linger too long in your car while you look for it, or the horns will start blasting.

Thus it was that at Bunwell I missed the turning to the village hall, which was first mooted in 1931 and finally completed more than half-a-century later, a triumph of patience and perseverance. And thus it was that at Tacolneston (ask for Tackleston if you get lost) I found myself swept along in the traffic so swiftly that I missed all three of the Big Houses and saw little but a blur of new bungalows. At Hapton I kept an eye open for a 250-year-old Presbyterian chapel, one of the oldest in the county, but only saw an electricity sub-station before I was bustled out of the village. When I did manage to pull up at what I thought was Rainthorpe Hall to look at its knot garden – I had never seen a bed of clove hitches or a clump of sheepshanks – I found I was actually at Tasburgh Hall, with not a running bowline in sight, just a notice saying 'Guard Dogs on Duty'.

Happily there are quieter corners to enjoy the scenery. Old Buckenham has a main road running through the common in the centre of the village, but the common is so vast that the road is quite lost in it, and the clusters of cottages around it are set so far apart they seem to be in separate villages. You can park your car on the grass and wander in safety. The thatched church is worth a look; it has a charity board featuring a benefactor called Mr Laughter (how well he would have got on with the Rev Fuloflove) and some impressive king-size hassocks, indicating that Old Buckenhamians must be very short in the leg. What I find more interesting, though, is the connection between Old Buckenham and New Buckenham, a couple of miles down the road.

Of course New Buckenham is not new, it is just newer. William d'Albini, a Norman notable, was given a castle at Buckenham, got bored with it and built another one. That was eight-and-a-half centuries ago. New Buckenham grew up beside the new castle, and it is much more compact than the original village. At its centre is a market cross, complete with whipping-post, and its green is of far more modest proportions. As for the castles, the old one has given place to a

21

Up and Down
the City Road

In the days when New
Buckenham really was
new, several centuries ago,
it acquired its Market
Cross. . .

. . . and the whipping post that was part of its essential equipment.

farmhouse and the new one is just a grassy mound. Instead New Buckenham can claim one of the latest structures to be listed as buildings of historical and architectural interest – a red telephone box. Thanks to the villagers' efforts it has been saved from the scrapyard or from conversion into a drinks cabinet (surely a fate worse than death), and proudly displays a gold crown above its door to demonstrate its special status.

This part of South Norfolk is flattish, if not actually flat, but nearer Norwich the undulations begin to appear, and if you find the right lanes you can come upon some delightful countryside within a few miles of the city. The villages along the River Tas have some pleasant corners, and if you feel sentimental about mustard you should pay your respects to Stoke Holy Cross, birthplace of John Jeremiah Colman, and to Dunston Mill, where he first turned his golden crop into gold.

A farm, a church and a ruined church tower – about all that remains of Shotesham St Mary. The old village street is now just a dent in the fields.

There is more open country, with real hills, around the Shoteshams. Shotesham St Mary is a cluster of cottages around a hilltop church with the ruined tower of St Martin's just below, and Shotesham All Saints has an elegant assortment of period houses on the far side of the valley. R.H. Mottram, the distinguished East Anglian writer, reckoned that All Saints 'has the character generally ascribed to Devonshire villages rather than Norfolk ones'. I am not sure I agree; in Devon there would be at least three souvenir shops and a quaint café selling cream teas.

You may well feel obliged to visit Caistor St Edmund, the site of the Roman town of Venta Icenorum, which they set up in Iceni country as a trading post and garrison town. At one time it was the most important Roman headquarters in East Anglia, and the reference books tell you it had public baths and a forum, an outer ditch a hundred feet wide and walls twenty feet high and eleven feet thick. Unfortunately to get a full impression of all this you need an aeroplane, very good eyesight and lots of imagination.

The east wall of the town is just beside the church, but it could be just another grass mound. The path to the church passes through the site of the Praetorium gate, but it could be just another path. The church itself has pieces of the old Roman walls built into it, but it could be just another old church. I did wander round the churchyard for a bit, trying to experience the feeling of a Roman town, but a young couple relaxing by the Praetorium gate obviously thought I was either a Peeping Tom or completely dotty, so I left them to experience the feeling on their own.

Between Arminghall and Trowse there is another frustrating antiquity, the site of a Neolithic temple dating back to 2500 BC. Again all the statistics are available: the outer circle had a diameter of 262 feet, there were eight oak posts buried to a depth of seven feet, each post was three feet across, and so on – a veritable Woodhenge. But I am afraid this too can only be detected from the air, just a few marks in a field. I wouldn't bother.

I suffered another disappointment at Trowse. For many years I have dined out (literally on some occasions) on the story of how

I planned to start a newspaper there and call it the Trowse Press. Ho-ho. Only when I visited the place did I discover that they pronounce Trowse to rhyme, not with 'douse' but with 'dose'. I have not told that story since.

We are within sight now of the Norwich suburbs and the skyline of Norwich itself. You can look in vain for the famous spire or the castle. From this angle all you can see are office blocks. It is not an area in which to linger. Norwich is a fine city, but only in the middle; ideally you need that aeroplane again to leapfrog Lakenham and Eaton and land in Cathedral Close.

There have already been many books written about Norwich, but there are one or two places of interest which have only recently become accessible. In fact 1989 was a bumper year for launching new projects in the city for the benefit of visitors. Some are still being developed as I write, but I trust they will be ready and waiting for you next time you are in town.

There is for instance an underground passage which the local Press hailed as 'The Tourist Trail Tunnel of Doom'. Every tourist knows Norwich Castle, and most of them know the Shirehall, but only recently have they been able to pass from one to the other through the tunnel which links them. Prisoners used it in the last century to walk from their prison cell in the castle to face their trial. It was closed for many years until a Norwich lawyer donated £10,000 so it could be used as an alternative entrance to the Royal Norfolk Regimental Museum, which is now housed in the Shirehall.

Once a royal Norman castle, later a prison, now a tourist attraction – Norwich Castle on its floodlit Castle Mound.

You will follow in the steps of notorious murderers like Henry Groom, who was executed in 1851 for killing his foreman to steal the men's wage packets, a matter of thirty-odd pounds. James Blomfield Rush went the same way a few years earlier for a double murder near Wymondham. When he returned through the tunnel he was hanged at the castle gate. If you relish such macabre memories then the Tunnel of Doom is the place for you.

Norwich Cathedral gets so much publicity one can forget that the city also has a long Nonconformist history, but the Nonconformists do not forget it and they recently erected a memorial stone to John Wesley, who preached regularly at the Tabernacle Chapel. It remained in use until 1924, when the congregation was so small they decided to sell it. The chapel served Mammon, in the form of the British Gas Light Company, until it was demolished in 1953. There was no reminder of Wesley's connection with it until the stone was erected and dedicated on Wesley Day 1989.

Another arrival on the tourist circuit is Dragon Hall, a fifteenth-century merchant's house in King Street, which went through a chequered career as tenements, a rectory and a pub until the city authorities took it over and restored it. I have a special affection for Dragon Hall because I was involved in launching a £650,000 appeal in 1989, which by now should have provided modern amenities in this ancient building. Watch out for the red dragon on one of the beams in the great hall, which they found during restoration work and which gives the hall its name. They found other things as well, but who would want to visit Woodworm Hall?

It is possible that, like me, you sometimes weary of the standard tourist attractions in a city, and I can offer you some havens of escape which also became available in 1989. Traditionally Norwich's 'green lung' has been Mousehold Heath, where Robert Kett sat under Kett's Oak (he had nearly as many oaks as the Devil had dykes) and assembled his rebels for the ill-fated assault on Norwich. It was also the Heath which George Borrow enjoyed the wind on, brother. Enthusiasts have argued that Mousehold is to Norwich what Hampstead Heath is to London, but of course there is no comparison in size and the traffic, let alone Norwich Prison, is never far away.

To provide more oaks to sit under and more heath to enjoy the wind on, the City Council has designated five new areas within its boundaries as nature reserves. Lion Wood is twenty-two acres of steep sloping woodland in Thorpe; Bowthorpe Marsh is a welcome patch of green in the middle of a massive housing development; Earlham Park Woods not only have woods but marshes and ponds; Danby Wood is an abandoned marl pit now specialising in ash trees; and Marston Marsh, alongside the river near the Ipswich road, has a two-kilometre nature walk named endearingly and for all too obvious reasons the Cow Pat Trail.

They must all be a great boon to those who have to spend their lives in Norwich. Mercifully I do not. So if you have had your fill of

Mousehold Heath, where
George Borrow enjoyed the
wind on the heath, brother;
he may have taken his dog
walkies too.

Tombland and Elm Hill and the multicoloured stall canopies in the
Market Place, all of which are immortalised alongside the castle and
the cathedral on umpteen postcards and calendars, I suggest we escape
to broader pastures on the alternative route back to Thetford, to the
west of the AII. We have only to negotiate the suburban villages of
Earlham and Colney first. Earlham Hall, once the home of Elizabeth
Fry, has been absorbed by the University of East Anglia, along with
much of Earlham itself, and the only architectural attraction I can offer
you is the Sainsbury Centre at the university, which looks slightly
better than it sounds. Colney has nothing to match a Sainsbury Centre,
not even a Bejam Corner, but it does have a medieval road warning.

Norwich Market, possibly
the most photographed collection of canopies in the
country. City Hall beyond
them was unkindly called
by its critics 'The Marma-
lade Factory'.

27

Some of the ingredients
that make up 'A Fine City':
top All Saints' church, one
of thirty medieval churches
in Norwich; *centre* the
postwar University of East
Anglia, on the city out-
skirts; *bottom* Doughty's
Hospital, a 'haven of rest' –
Mr Doughty's phrase, not
mine – since 1687; *below*
Chapelfield Gardens, the
oldest public park in the
city, once the grounds of a
priests' college; and *far
right* the city's most familiar landmark, seen from an
unfamiliar angle, end-on.

If you can park by the church without being hit up the bumper you will read over the porch how John Fox, in the 79th year of his Age, was thrust down and trampled on by the horses of a waggon. 'Reader,' the notice exhorts, 'if thou drivest a team be careful, and endanger not the Life of another or thine own.'

Unfortunately not many drivers seem to take much notice, and you are well-advised to take the road to Bawburgh, renowned for a more leisurely form of transport. St Walstan was the son of a noble family who spent all his days toiling in the fields, doing good to all and ill to none, and being generally saintly. He asked that when he died his body should be put in an ox-cart and buried wherever the oxen stopped. (The traffic was lighter in those days.) They wandered for miles before finishing up at Bawburgh Church. St Walstan's shrine there was a centre of pilgrimage until Henry VIII put a stop to that sort of thing and demolished it. Walstan sank into obscurity for centuries, but lately he has been adopted as Norfolk's Saint of Agriculture, and 1989 was designated the Year of St Walstan. Was it just a coincidence that we had the best summer for a decade?

Hethersett is too close to the A11 for comfort, which perhaps is why Temperance Flowerdew decided to emigrate to America; it may have been a little noisy even in 1609. Ms Flowerdew is worth a mention if only for her delightful name, but she achieved further distinction when she arrived in Virginia. She married the Governor, Sir George Yardley, and became the first titled lady in the New World.

While we are so close to the A11 it is well worth a stroll around Wymondham, which has happily been bypassed, though the traffic continues to grow so fast there is now talk of a bypass to bypass the bypass. In 1989 attention turned from the traffic to the Market Cross, which is not actually a cross but a seventeenth-century timbered room on stilts. After restoration work the ratepayers were reported to be 'incensed' when the covers were removed and they saw the familiar oak frame timbers, which used to be stained black, were now painted with limewash.

Their protests provoked a scathing letter to the local Press from an architect who said they must live in modern houses 'with softwood "beams" stuck in the walls, pseudo Georgian doors, "Elizabethan" double-glazed leaded-light bay windows, and sliding patio doors leading to plastic "Victorian conservatories".' All he left out was the imitation coach lamps by the front door. The Market Cross architects knew what they were doing, he said. 'Leave well alone and don't interfere.' He could almost have been addressing Prince Charles.

I nearly got embroiled in this argument myself, since the Town Council had kindly invited me to perform the re-opening ceremony. But a typical British compromise was reached: the architects agreed that the beams should be wirebrushed so that most of the limewash was removed, leaving the timbers in virtually their natural colours.

The result, I think, was most effective and seemed to please everybody. If you still yearn for black-painted wood there is any amount of it inside.

You will also find the floor slopes quite alarmingly from the centre post down to the octagonal walls. Apparently the Victorians inserted a central pillar to provide added support, and while the eight pillars holding up the outside walls continued to subside gently the central one on its solid new foundation stood firm, forcing the floor upwards. The ingenious burghers of Wymondham overcame this hazard by shortening the front legs of their chairs, so that as they sat around their central council table their seats remained horizontal! These days the meetings are held elsewhere and the chairs have gone into store, while the Market Cross is given over to the tourists.

The nearby Chapel of St Thomas à Becket has also experienced a change of use since it was built, in the same period as the better-known Wymondham Abbey. It became a grammar school and more recently a county branch library. There were thought to be secret tunnels between the chapel and the abbey, but they turned out to be disused Victorian sewers.

Wymondham – pronounced Windham, as many a BBC announcer has discovered too late – is a busy little town which no amount of bypassing is likely to alter. But you only have to travel a mile or two away from the trunk road to find quiet little villages which do not seem to have stirred for centuries. There are two on the edge of the nearby Kimberley estate; both have enjoyed the benefit of the healthy income from those famous South African mines.

One is Kimberley itself, immaculate thatched cottages among immaculate oaks and beeches around an immaculate village green. By the immaculate park gates is the immaculate little church. The Wodehouse family, who became Earls of Kimberley, kept the village looking like this for about five hundred years, and although they sold the Big House and moved to Wiltshire in 1958 – fancy wanting to move from Norfolk to Wiltshire! – the estate remains, yes, immaculate.

On the far side of the park by a Regency gatehouse is Carleton Forehoe, just as trim but mostly elegant houses instead of pretty cottages, surrounded by meadows and parkland and paddocks, with hardly a root of sugar beet or an ear of barley in sight. Kimberley House is well concealed from the public eye, as is only right and proper. This is traditional gentry country; even the name Carleton Forehoe sounds like the hero of a Barbara Cartland novel.

Barnham Broom, a couple of miles away, sounds much more workmanlike. It caters for a different kind of gentry, who like to combine business conferences with a few rounds of golf or a game of squash. In recent years Barnham Broom Conference Centre and Country Club has expanded so greatly one almost forgets the modest village on which it is based, but if that story of St Walstan took your

When Wymondham Market Cross was restored in 1989 the familiar black-stained timbers were lime-washed, almost as white as the walls. The citizens were incensed, and a classic compromise was reached. The limewash was brushed off and the beams are virtually their natural colour.

31

fancy you will find a painting of him in the church. He is still revered in the village, though his wandering oxen would not be too popular with the golfers up the road.

Attleborough, like Wymondham, no longer has the A11 to cope with, but the bypass was only recently built and the town still seems to be recovering from the shock. No doubt it will regain its pre-A11 character, whatever that was, but meanwhile I much prefer Hingham, which had the good fortune to avoid any contact with the trunk road and remains an unspoilt little Georgian market town. I first saw it on a Bank Holiday. The A11 only five miles away, was a solid mass of traffic in both directions, but in Hingham the little market place snoozed in the sunshine, the mellow old houses looked as though they had never sniffed a diesel fume, and I almost expected a coach and pair to come trotting round the corner.

The houses were built as winter quarters for the folk in the Big Houses, out on the neighbouring estates. Living in the middle of a park at the end of a long drive must be delightful in summer, but when winter gales are blowing unchecked across the park, the drive is under three feet of snow and nobody has yet invented central heating, even the hardiest Lord is likely to forsake his Manor for the cosier comforts of town – and no town in mid-Norfolk is cosier than Hingham. It is not just the town centre; I wandered round the lanes which lead off the market place and they looked just as attractive. Even the wartime pre-fabs on the road to Norwich are starting to look homely.

Hingham's town sign depicts the departure of the local Pilgrim Fathers for the New World...

In the days before Hingham became a rural Georgian fleshpot it was the home of the Lincoln family, who joined in the general exodus to the New World and in due course begat a President of the

United States. Had they known what a pleasant place Hingham was going to be, they would probably have stayed put – and changed the course of American history.

IN·THIS·PARISH·FOR·MANY·GENERATIONS
LIVED·THE·LINCOLNS
ANCESTORS·OF·THE·AMERICAN
ABRAHAM·LINCOLN
TO·HIM·GREATEST·OF·THAT·LINEAGE
MANY·CITIZENS·OF·THE·VNITED·STATES
HAVE·ERECTED·THIS·MEMORIAL
IN·THE·HOPE·THAT·FOR·ALL·AGES
BETWEEN·THAT·LAND·AND
THIS·LAND·AND·ALL·LANDS
THERE·SHALL·BE
"MALICE·TOWARD·NONE
WITH·CHARITY·FOR·ALL"

. . . and this is what the New World sent back to Hingham – a bust of Abraham Lincoln, one of their descendants, presented by Hingham, Mass.

Between Attleborough and Hingham is Great Ellingham, a much-developed village notable mainly for the bright golden cockerel which perches on top of the church spire. Spires, as I have said, are rare in Norfolk, and this one is so modest compared with the sturdy tower beneath it one wonders why they bothered, but the cockerel makes it all worth while. Alas, when I last visited the village the unfortunate bird was leaning at a drunken angle, victim no doubt of a winter gale. I trust by now it is in a fit state to crow again.

Little Ellingham cannot claim a cockerel, drunk or sober, but it does have a very substantial clock tower for a small village – so substantial that it has living accommodation in its base. No doubt the occupants would hope that time never weighs too heavily upon them.

A few miles away is Scoulton Mere, the biggest expanse of water in the area but not easy to find, as there are no signposts off the main road and the entrance is disguised by 'Private Fishing' notices. At a quick glance I found it uninviting, even without the notices. The trees come down to the water's edge and though the sun was shining it looked dark and forbidding. No doubt the private fishermen view it differently.

Up and Down the City Road

It may have been the trees more than the mere which influenced me because this is babes-in-the-wood country, where the two infants fell foul of their wicked uncle Robert de Grey of Griston Hall. The village sign at Griston portrays them languishing in the wood with Uncle Robert lurking nearby. It was unveiled, ironically, by his direct descendant Lord Walsingham, who no doubt expressed the family's regrets.

The sign is not the only reminder of that sad incident. Wayland Wood gets its name, so they say, from the Wailing Wood where the cries of the babes can still be heard – particularly when there are seagulls on Scoulton Mere.

After babes-in-the-wood country you come to road-closed-ahead country. This is the edge of the Stanford battle area, a vast blank on the map of Norfolk where the military play their war games and nobody is allowed to watch. They do, however, take parties of conservation experts into the area to show what a splendid job they are doing in conserving the countryside while in the process of thumping each other. Explosives and Army boots are apparently not nearly as damaging to the flora and fauna as a dose of agricultural chemicals.

One might assume that the neighbouring villages are not the most restful of places, but the Army has over forty square miles of empty terrain to rush about in, and they rarely get too close to the edges. Apart from the road-closed signs and the out-of-bounds warnings, these villages are no different from any other in South Norfolk, and in some cases they are a lot more attractive. Merton, for instance, has built itself a little flint-and-thatch bus shelter on the green which is a great improvement on the graffiti-covered concrete some villages prefer, and its park with the church overlooking the Big House, its lake and paddocks is as peaceful a scene as you could wish.

The Big House is not as big as it was, thanks to two major fires, but it still looks a sizeable home for the de Greys, who inherited the estate by marriage in the fourteenth century and have owned it ever since. It has not been on the market, in fact, since it appeared in the Domesday Book.

The de Greys have lived at Merton Hall since the 14th century – and throughout those 600 years their view of Merton Church across the park has hardly changed.

Thompson is another quiet village by the battle area which actually benefits from all those road-closed signs, since they keep away any through traffic and the thatched cottages in its main street are left in peace. The only curious feature of Thompson is its name. Some surnames sound appropriate for villages – we do not think twice about neighbouring Merton, and we have Houghton and Ingham and Eaton and Melton, and many more villages which bear people's names, but Thompson seems almost as incongruous a name for a village as, say, Timpson. A college of priests was founded here by Sir Thomas Shardelowe in the fourteenth century, and perhaps Tom's son had a hand in christening it. But why not call it Shardelowe? It sounds a much more salubrious place to live.

The Norfolk Naturalists' Trust has taken over some of the heathland and meadow which the Army missed, and Thompson Common is one of its acquisitions. Its local showpiece, however, is East Wretham Heath, also on the edge of the battle area but a peaceful haven for birds and people alike. There is even a nature trail for the physically handicapped, with guide ropes to help the blind and recorded commentaries at each stopping point – an unusual amenity which other conservation bodies could copy.

East Wretham has another distinction which is now just a part of history. Wretham Hall was the home of Sir John Dewrance, who went coal-prospecting in Kent and developed the Kent coalfields. He lived to see them provide many thousands of tons of coal and many hundreds of jobs. He did not live to see the coal and the jobs dwindle until the last mine was closed in 1989. Wretham Hall has been demolished, the Dewrance family have moved away and the words on his tombstone are almost obliterated, but Sir John is still remembered by the older villagers – and perhaps by some of the older ex-coalminers of Kent.

East Wretham itself is pleasant enough; there is a very grand rectory and the church tower has a sloping red-tiled roof which makes it look like a very tall cottage. But the village is flanked on one side by chicken-houses and on another by Army huts, and I cannot decide which look the less inviting.

We are nearly back to Thetford and you may wish to rejoin the London road and keep going. But this circuit of the AII in South Norfolk is only one aspect of what the county has to offer. There are the Broads in the east, the coast to the north, and High Norfolk, the hinterland where tourists rarely roam. For those arriving from the Midlands and the North there is an area quite different from any of these. It was once part-fen, part-marsh, part-water. Now the water has been drained and the fens and marshes are fields, but it still has a strange air of remoteness and it still leads a life of its own. Officially this is part of West Norfolk, but it is quite unlike anywhere else in the county.

2 In and Out of the Sea Walls
The marshland and fenland of West Norfolk

In the 1987 General Election a Conservative candidate ventured into the Norfolk Fens in search of voters, and came upon three Fenmen working on the roadside in the middle of nowhere. Two of them, when pressed, confirmed they were Conservative supporters; the third revealed he was Labour. As the candidate prepared to drive off, one of the two Tory Fenmen leaned through the car window. 'Don't you worry,' he said. 'As soon as yew've gone, we'll hang 'im.'

I am still not sure if he was joking. Fenmen have a history of being a law unto themselves, dispensing and receiving rough justice. In the days when the Fens were being drained, anybody who broke down one of the new embankments was staked in the gap and buried alive. It was the local version of the little Dutch boy only instead of plugging the breach with a thumb they used an entire Fenman.

The battle against the twin onslaughts of fresh water overflowing from the rivers and salt water flooding in from the sea was going on long before the Dutch engineers were hired in Jacobean times to make a professional job of it. The Romans were digging dykes and building sea walls sixteen centuries earlier. Traces of their sea walls still remain, miles inland from those of the present day. There is one on the outskirts of Terrington St Clement and presumably there was another on the outskirts of Wisbech, because its close Norfolk neighbour bears the Roman name of Walsoken. In spite of the wall the Romans were still, as it were, soken; the waters poured in and out of the old walls almost as easily as we can walk or drive through them today.

Now at last the rivers seem under control and the sea has been driven back to uncover more arable land, but anyone who has seen those floodwater marks on St Margaret's church in King's Lynn, with dates ranging from 1883 to 1978, will appreciate that sea walls are still not impregnable. The Wash can be an uncomfortable neighbour.

Only a small section of the Fens lies in Norfolk and Suffolk; a much larger area lies in Cambridgeshire and Lincolnshire. Indeed for many years after I came to East Anglia I assumed that Norfolk stopped at King's Lynn. The Great Ouse seemed such an obvious boundary, and with the Little Ouse and the Waveney cutting it off from Suffolk to the south, and the North Sea on the other two sides, it would have meant that Norfolk achieved what many Norfolkmen would have liked, and became an offshore island.

It was quite a jolt, therefore, the first time I drove from Peterborough to King's Lynn, to see a sign on the Wisbech bypass which told me I was already entering Norfolk. This may well have been the road that Noël Coward took, because, no doubt about it, the area of Norfolk between Wisbech and the Ouse is very flat. He would have got the same impression if he had arrived on the A17 from Newark, the main entry route from the North, or on the A10 from Ely in the south. Flatness abounds.

Many Norfolkmen in other parts of the county are very happy about this and hope that visitors will find the terrain so boring they will turn round and go home again, as presumably Noël Coward did. Of all the assorted areas of East Anglia this would seem the least likely to harbour any attractions for the traveller.

Not so. There are many strange and wondrous things to be found in this apparently characterless corner, where you might think that the only mystery is why such a flat countryside with so few natural obstacles should have such narrow and winding main roads. It is actually another attempt to discourage visitors, this time by the Department of Transport, but the unending cavalcade of caravans in the summer months proves they have not yet succeeded. Indeed there are indications they have thrown in the sponge and plan to build dual carriageways on these Western Approaches, but it could be many years yet.

Meanwhile it is worth turning off the congested trunk roads to explore the deserted lanes that lie between. But be warned. Arm yourself with a very good map, a lot of patience, and haversack rations for three days. Fenland lanes are liable to end abruptly at a twenty-foot embankment, beyond which lies a forbidding barrier which may be the Old Bedford River or the Middle Level or the Sixteen Foot Drain. The lane will have dykes on each side which prevent anything less than a ten-point turn, and fainthearted drivers have been known to tour much of the Fens in reverse. It can be all the more exasperating when the church you may be seeking is clearly visible across the fields, but the only way to reach it is to drive five miles back to the main road and start again . . .

It is the churches, of course, which make all the effort worth while. In particular the marshland churches, which are among the finest in East Anglia. To the casual visitor the marshlands and the

In and Out of the Sea Walls

Fens may look much the same; just flat. They are actually quite different. The Fens in their present form were only created when the land was drained; there were no permanent communities there before. The marshlands nearer the sea have always been there in spite of the constant threat of flooding, and their villages and churches date back much further, to the twelfth and thirteenth centuries, when building in the Fens was limited to islands such as Ely.

The marshland churches were built with great strength to withstand the attacks of wind and water, and, thanks to the profits from the sheep which grazed on the marshes, they were built on a very grand scale. As a result they are among the most majestic churches in East Anglia, and their flat setting makes them look all the more dramatic. In spite of this it is estimated that, for every visitor who makes a tour of the marshland churches, probably a thousand tour the wool churches of West Suffolk. The reason I suppose is fairly obvious.

A typical marshland village: big church, small cottages, lots of rich black earth under a vast sky. Wiggenhall St German's has the Great Ouse too.

Most tourists do not live by churches alone. West Suffolk villages are picturesque, marshland villages are rather dull; the West Suffolk countryside is hilly and wooded and varied, the marshland countryside is, indisputably, flat.

So once you cross the Great Ouse from King's Lynn, if that is your starting-point, do not expect too much picture-postcard scenery. West Lynn, on the opposite bank, could be a suburb of almost anywhere; one cynic observed that the nicest thing about it was its view of King's Lynn across the river, and even that is mostly obscured by warehouses and factories. However there is a little boat that ferries foot passengers to the town, and it must be quite a civilised way to go shopping or commute to work during the summer, when the road bridge further upriver is clogged with traffic. In the winter, of course, it is a different story; the Great Ouse in a small open boat with an east wind howling in from the North Sea makes London Underground in the rush hour seem like a haven of peace.

On the road to Clenchwarton there are some tempting lanes heading seaward but I would not recommend them. They will either lead you into a farmyard or back past the sewage works into West Lynn.

Both these villages have a parish church but they are not the ones we are looking for. Even Lady Harrod, president of the Norfolk Churches Trust and an enormous enthusiast on the subject, can find little to say about them, and Arthur Mee, who could generally dig up some sort of information about almost anywhere, ignores Clenchwarton altogether. But there is better news in store.

The next village up the road is Terrington St Clement, again an unremarkable semi-suburb with the standard allocation of chalet-bungalows, redbrick 'luxury homes' and petrol stations. One guide describes it bluntly as 'a big, very ugly village . . . with hardly a nice-looking building.' But it has two great attractions, both as it happens run by clergymen – its African-violets nursery, founded and developed by a former parish priest, and its marvellous church, 'The Cathedral of the Marshes'.

This is not to be confused with 'The Queen of the Marshes' at Walpole St Peter. I wonder who coined these evocative and slightly over-the-top titles, and which indeed was coined first. Did a pushy parson at Terrington decide that his church deserved cathedral rating, and then an envious incumbent at Walpole, not to be outdone, conferred his own with royal status? Or were they both dreamed up by a medieval public relations consultant to raise an extra groat?

Neither church really needs this kind of hype. Of the two I prefer St Peter's, perhaps because it is not only grand but in some respects odd. St Clement's is just grand. But its grandness is enough to keep any tourist happy. There are the pinnacled turrets and flying buttresses outside and, inside, the soaring arches and fine carvings and the massive font cover which opens to show New Testament scenes. The arches were meant to support a central tower, but the architect changed his mind when he rechecked the foundations. He found that the weight of the church and the tower together would be too much

39

In and Out of the Sea Walls

for the marshy subsoil, and the whole lot was likely to capsize with a very loud squelch. He cut his losses, left the arches where they were, and built the tower alongside the church instead.

The villagers of Terrington had good reason to be thankful for his caution. When a dyke broke its banks in the seventeenth century and the waters came rushing in from the Wash, the tower stood firm and they took refuge in it until the water subsided, subsisting on supplies brought by boat from King's Lynn.

Looking at the vast expanse of fields which now surrounds the village it is difficult to visualise how a flood could reach this far. You have to drive quite a way to get even a glimpse of the Wash and only one of the marshland lanes goes anywhere near it, at a tiny settlement with the unlikely title of Ongar Hill. It seems unlikely because the Ongar you probably know is a hundred miles away in Essex on the end of the Central Line, and if there was ever a hill at Ongar Hill it is certainly not there now.

Elsewhere in East Anglia a field of yellow would probably be rape or mustard, but here in the rich marshland near Clenchwarton it's daffodils.

The lane from Terrington takes you out across the marsh, past isolated cottages and vast fields of grain and potatoes. It was on one of these cottages that I spotted my first satellite dish, a hi-tech intrusion which looked even more incongruous in this remote landscape than it does in that other Ongar. But who can blame the occupants, faced with the long lonely evenings of a bleak Norfolk winter, and not another soul for miles?

On my last visit there, winter could not have seemed further away. It was the height of the 1989 heatwave; the tar was melting on the roads, the barley had been harvested early and the wheat was well on its way. Inland there was not a breath of wind, but as I neared the coast the breeze strengthened. At Ongar Hill there was a field of gladioli ready for gathering, and on the opposite side of the lane a garden gate bore the legend 'Coastguard Cottages', though there was still no sign of the sea. The lane ended, as so many do in this area, at a high embankment, and here the breeze was so brisk I visualised the waves breaking on the far side. But there was just another vast field, this time of peas, and a half-mile walk to a further embankment before the Wash came into view. Had I come there years earlier I could have watched boats sailing where the peas were now growing. The coastline of the Wash has been reshaped and the land reclaimed, to the confusion of the map-makers and any odd Roman who might return.

Terrington St Clement has a junior partner four miles away, Terrington St John, but you are unlikely to confuse the two. On the other hand Walpole St Peter and Walpole St Andrew adjoin each other so closely it is difficult to tell where one parish ends and the other begins. I have a soft spot for St Andrew, which rarely gets more than a couple of lines in the guidebooks and has to exist in the shadow of its famous neighbour. If it were anywhere else St Andrew's church would rate a visit in its own right, if only to inspect the hourglass which stands by the pulpit as a reminder for over-eloquent parsons. There is also a theory that King John left his treasure at Walpole St Andrew before he set off across the Wash, which at that time was not far away. If it is ever discovered the tables will be turned and we shall see the village emblazoned on the front pages with never a mention of its big brother.

Meanwhile it is the massive church of St Peter's, a bare half-mile away, which draws most of the visitors and whatever publicity is going. It sits in much more attractive surroundings than Terrington St Clement. There are nice old houses surrounding it in a backwater away from the newer part of the village, though the red brick has marched up close to the churchyard wall on one side, under the guise of a new Rectory. It must have been in this original part of Walpole St Peter that the family lived who borrowed or gave it the name (one can never be certain which way round it happened). The Walpoles had the sense to get out long before the newcomers came in. They went off to provide England with its first prime minister, and built an assortment of stately homes in more scenic corners of Norfolk.

I mentioned the church has oddities and you will find one of them if you venture past the main door to the east end, avoiding an enormous copper beech which spreads a good twenty-five yards across the churchyard. Under the church is the Bolthole, an arched passage barely the height of a man, with rings in it for tying up your horse. This is directly underneath the high altar, which makes it so high the priest has to mount nine steps to reach it.

Views differ about the Bolthole. The church guidebook says it was an ancient right of way. Arthur Mee agrees and says it is

The marshland and fenland of West Norfolk

Flaking walls and a perspex-covered window – marshland churches take a lot of maintaining. This is at Walpole St Andrew's.

'unique in our experience'. Lady Harrod declines to speculate. But it does look very like the archway under the church at Metton in north-east Norfolk, and the reason for that was because the church was built hard up against the wall of the farmhouse next door, and the arch was to allow processions to pass right round it. The same surely applies to Walpole St Peter.

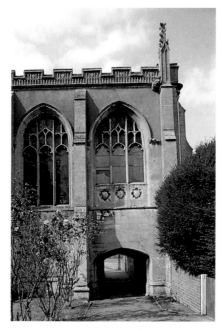

A couple of curiosities at Walpole St Peter's: the passage under the high altar, known locally as the Bolt-hole, and the portable sentrybox which protected the parson at draughty graveside funerals. . .

If the church had been a bit smaller the problem would not have arisen, and indeed the church guide notes that visitors often ask why it is so big. It replies rather loftily, 'Men built an immense Church to the greater glory of God, who is immense.' To which one feels like responding, 'Yes I know, but . . . ' The more mundane explanation – and, to be fair, the guide comes to it later – is that the sheep farmers made so much money in the fourteenth century they decided to show their gratitude in as ostentatious a fashion as possible. The original Norman church, incidentally, was completely destroyed except for the tower by floods coming in from the Wash, though it is now ten miles away. One can imagine what precarious lives they used to live in the marshlands; Noah would have felt very much at home.

In the entrance porch a faded sign requests worshippers to remove their pattens before entering the door, and to make sure there is no mistake a pair of pattens hangs above it. These were the wooden-soled sandals which preceded the gumboot as standard wear on the farm, and very inadequate they must have been when the weather turned inclement. The parson however was given special protection if he had to take a funeral at such times. In the church is a sort of portable sentry-box with handles. It is described as 'a shade of wood to cover the minister when he burieth the corpse'. A couple of husky parishioners carried it out to the graveside ahead of him. I tried to lift it and it hardly budged, but they come tough in the marshlands.

The parson does not receive so much consideration when he climbs into the pulpit. The open-plan stairs winding round a stone pillar have no protective railing. It takes a steady nerve to mount them, and an even steadier one to come down.

St Peter's has other unusual features – an ancient alms box, a wooden cradle at the back of the pews (part of a medieval creche?), and two ornamental crooks 'laid up' by the Marshland Shepherds Club, which was formed in 1841 'to relieve the sick, bury the dead, and assist each other in all cases of unavoidable distress'. It seems to have been a pastoral version of the Masons. The crooks are a reminder, not only of the community spirit of the marshlands, but of the original source of their wealth, though it no doubt passed the shepherds by.

... and a couple more: the ancient alms-box on a pillar (an original pillarbox?) and the wooden cradle behind the pews, perhaps part of an early crèche.

There is a third Walpole village, Walpole Highway, and that is basically what it is, a congested section of the A47 trunk road. On another stretch of the same road is Walton Highway; you will not wish to linger here either. The place to head for is West Walton, not to see its rows of chalet-bungalows but to visit what Lady Harrod calls quite simply the finest thirteenth-century church in Norfolk. It also has the finest church tower in the marshlands, separate from the church and built right over the entrance to the churchyard, the biggest lych-gate in the business. It seems in rather better shape than the church, probably because it is cared for by the Redundant Churches Trust, while the church still has to survive on the efforts of its parishioners.

Judging by the plaque inside the church it is remarkable it has survived at all. It records how in November 1613 'the sea broke in and overflowed all Marshland, to the grate danger of men's lives and loss of goods'. Four months later all marshland was overflowed again, this time from the rivers. And in 1670 it was flooded a third time, thanks to 'the Violence of the Sea'. Even Noah would hardly have known which way to turn. In more recent years the process has been repeated: the rivers burst their banks in 1947, and six years later the marshlands were inundated again, as was most of the Norfolk coast, by the great sea floods of 1953.

With so much water washing around West Walton over the centuries, small wonder that one of the local family names is Mudd. Somewhere in the churchyard, though I failed to find it, a tombstone proclaims: 'Here lies Matthew Mudd, Death did him no hurt. When alive he was but Mudd, and now dead he's but dirt.'

Presumably to avoid vandalism or theft, West Walton church, like so many others in East Anglia, is kept locked. That is the bad news. The good news is that the key is kept in the King of Hearts next door. I had an excellent lunch of steak and kidney pie, peas and chips, a traditional pub lunch but cooked to perfection. The peas even tasted like peas. I remember that meal with as much pleasure as I remember the fine church next door; each in its own way is a part of our English heritage.

Incidentally the landlord confessed that he had only entered the neighbouring establishment twice in nine years, and was quite unimpressed by its historical significance. No matter; he is doing a great job where he is.

I could not arouse such enthusiasm over Walsoken, the last of my marshland churches. Here again the door was locked, and this time there was no King of Hearts to tempt me in search of it. I am assured that the church has fine Norman arches and a splendid font, and certainly from the outside it looks as imposing as Terrington and Walpole St Peter, but its surroundings, alas, are not inspiring. Walsoken is a suburb of Wisbech, full of Victorian villas and postwar housing estates, with such urban delights as a fish bar, a video shop and a Chinese takeaway.

Nevertheless the spirit of Nelson lives on in this distant outpost of Norfolk. In 1989 the Boundary Commission recommended that Walsoken should be transferred into Cambridgeshire. It must have seemed logical. As you drive down the village street it is difficult to know where Walsoken ends and Wisbech, already part of Cambridgeshire, begins. But the good folk of Walsoken thought differently. Three hundred of them registered objections and they were backed by the county council, the borough council and the local MP.

The Environment Secretary, at that time the much-reviled Nicholas Ridley, confounded his critics by bowing to their wishes.

'He is not convinced,' said the Ministry letter, 'that on the evidence he has received the proposed transfer is so desirable . . . that the strong and widespread views of those affected be over-ridden.'

Walsoken's ancient font and late-Norman arcade – but the first problem is to get inside the church.

It was a famous Norfolk victory. A notice was posted on the church door headed triumphantly, 'The Parish of Walsoken (*Norfolk*)'. If I had been anywhere near Trafalgar Square and happened to glance up at the figure on top of the Column, I am sure I would have detected a faint smile.

And so, well done, Walsoken, regardless of your video shops and Chinese takeaways. And well done, Emneth, which was also under threat from the Commission, and shared in the protest. Emneth cannot claim a church as grand as Walsoken nor a name dating back to the Romans, but it does have a brass in memory of John Chafto who helped to preserve the thin red line at Balaclava, and his successors have helped to preserve the thin black line which is the Norfolk county boundary.

We know where we stand, then, with Walsoken and Emneth. I am not nearly so confident about Upwell and Outwell. They lie along both banks of the Wisbech Canal and the old River Nene, forming what was once considered the longest village in England, but that was before the invention of ribbon development. Originally Upwell and Outwell were single parishes, then the houses on the east bank were ruled to be in Norfolk and those on the west bank in Cambridgeshire. But in 1989 the Boundary Commission took its mind off Walsoken for a moment to propose that the Cambridgeshire parishes of Outwell (Isle) and Upwell (Isle) should be merged as single parishes with their

In and Out of the Sea Walls

The distinction between Upwell and Outwell has never been too clear to non-natives, but this I am assured is Outwell.

namesakes. The parish councils, who presumably understood what the Commission was talking about, agreed to co-operate and the proposal has gone through.

But I am still not clear where the county boundary lies. I drove up and down both banks, and just when I thought I was leaving Norfolk I found a notice saying I was entering it. I am sure the locals know which county they are in, if only from the name on the dustcart, but for visitors it is perhaps simpler to keep off the subject and just enjoy the scenery.

This is one corner of the fens where there is scenery to enjoy. Some writers compare it with Holland, and although the architecture is undistinguished there is always something pleasant about houses along a river. It looks a lot more peaceful now than it did in 1774 when Lord Orford led a fleet of nine ships through what he called 'these populous towns'. And it was still pretty busy in 1883 when the Great Eastern Railway built the Wisbech and Upwell Tramway. A wooden-sided steam engine trundled alongside the river, criss-crossing the road, at a steady eight miles an hour. it was replaced in 1953 by a diesel engine, but not before the vicar of Emneth had taken note of it to include in his children's books. 'Toby the Tram Engine' lives on, thanks to the Revd W. Awdry. The tramway, alas, does not.

However there is one feature of Upwell's history which has been revived with enormous success. It originated among thirteenth-century monks and is now the most profitable enterprise in the area, famous well beyond the borders of East Anglia. The owner of Welle Manor Hall, Eric St John Foti, discovered the monks' recipe for a punch which rolls off the tongue as smoothly as his own name. He made a few bottles for a local charity event, the taste caught on, and he now sells one-and-a-half million bottles a year.

Norfolk Punch is based on herbs and other natural ingredients, and in spite of its name is completely free of alcohol. In fact Mr Foti does have a licensed still but only to remove the alcohol from the ingredients. The taste is just what you would expect. Barbara Cartland has commended it, which you would also expect, and I suppose one-and-a-half million bottles can't be wrong, but I am a little sad that a punch bearing the name of Norfolk does not have a little more, well, punch . . .

Welle Manor, where a 13th-century recipe for Norfolk Punch has become big business.

Not far from Upwell and Outwell is the curiously named village of Three Holes. From what I saw of it, one would have been sufficient. There is also a village called Nordelph and an old drainage system called Popham's Eau. Nordelph sounds Dutch and probably is. It must have looked even more so before 1865, when churchgoers used to travel upriver by horse-drawn barge to attend church at Upwell before their own was built. Popham's Eau on the other hand sounds French, but probably isn't. I gather this eau is Anglo-Saxon, pronounced not 'o' but 'ee'. Who Popham was and why he should wish to confuse us in this way remains a mystery.

Once we have negotiated these linguistic hazards we can encounter a more familiar name, to American as well as British travellers. This is Denver, at the junction of the Bedford River and the Great Ouse, the focal point of Fenland's drainage system and the home of the Denver Sluice.

I can no longer postpone a mention of the man whose fame in connection with the Fens is second only to Hereward the Wake, whom

In and Out of the Sea Walls

I have also miraculously avoided. Cornelius Vermuyden was brought from Holland in the seventeenth century to supervise the draining of this vast tract of boggy nothingness. He dredged the old rivers and dug new ones, and pumped the waters into them by windmills which were replaced by steampower, then diesel, then electricity. He made a fortune for his backers and a lot of enemies for himself, as the Fenmen saw their hunting and fishing grounds destroyed. Out of it all emerged some of the richest farming land in Britain.

A vital key to it all is the Denver Sluice, built by Vermuyden across the Great Ouse in 1650 to stop the tide sweeping up the river and bursting its banks. The Sluice suffered much damage from storms and saboteurs, but it was repaired and enlarged and strengthened over the years. Vermuyden's Old Sluice and the adjoining New Sluice across the cut-off channel present an unexpected and impressive sight as you drive a mile out of Denver village and suddenly see the superstructure towering above the flat Fenland countryside.

The Denver Sluice, built to protect the Fens, now protects holiday craft too. It was not always so peaceful – the Fenmen tried to wreck it.

There is a pleasant old pub on the riverbank, almost under the shadow of the Sluice, which still bears a notice showing the list of bridge tolls imposed by the Great Ouse River Board. Horses, cattle, sheep and pigs cost a penny, a two-wheeled cart was sixpence, and it went up to half-a-crown for a threshing engine or a steamroller. As a gesture to the Almighty parishioners on the west bank could cross the river to attend Denver church for nothing. The tolls were only discontinued in 1963, and I wonder if churchgoing fell away as a result, since you can now go anywhere for nothing.

There is more to Denver than the Sluice. It has a fine old windmill, well restored and one of the showpieces of the Norfolk Windmills Trust, to whom a Sluice is just a sluice but a mill is a joy for ever. It was the birthplace too of a schoolfriend of Nelson who also

Denver Mill, restored by the Norfolk Windmills Trust, to whom a Sluice is just a sluice but a mill is a joy for ever.

went to sea, but his interest was in how to save the lives of sailors, not how best to dispatch them. George William Manby invented the rocket life-saving apparatus which is still used to rescue crews from stricken ships.

Denver also was the home of Canon St Vincent Beechey, whose legacy to mankind was not a life-saving rocket but a modest tin hut. Nevertheless, this hut, which he presented to his parishioners in 1903 as a reading room, has earned its own place in history. In 1988 it came under threat from the developers, and the people of Denver applied for it to be listed as a building of historical and architectural interest.

It would be the first tin hut to achieve such a status, but actually it is quite a handsome structure, albeit made entirely of corrugated iron. In Canon Beechey's day this material was very new, quite exciting and perfectly acceptable. This little building may be the earliest of its kind, and if it were the first building made of flints or bricks or even concrete it would soon get on the list, along with all those telephone kiosks, so the application was not as eccentric as it may sound. As I write, the hut still stands, and long may it do so.

Certainly there would be no problem if it were cast iron, which now has a keen following among industrial archaeologists. They would doubtless be delighted with the cast-iron neo-Gothic clocktower in nearby Downham Market, the only slightly incongruous note in a pleasant little market town where Norfolk carrstone is the more common building material. It was erected in 1878 and I am assured the townsfolk are delighted with it.

Downham is the only town in this corner of Norfolk, and for motorists entering the county from Cambridge and Ely its town sign by the A10, which now bypasses it, is the first evidence that you have arrived anywhere. There was a time when town signs were decorative affairs depicting aspects of local history, and Downham has one of these too. It portrays St Winold ringing his bell to charm the fish from the river (could he be the patron saint of fly-fishermen?), a youthful Nelson playing with a toy boat (what else?), two horses to recall the annual horse fair, a butter churn, and the initials of the Women's Institute which presented it. The town sign beside the A10 is rather more prosaic. It depicts a petrol pump, a bed, and a knife and fork. Instead of 'WI' it says 'WC'.

You will find all these worthy items in Downham Market, and you will also find a railway station, not as young as it was but still functioning. When Dr Beeching had finished his massacre of our rural railways only two lines were left in Norfolk, extending up from London like two mocking fingers. One went up the eastern side to Norwich, with minor offshoots to the coast, and the other went up through Cambridge to Downham Market and King's Lynn. Not even royal patronage could keep it open a little further to Wolferton, the station on the Sandringham Estate.

The cast-iron clock tower at Downham Market presides over the market stalls, surrounded by its more indigenous carrstone neighbours.

51

I have always regarded this line as a convenient back door to the county, without the problems of parking and traffic congestion which Norwich offers, and only a twenty-mile drive from home instead of thirty. But it has been a tedious journey, with a long pause at Cambridge either to change the engine from diesel to electric or to change trains altogether. Now the whole line is being electrified and we are promised a faster and more efficient service. If it is like the fast, efficient, electrified service from Norwich then we were probably better off with the diesels, but one must hope for miracles. As I write, there is a bus service only between King's Lynn and Ely while the work is carried out, and even the Norwich line is better than that.

Even when the trains are running on this stretch of line it is not the most attractive of journeys, making you feel as isolated from civilisation as the Trans-Siberian Express – and when the heating has one of its regular hiccups it can be just as cold. The villages which do exist in this remote corner are out of sight of the railway, though they should not be entirely out of mind.

Fordham, for instance, has the soothingly named Snore Hall, where Charles I is said to have hidden in a secret chamber before his final surrender at Newark. Hilgay is where Captain Manby, of life-saving fame, came to live when his father became lord of the manor, and he is said to have tested his rocket-fired lifeline from the tower of the church; his tombstone bears a carving of the mortar he used. Ten Mile Bank is – a ten-mile bank.

Blurred with age now, but Captain Manby's tombstone at Hilgay depicts his life-saving rocket-firing mortar.

As the line continues northwards into Norfolk there is just one station in this vast flat countryside. It is more of a halt than a station, called Magdalen Road for many years, after the little lane that crosses the railway at that point. With the coming of electrification

British Rail decided this did not sound grand enough and renamed it Watlington, after the nearest village, but that is well away from the station and all you see from the train is still just the Magdalen road.

The rechristened Watlington station, still waiting for electrification to reach it on the long lonely line from Ely to King's Lynn.

It leads to Wiggenhall St Magdalen, one of a series of Wiggenhalls scattered along the banks of the Great Ouse.

The river always strikes me as rather forbidding on this stretch, broad and muddy-brown with high bare banks, but the villages are not as depressing as you might expect. It is true they are not your average picture-postcard riverside scenes, with immaculate green lawns running down to the water, quaint old bridges crossing it, and sailing boats dotted about on it. A towering embankment stands between the cottages and the river, the bridges are strictly utilitarian and any sailing boat which ventures on these strongly tidal waters is in danger of finishing up in the North Sea.

Nonetheless the Wiggenhalls are more attractive than most marshland villages. St German's, for instance, has a pleasant village square with eighteenth-century buildings surviving among the modern shops and garages. In the 1970s Ion Trewin, then literary editor of *The Times*, bought a tumbledown cottage in the village and wrote a delightful book about the tribulations of restoring it. He became as devoted to his corner of Norfolk as I am to mine, and he took me there hoping to convert me as successfully as he has converted his cottage.

Certainly there are some striking features. The ruins of St Peter's church, abandoned between the wars but now preserved against further collapse, offer a dramatic sight on a winter evening as you approach it along the river bank. St German's church has its hourglass by the pulpit,

53

In and Out of the Sea Walls

The ruins of Wiggenhall St Peter's standing sentinel beside the Great Ouse. . .

. . . and an elegant courtier stands sentinel in a pew-end in Wiggenhall St Mary's.

More modern sentinels – the sugar beet factory silos loom over the Fens at Wissington.

although as Ion noted with perhaps some regret it is no longer in use. And the church of St Mary the Virgin has carved benches reputed to be the finest in England, though many others contest the claim. In recent years St Mary's was made redundant but it is protected, one hopes, from falling into the sad condition of St Peter's.

Dominating everything in this area is the broad sweep of the Great Ouse, at low tide a rather dismal expanse of grey mud for much of its width, at high water a much more formidable spectacle as the powerful current sweeps under St German's bridge. I am used to the bleakness of a Norfolk winter but in the Wiggenhalls it must be bleak indeed, with that mass of grey water flowing through the villages and the flat marshland stretching away on every side. But it must have a fascination about it too, or Ion and others like him would long since have forsaken it for cosier climes.

Between the Wiggenhalls and King's Lynn there is nothing but the sugar beet factory, another treat for train passengers as they near the end of their journey. They will know when it is operating by the plume of white smoke from the chimney and the quite unmistakable

smell of boiling beet. If they are connoisseurs of these refineries there is a much more spectacular one further south on the banks of the Wissey. At Lynn there are other buildings visible in the distance, but the one at Wissington stands alone and almost sinister, looming up incongruously out of the deserted countryside as if dropped from another planet. If there is a mist rising over the Fens and only the tips of its silos and chimneys are visible it is all the more eerie. But the smell is just the same.

It was a few miles from this factory that I at last discovered West Dereham. I worked in East Dereham for eight years without any idea of where its western partner was located, and as East Dereham came to be known simply as Dereham it was easy to forget that the other one even existed. But there it is, a modest village in that lonely corner of West Norfolk twenty-odd miles from its big brother, the congested and fast-developing market town on the main road from Norwich to Lynn.

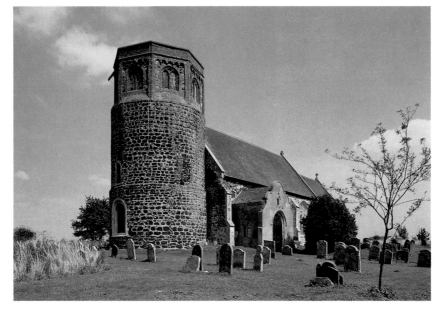

West Dereham church may be much smaller than its East counterpart but its Norman carrstone tower and Tudor brick belfry do catch the eye.

The reference books do not explain why they share the same name. East Dereham dates back to the legend of St Withburga being saved from starvation by the milk of some friendly deer, but she never wandered as far as West Dereham; nor, I imagine, did the deer. On the other hand, when the abbey at West Dereham was destroyed during the dissolution of the monasteries, it was the Dereham family who got the lands, and their tombs are much in evidence in the church. Did they name the village, or did they take their name from it, or was this one of history's more remarkable coincidences? I could find nobody in East or West Dereham who could tell me, or indeed who cared either way.

**In and Out
of the Sea Walls**

Mentioning East Dereham encourages me to emerge now from the marshlands and the fens and head for what I think of, with apologies to my friends on the other side of the Ouse, as Norfolk proper. You get a clear idea of the transition if you drive along Barroway Drove, one of the many dead straight, very narrow and generally bumpy roads that criss-cross the flatlands, to Stow Bridge. You may like to pause here to see the folding altar table which was used during the Afghanistan Campaign by the Revd James Adams, the first Army chaplain to win the Victoria Cross. Then head over the river, across the railway and the A10 beyond it, and you will find the cottages begin to look more flinty, the fields are smaller and more undulating, and there are actually woods and hedges.

Again you may like to call at Stow Bardolph church to marvel at the unnervingly lifelike wax effigy of Sarah Hare, who, it is said, used to sew on a Sunday and as punishment died from pricking her finger. Her father is there too in more orthodox marble but dressed unaccountably as a Roman emperor. Now lose no time in heading for the hills, or at least the undulations, where you will come upon two delightful villages. Shouldham was once a market town with two annual fairs and it still has its spacious green surrounded by fine old pantiled houses. Its smaller neighbour Shouldham Thorpe has plenty of trees and attractive cottages and a neat little church by the duckpond. This is the start of the unexpected Norfolk that Noël Coward never knew. We need not delve deep into the county at this stage to find it; there is plenty of little-known territory within a few miles of the holiday route around the coast.

3 That's the Way the Coast Road Goes
The Norfolk coastal area from King's Lynn to Yarmouth

If you were ever asked in a geography lesson to draw a map of
the British Isles the easiest bit was the Norfolk coast. It is that
boring-looking bulge on the backside of Britain. It looks boring on a
map because there are no broad estuaries or jagged cliffs to interrupt
the smooth arc from King's Lynn to Great Yarmouth. It can look boring
from the seat of a car, too, because the so-called coast road is almost
entirely out of sight of the coast.

The only place between Lynn and Yarmouth that can take
boats of any size is advisedly called Wells-*next*-the-Sea, because it
is a mile away from it up a narrow winding channel. The days when
great fighting ships sailed out of Blakeney and Morston and Cley are
long since gone; the sea has retreated and the harbours are clogged by
centuries of silt. Only the occasional spit of shingle jutting out into
the North Sea, where navigable rivers used to flow, recalls Norfolk's
more active maritime past.

Yet this hundred-mile stretch of coastline offers some unique
and unexpected attractions; they just take a bit of finding. There
are the obvious holiday centres, from Yarmouth at one end – very
obvious indeed – to Hunstanton at the other, with Sheringham and
Cromer midway between. And there are the vast caravan parks and
holiday camps north of Yarmouth, which have about as much Norfolk
character about them as the turkey in British Rail sandwiches.

But the Norfolk coast has much more than candy floss and
caravans. There is sailing: wherever you see a staithe marked on
the map you should find safe moorings. There are miles of empty
beaches beyond the saltmarshes, and the marshes themselves are a
birdwatcher's paradise. For walkers there is the uninterrupted coastal
path and some of the highest hills in Norfolk. They are only three
hundred feet, but enough to put Noël Coward in his place. And just

One man and his dog is a
crowd on the North
Norfolk coast. This is at
Thornham.

inland there are wooded valleys and quiet streams, stately homes and flintwalled cottages, rolling parkland and gorse-covered commons – not at all the popular vision of Norfolk as an intensely agricultural county where every acre is under cultivation and the combine harvester rules.

Admittedly there are places where the barley fields come close to the sea, but on long stretches of the North Norfolk coast there is a belt of undisturbed countryside, perhaps five or ten miles deep, where there are just meadows and woods, secluded villages and empty lanes. If you are looking for a picture-postcard Norfolk this is one place to find it. If you are looking for actual picture-postcards, you may as well start in King's Lynn.

When the first Norman Bishop of Norwich founded a priory in the far west of his diocese on the banks of the Wash he staffed it, so the story goes, with some of his more troublesome colleagues, to keep them out of his tonsure. Bishop's Lynn, later to become King's Lynn, has been pretty stand-offish about Norwich ever since. It considers itself the capital of West Norfolk, and West Norfolk regards it in much the same way. While all Norfolkmen like to 'du different' from the rest of England, West Norfolkmen like to du different from the rest of Norfolk.

This may be why Lynn was the only sizeable town in Norfolk to support the King during the Civil War – and got severely thumped as a result. It has also been thumped frequently by the sea, and in more recent years, on a much larger scale, by the developers. As a result, between the medieval riverside area and the pedestrianised town centre there is an uninspiring vista of service roads, warehouses and car parks. The trick is to avert your eyes from these areas, and close them altogether if you are arriving by train, because the expanse of rusting sidings left derelict since the Beeching area is the final gambit by British Rail to depress new arrivals. If you approach the town centre by road try to ignore the mundane modern buildings and concentrate on the Greyfriars Tower, part of a Franciscan friary which was allowed to remain standing after the Dissolution only because it was useful as a navigation point for ships coming up the river. May the developers show it equal respect.

There are two areas of Lynn which have survived fairly unscathed, based on the two market places – the vast Tuesday Market with its old Corn Exchange and its coaching inns, and the more modest Saturday Market, little more than a parking area opposite the ancient Guildhall. One might have thought that Saturday was a more important trading day than Tuesday, but this is West Norfolk, where they du different. The Tuesday Market is also the site of the Lynn Mart, the first major event of the year in the showmen's calendar. When they set up their roundabouts they may not appreciate that this was where they were invented.

far left The Greyfriars Tower, which survived the Dissolution because it was a useful navigation guide for mariners.
left The ornate Corn Exhange in the Tuesday Market, which survives through the benevolence of the District Council.

In 1885 a young engineer called Frederick Savage began by producing a mechanical winnowing machine and finished up with the first steam-powered roundabout. They made him Mayor, though probably because of the winnowing machine rather than the roundabout. Even so, it would be nice to think that instead of the routine mayoral procession Mayor Savage and his aldermen, in full regalia, took a whirl on the wooden horses . . .

If you take the wrong turning out of the Tuesday Market you can finish up in the shopping precinct, where the name of the Vancouver Centre is the only reminder that you are in a historic seaport and not South Croydon; or you could get lost in the wasteland behind it, among the back entrances to Bejam and Sainsbury's. Aim instead for the Globe Inn, once a notable coaching inn, now an outpost of the Berni empire. Beyond it are the old merchants' houses backing down to the river, and looming behind one of them is a five-storey Tudor tower where the servants kept watch for returning ships. There is also St George's Guildhall, where there must have been some complacent smiles during the hubbub over the Rose Theatre site in London because Shakespeare's touring company played in the Guildhall, and even the most cautious experts concede that the Bard was there too. So while the nation's most distinguished Thespians were in a lather about a hole in the ground in London, King's Lynn was still using an actual building where Will and his friends trod the boards. They are trodden today by more esoteric performers in the annual Lynn Festival.

In 1988 the Customs and Excise moved out of the splendid Custom House on Purfleet Quay and in spite of strong local protests it was put up for sale. The Custom house was not Custom-built; a

That's the Way the Coast Road Goes

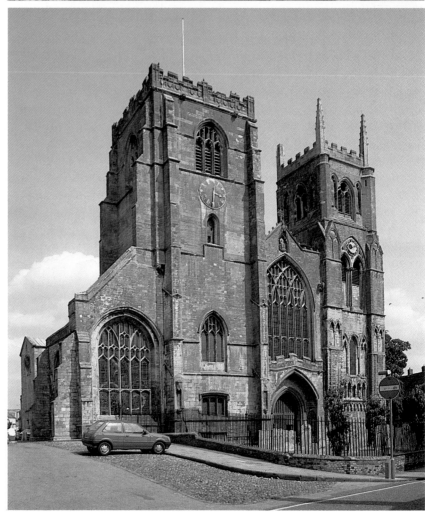

Two more King's Lynn survivors: the Custom House on Purfleet Quay, used as such for 300 years, now sold to a development company...

... and St Margaret's church, with its 'tide clock' on the far tower, and marks on the porch to show how high the tide actually came.

Lynn merchant and architect called Henry Bell, who also built the Duke's Head Hotel in the Tuesday Market, designed it as a merchants' exchange. It was taken over by the Excisemen early in the eighteenth century and they occupied it for the next 270 years. The King's Lynn Preservation Trust put in a gallant bid when it was put out to tender but it was bought by Melton Developments, who also own another historic piece of Norfolk, Melton Constable Hall. The Hall has been converted into a multi-million-pound arts and culture centre, but as I write the future of the Custom House is not known. It is a bit small to become another multi-million-pound centre; maybe it will be just the booking office for Melton Constable.

Charles II is perched on the Custom House and his father is not far away on the nearly-as-splendid Bank House. Both of them had grandstand views for the filming of *Revolution*, which may have slumped at the box office but did very nicely for the residents of riverside King's Lynn. The clock was put back a couple of centuries; cars were cleared from drives, aerials were removed from roofs, lawnmowers were silenced, bicycles hidden, transistor radios suppressed. It was all of course at a price. The film crew even found a way of disguising the massive grain silo that looms by the river, while the inlet known as the Purfleet, silted up for years, was dredged so that three-masters could sail up it. The producers lost millions, and the locals wept all the way to the bank.

Further up the quayside, well back from the present riverbank, is Thoresby College, which has a mark in the courtyard where the original quay wall used to be. Thanks to centuries of silt and a fair amount of rubbish dumped by the townsfolk the Ouse now takes quite a different course from medieval times. However the floodmarks on the porch of St Margaret's church, even further from the river than the College, show how it can come back again. Small wonder that instead of a clock on its tower St Margaret's has a high tide indicator, inscribed around its face 'Edith Gihnnyl' – or if you read it the other way, as I eventually did, Lynn High Tide.

St Margaret's has other unusual features: the two largest brasses in Britain, for instance, and a sanctuary handle on the west door which had only to be touched by a fugitive to gain the church's protection. And just across the road behind the chequerboard flint and stone frontage of the Guildhall are more goodies, including King John's Cup, King John's Sword and King John's Charter, of which only the charter is actually his. The cup was not salvaged from the Wash but dates from a hundred years later, and the sword has a sixteenth-century handle and a seventeenth-century blade. In spite of all this fascination with King John it was not he who gave Lynn its royal status. That came during the Reformation, when the existing bishops went out of favour. The Town Clerk must have got very fed up with crossing out 'Episcopi' on all the notepaper and putting 'Regis' instead.

The Norfolk coastal area from King's Lynn to Yarmouth

Two kings in King's Lynn: Charles II on the Custom House. . .

. . . and James I on nearby Bank House, both featured in the filming of *Revolution*. They look even less impressed than the film-going public.

61

That's the Way the Coast Road Goes

If all this royal memorabilia, genuine or otherwise, has given you a taste for peering into glass cases you should not leave the environs of Lynn without paying a call, in more than one sense, at the Butterfly Inn, alongside the terrifying roundabout where all the main roads in West Norfolk converge. Ladies, I am afraid, are excluded because these exhibits are in the gentlemen's convenience. Instead of being confronted by unsavoury graffiti it is possible to read the news of the day; copies of the quality newspapers are encased in glass frames above the stalls.

To get the full benefit of these wallsheets one has to be rather shortsighted and a very fast reader. It can also be exasperating if the story is continued on page two. Nonetheless this is an innovation which I have not observed elsewhere. Rural Norfolk is not renowned for sophisticated sanitation but here at least it leads the way.

For an attraction of more general appeal there is always Castle Rising on the other side of Lynn. It has one of the best preserved castles in East Anglia, dating from William the Conqueror's brother-in-law, Bishop Odo. Odo's loyalty was only so-so, and William gave Castle Rising to the royal butler, a Mr d'Albini, who also acquired the castle at Old Buckenham. These seem rather extravagant perks for a butler compared with the odd bottle of port, but the title was more illustrious in those days. Castle Rising has changed hands a number of times since, but the present owners, the Howard family, are distant descendants of the fortunate Mr d'Albini.

It was a Howard who built the Jacobean almshouses in the village which are still in use. The ladies go to church on Sundays wearing long red cloaks and pointed black hats, giving a rather Welsh flavour to this very Norfolk village. It was once a major port, but the sea has now receded for two or three miles. While the water at Rising was falling, at King's Lynn it was rising. Hence the little verse which no self-respecting book on East Anglia can bear to be without:

> *Rising was a seaport when Lynn was but a marsh,*
> *Now Lynn it is a seaport town and Rising fares the worse.*

May I add a second verse which future books are welcome to copy:

> *But much of Lynn is modernised, a place for the go-getter,*
> *So maybe in the long run Castle Rising's fared the better . . .*

When you rejoin the coast road from Castle Rising make the most of the broad carriageway; it does not last for long. While it does you may flash past the crossroads at Babingley where a village sign depicts a beaver in a bishop's mitre, grasping a bishop's crook. St Felix sailed up the Babingley River after crossing from Burgundy to bring Christianity to East Anglia. His boat got into difficulties and he was saved from drowning, so it is said, by a colony of beavers. In gratitude he made the head beaver a bishop. The river is now a mere trickle and the village just a handful of cottages and a disused tin church, but the ecclesiastical rodent lives on.

You may also miss the turn to Wolferton, much to the chagrin of the proprietor of Wolferton station museum, who used to complain bitterly about his direction signs being banned on the Sandringham Royal Estate. At one stage he threatened to close if the ban was not lifted. If you do spot a sign then his ploy will have succeeded.

I hope it has, because I find Wolferton station just as fascinating as Sandringham itself, and indeed one gets a much more intimate slant on the earlier royals from the station waiting rooms than from the House itself. Not that they ever had to wait for a train; woe betide the stationmaster if they did. But Prince Edward, the future King Edward VII, and his wife Princess Alexandra often met their guests at the station and entertained them while the luggage was sent on ahead.

The Norfolk coastal area from King's Lynn to Yarmouth

Wolferton's sign depicts the Norse wolf Fenrir – 'when he gaped one jaw touched earth and the other heaven' – but the connection is obscure.

Wolferton station, once frequented by the Royal Family, is now royal-less and nearly rail-less, and has no connections with British Rail at all.

The menfolk played cards in the Prince's oak-panelled snug, took a glass or two of wine, and if it had been a long journey availed themselves of his private facilities, which must be the only railway toilet with royal blue and gold decorations. Meanwhile across the passage the ladies took tea with the Princess in her sitting-room, upholstered in her favourite shade of blue. If it was fine they might stroll in the station garden, still concealed from public gaze. All the station windows are opaque to ensure privacy, except the one looking on to the garden.

That's the Way the Coast Road Goes

Five generations of British royalty and most of the crowned heads of Europe used Wolferton Station. So did Rasputin, but only briefly. The sinister Russian monk turned up on a train from London demanding to see the King. Discreetly but firmly he was put on the next train back. When the line was closed in 1966 British Rail wanted to demolish the station and build houses instead, but happily the application failed and it was bought by an enthusiast who restored it to something of its former glory. But if you have travelled far, be warned: Prince Edward's blue and gold loo is no longer in use.

I must loyally mention Sandringham itself, though one guidebook is honest enough to describe the house as 'very ugly, like a huge and grandiose Victorian seaside hotel'. It was largely the creation of Prince Edward, who spent much of his time there. He made a rather better job of the estate, which started off, according to one of his contemporaries, as 'windswept, barren, sandy moorland, the wildest and most out-of-the-way place imaginable'. It is now a highly efficient estate with large areas of attractive woodland and some of the best maintained villages in Norfolk – Anmer, West Newton and Sandringham itself. The Prince's choice of cattle breeds showed a nice sense of diplomacy; his Shorthorns represented the leading English breed, he brought Highland cattle from Scotland, and his Dexter-Kerries came from Ireland. Wales of course was already represented in his title.

It was a Norfolk winter at Sandringham which helped to alter the royal succession. A few days before Prince Edward's fiftieth birthday Sandringham House was badly damaged by fire. He insisted the celebrations should go ahead, under a temporary roof of tarpaulins, but it is not wise to take such liberties with the Norfolk climate in November. Prince Albert Victor, his heir, contracted a chill which turned to influenza and proved fatal. So in due course it was the younger brother George who succeeded to the throne.

Nevertheless Sandringham is still popular with the royals, even in winter. Prince Philip enjoys his shooting, the Queen enjoys her riding, the Queen Mother seems to enjoy just about everything. The locals have grown used to them and are not the sort to intrude; nor are they easily overawed. The Queen Mother has long been a member of Sandringham Women's Institute, and I suspect that if she entered a pot of jam for the monthly competition, there is no certainty it would even be placed.

Back on the coast make all speed, which won't be much, through the three 'hams', Dersingham, Snettisham and Heacham. I first visited these villages just after the 1953 floods, when the sand dunes and beaches were a scene of appalling desolation. Bungalows, beach huts and caravans had been smashed up and scattered all along the coast. The authorities did not take advantage of this disaster to plan a more elegant beach area, but merely allowed the wreckage to be replaced with more bungalows, more beach huts and many, many more caravans.

You may well be able to avoid Dersingham altogether, as a bypass round the village has been approved. There were great objections from the conservationists because the new road crossed Dersingham Bog, home of a rare moth. It is so rare that nobody has actually seen it for years. The planners looked at the traffic pouring through the village and they looked in vain for the moth. They decided, understandably, to let the new road go ahead. But if you get a lot of messy blobs on your windscreen, they could have been wrong.

While Dersingham claims an elusive moth, Snettisham claims an elusive ghost. Locals tell the tale of Mrs Goodeve, a lady from London who in 1893 received instructions from the spirits to visit Snettisham, which she had never heard of before, and wait at midnight by the tomb of Robert Cobbe in the parish church. She would receive a message from a Mr Henry Barnard, also deceased, for his daughter. The game Mrs Goodeve did as instructed and emerged from the church 'newly calm and distant – as if she had been witness to something beyond normal understanding'.

Unfortunately we shall never know what it was. She had been sworn to secrecy by her ghostly messenger and Henry Barnard's daughter was not talking either. But whatever it was, her mission must have been successful. Nobody has seen a ghost there since.

If a message came from Heacham's most famous ex-resident it would probably be a spectral smoke-signal. In 1614 the Red Indian princess Pocahontas married an early colonist, John Rolfe, whose family owned most of Heacham. He was the first successful planter of tobacco, and thus has much to answer for, but it seemed a good idea at the time and he returned home in triumph with his bride. Pocahontas lived for a time at Heacham Hall as the squire's lady, and the villagers must have wondered whether to touch their forelock or raise a hand and cry 'How!' She died of consumption three years later and her husband returned to America, but there are still Rolfes in Heacham and a monument to Pocahontas, elegantly dressed as an English lady with high hat and fan.

Further up the coast road you will come to the Heacham lavender beds, in this case not a euphemism for a sewage works but the real thing, a mass-production lavender farm where the flowers are not sold by little old ladies in shawls but are distilled into oil for perfumes and soaps. And then comes Hunstanton, which I am glad to say is the end of the road for many holidaymakers, so the traffic thins out before it reaches my favourite part of the North Norfolk coast that lies beyond.

Hunstanton might have followed the example of Southwold and remained an unspoilt Victorian watering-place, but it plumped for a more up-to-date image and seems to have fallen somewhere between the two. Nobody however can complain about its fine sands and its

The Norfolk coastal area from King's Lynn to Yarmouth

curious cliffs. Cliffs in Norfolk are a curiosity in themselves, but these look like slices of layer cake, with strips of red and white chalk and brown carrstone. Odder still, they face west, the only holiday resort in Norfolk to do so.

Incongruous colours: Heacham's lavender beds are an unexpected splash of blue in the greens and golds of the Norfolk landscape. . .

. . . and Hunstanton's striped cliffs have layers of red and white chalk in the brown carrstone.

Although most of Hunstanton looks less than a century old it is the home of the Lestranges, one of the most ancient Norfolk families, who have lived there for over eight hundred years; their family seat still has one wing and the moat intact. Sir Hamon Lestrange commanded the Royalist forces defending King's Lynn. When he lost it Roger Lestrange tried to win it back. When that failed he took to writing pamphlets of such inaccurate virulence that he was nicknamed Lying Strange Roger. The family has taken a more discreet approach to politics ever since.

Beyond Hunstanton the coast road turns the corner of Norfolk and heads eastward past the deserted saltmarshes and beaches that still evade the main holiday onslaught. I fear they will not evade it much longer. I can only emphasise what they lack, so that fainthearts will be discouraged and seekers after bright lights and bingo will seek them elsewhere.

There are very few car parks for a start, and car parks are essential because the most delightful stretches of beach are only accessible on foot. You need to carry food and drink with you, because there are very few pizza houses or bars among the dunes. (I hope you will take the cartons and bottles away again, but even in the remotest corners these days it is difficult to escape them.) There are also no deckchairs for hire, no beach huts, no ice cream stalls. It is just you, and the sand, and the sea.

The Icknield Way, the chalk ridge which acted as a prehistoric motorway for tribes venturing into the forests and fens of East Anglia, terminates along this coast at Holme-next-the-Sea. Presumably the

67

That's the Way the Coast Road Goes

first settlers had never seen the sea before and called this Holme because there was no place like it. Peddars Way also ends here, but this was much more purpose-built and has all the hallmarks of a Roman road as it cuts straight across West Norfolk. The theory is that the Romans built it after their unfortunate experience with Boadicea to ensure easier access for their troops, and they ran a ferry service across the Wash from Holme to Lincolnshire. They built a signal station a couple of miles away at Thornham to send warnings to the Lincolnshire Legion if the Iceni got too restive, and at Brancaster they had a fair-sized fort called Branodonum to fend off any invasion from the sea.

So there was quite a bit of action along this coast in Roman times, but there is no indication of it today, except that one of the roads in Brancaster is called Branodonum Way. Its most famous listed building is not the fort but a yellow AA box, which has become even scarcer. The main occupations are sailing, strolling and supping, and if you sup at the Lifeboat Inn at Thornham you can also try tossing the penny. There is a venerable bench with a hole in it which looks like an inadequate commode, and the idea is to toss thirteen pennies into the hole – the pre-decimal sort, specially preserved for the purpose. Only one player in the last forty years has tossed them all in without a miss; a gallon of whisky awaits the next.

Scavenging gulls have the shore to themselves near Thornham. . .

If you are more used to hitting golf balls than tossing pennies then Brancaster offers one of Norfolk's more adventurous courses. The Royal West Norfolk lies between the beach and the marshes, and the clubhouse is the only building on the seashore for miles. The marshes are flooded several times a year, cutting off both the clubhouse and the course at high tide. On such occasions the members take pride in completing a round between tides. Even when a spring tide flooded the eighth and ninth holes recently, some intrepid players rose at dawn, breakfasted in the clubhouse while the waters encircled them, then timed their round to play those two holes during the brief period they were above water. I am not a golfer myself – why spoil a good walk? – but I have to admire their dedication.

Brancaster and its staithe are over-run with hearty sailing folk as well as dedicated golfers in the summer, but there is a vast stretch of saltmarsh and sand between Holme and Titchwell with hardly a yachting cap in sight (though Holme has a golf course as well). There is an RSPB reserve to occupy the 'twitchers', so most of the beach is available for the likes of me, miles and miles of it. There is enough sand for everyone even at high tide, and at low tide the sea is almost out of sight. I have stood on the beach at Titchwell on a summer morning, with the sands and the sea and the marshes stretching away to the horizon, and I have not seen another soul, just the gulls and the oystercatchers and the occasional flash of a kingfisher over the marshes. It will serve me right if next time I see you there too . . .

. . . and on the sands at Brancaster there are just two distant figures and a dog to watch the solitary wind-surfer sail by.

The Burnhams on the other hand are tourist country, mainly because of Burnham Thorpe, birthplace of Lord Nelson. I became a little disillusioned with The Hero (as he is named by several Norfolk pubs) when I found he never actually composed that famous signal, 'England expects . . . ' He wanted it to read, 'Nelson confides . . . ' It was Hardy who boldly suggested that 'England' might be a little less immodest, and it was a signals officer who pointed out that there was no stock signal flag for 'confides', and 'expects' would be a lot quicker. Happily it still worked.

Nelson was not much of a prophet in his own country in his early days. When he went shooting in Norfolk as a young man he disconcerted the locals by carrying his gun at full cock and shooting from the hip, Clint Eastwood style. They considered his most remarkable achievement was not winning all those naval battles but actually hitting a partridge from this angle.

69

That's the Way the Coast Road Goes

Since then, however, they have discovered his tourist potential and Nelson enthusiasts have a real ball at Burnham Thorpe. They can drink at the Lord Nelson, look round the Nelson Memorial Hall and shop at the Trafalgar Stores. The church seems as much a museum as a place of worship: Nelson's battle flags are round the walls, his bust is in the chancel, his name is on the kneelers, pieces of oak from the *Victory* are in the lectern. There is even a picture of his medicine chest. I am afraid I find it slightly ludicrous that a parish church should devote such a large proportion of its space to one man, however illustrious. I think of it as the Ho(ho)ratio.

By sad contrast the church at Cockthorpe, ten miles away, became so dilapidated it had to be rescued by the Norfolk Churches Trust, yet in terms of admiral population Cockthorpe knocks Burnham Thorpe – forgive me – into a cocked hat. It produced two of them, both with distinguished careers and a fine record for thumping our enemies. Sir John Narborough subdued the Tripoli pirates who harassed our merchant ships in the Mediterranean during the 1680s, and Sir Cloudesley Shovell dealt with the Dutch until England got a Dutch king, then he dealt with the French instead. They are hardly remembered in Cockthorpe today. Narborough does have another village in Norfolk which bears his name, but you would have to dig deep to find a Shovell.

Burnham Market is the most attractive of the Burnhams, but its pleasant green is now surrounded by antique shops, art galleries and bijou cottages. Burnham Overy Staithe is another sailing centre, and Burnham Deepdale is full of people on their way to the other Burnhams. The quietest is Burnham Norton, tucked away on one side of the coast road while its church is a mile away on the other, set on a hill overlooking the saltmarshes and the sea, a splendid vantage point for enjoying this broad expanse of coastline. It has one of the finest wineglass pulpits in the country, presented as a penance by a man who was caught stealing oysters from the marshes. It is so fragile after five hundred years that a reserve pulpit, only three hundred years old, is used instead.

A lonely windmill presiding over an empty landscape. It could be anywhere on the North Norfolk coast; this happens to be Burnham Overy Staithe. . .

If you are into stately homes then Holkham Hall is as stately as they come. This was where, according to local legend, the famous Coke of Norfolk saw two rabbits fighting over a blade of grass, such was the poorness of the soil, and it inspired him to turn thousands of acres of barren heathland into fertile farming country, while preserving a fair chunk of it for his personal enjoyment as a garden and deer park. Today the estate produces annually enough wheat to bake 712,000 loaves, more than a million pounds of beet sugar, sixty thousand pounds of lamb and enough malting barley to brew five million pints of beer. Even the park is productive these days: five thousand pounds of venison and 150 live hinds are sold each year. It must be the prettiest production line in the country.

It was in this park a couple of centuries ago that Coke started the Holkham sheepshearings, great gatherings of the gentry at which the socialising was as important as the sheep. This was the foundation for all the agricultural shows which now take place all over the country. After a long gap the Holkham country fairs have now been resumed, and although these days they feature as many skydivers as sheep, most of the traditional rural activities are still represented – particularly the socialising.

Thomas Coke was not only a remarkable farmer, he was a liberal in every sense. His grandfather warned him as a lad, 'Never trust a Tory,' and he duly became a Whig MP. He also backed the American colonists against George III, sympathised openly with the French Revolution, and looked after his tenants so well that Holkham was one of the few places in Norfolk which had no need for a poorhouse.

It is recorded that at the annual tenants' dinner the chief tenant rose, mug in hand, and proposed a notable toast: 'Here's to Mister Cewk and his tenants. And if they dew as he dew they 'ont dew as they dew dew!' Which means, I think, 'If they farm the way he shows them they'll do better than they do now.' And so they did.

The Cokes became Earls of Leicester, so they no longer had to keep telling people how to pronounce their name (the chief tenant got it just about right). It also avoided confusion in later years with another Cook family in Norfolk, who achieved fame and a useful fortune by inventing the package tour. The present Thomas Cook lives twenty miles from Holkham, rather more modestly, in another great park at Guist, which has its own pronunciation problem. It rhymes with cut-priced.

Wells-next-the-Sea is also Wells-next-to-Holkham, just outside the estate. It is still a fishing port and they still boil whelks not far from the quayside, but the quayside itself is now lined with cafés and souvenir shops. Its real charm lies in the narrow lanes and alleys between the quay and the Buttlands, where pleasant old houses surround the green on which archers used to practise. Wells is a busy place in the summer but in the winter it seems almost deserted, because a large number of its cottages, some say as many as a third, are holiday homes. So are many of the former shops in the High Street. This is the 'incomer' problem at its most acute. On the

The Norfolk coastal area from King's Lynn to Yarmouth

That's the Way the Coast Road Goes

other hand, with no local industry to speak of, would anyone else live there permanently? Not everyone wants to be a whelk fisherman . . .

Between Wells and Sheringham there is a succession of delightful little villages, which unfortunately have the main coast road passing right through the hearts of them. Stiffkey, Morston, Cley, Salthouse, Weybourne; in the summer months you wander in them at your peril. Cley in particular, with the road narrowing and bending sharply through the village, offers little chance to stand and stare at the famous windmill which features on so many book covers and postcards, but you can escape on to the marshes and view it from there. At Morston you can escape more dramatically by taking a boat from the staithe, if the tide is right, and going out to see the seals off Blakeney Point. And at Weybourne you can exchange one kind of traffic for another by visiting the Muckleburgh collection of military vehicles, based in an old Army camp.

. . . and here's another, guarding the marshes instead of the fields. This is Cley Mill, best known of all – no Norfolk book is complete without it.

My own favourite escape route along this stretch is up on to the common behind Salthouse. There is a birdwatching centre here too, but if you do not take birdwatching too seriously you can drive on to the common and park among the gorse bushes, overlooking the sea. Below you are the pantiled roofs of the village and the duckpond by the main road where a quite phenomenal number and assortment of ducks gather to gorge themselves on the bread and biscuits that rain down upon them. Ahead of you are the saltmarshes and the distant line of breakers. And over it all is this vast Norfolk sky . . .

Not many people know about the common but everybody seems to know about Blakeney. It is on a loop off the main road so it escapes the through traffic, but it gets plenty of everything else. The narrow lane runs down to the quayside, along it, and back up to the main road again. Shops and cottages open straight on to it, there is no pavement, and a great many people. I sometimes wonder why it is not one-way, but I suppose this would merely speed up the traffic and knock down more people.

You are safe once you are down on the quay. Blakeney was once a major seaport but the tide went out several centuries ago and never came back. It left behind a winding channel just deep enough for small sailing craft at high tide, set in a typical North Norfolk panorama of saltmarshes, water meadows, and reed-filled pools, ideal for wildlife and walkers. There is also a great deal of mud.

Beware of shortcuts. I tried it once, where I could see footprints emerging from the mud. I took two steps and sank up to my knees – and I have been wondering about those footprints ever since. It could have been a variation on the Norfolk technique for testing the depth of a flooded road. You back your car a little way into the water, then drive out and wait round the corner. The next motorist to arrive will be reassured by the emerging tracks and drive in. If he gets through, so can you. If not . . . Perhaps I had fallen for it again.

For more peace and quiet, and less mud, turn inland off that clogged-up coast road. Just a mile or two away you will find deserted lanes, peaceful village greens, pleasant pubs – and hardly a tripper in sight. There are a few discreet tourist operations; Langham has a glass factory in converted farm buildings, and Cockthorpe, after slumbering for centuries since the last admiral left, now has a toy museum. But in the main these peaceful communities so close to the main holiday route – Warham and Wighton, Saxlingham and Field Dalling, Wiveton and Glandford, Binham and Bale – do not expect to spy strangers from one day to the next. Yet they have marvellous churches, from Warham St Mary with its towering three-decker pulpit, far too big for the church, to Binham Abbey, a majestic ruin of which the nave is used as a parish church – and like so many Norfolk churches, is far too big for the village.

I have spent many hours puttering around this delightful corner of North Norfolk, and there is always something fresh to discover. What I have yet to find, I am rather glad to say, is a teashop or a café. For that you must visit Holt, which in my view competes with Hingham as the most attractive little market town in Norfolk.

Most of the original town was burned down nearly three hundred years ago, but the people who rebuilt it did an excellent job and it has not changed too much since. In spite of a new bypass it still gets plenty of traffic but there are enough back lanes and alleys to wander in safety. My wife assures me it has some excellent dress shops, and judging by the bills I hope she is right. It is also very strong on antique shops, the better kind of craft shop, traditional butchers and grocers, cheeses – and bells.

The church porch advertises a special offer: 'Let everyone know your Granny is a hundred . . . It's your golden wedding . . . Your son/daughter is 18 . . . Get us to ring out the glad news: 1260 changes = 45 minutes = £20!' Thanks to this enterprising offer and other activities the church now has eight bells instead of six, the last two in memory of a renowned local ringer called Billy West, who rang his first peal in 1911 for what he called the Coronairshun, and was still ringing when they filmed *The Go-Between* in this area in the 1970s.

The Norfolk coastal area from King's Lynn to Yarmouth

That's the Way the Coast Road Goes

'That were a quare dew, boy,' he once recalled. 'There were the fillum ringers hauling away with their ropes tied to a beam, and we wus ringing the bells fifteen miles away.'

Holt was rebuilt by the Georgians and has changed little since, except for the double yellow lines; but you need to rise very early to catch it like this.

He was a great raconteur, and the story I like best was his initiation into a new team of ringers at Wiveton. All went well until the captain gave the instruction to change the peal: 'Go Dick!' 'Now if he'd said Kings or Queens or anything like that, all well and good,' said Billy, 'but Dick were a new one on me and I got it all wrong. So they stop and he say, "Billy," he say, "you want to follow the treble"; and that turns out the treble ringer was called Dick, and thass how they knew how to change: "Go Dick." They'd never been taught, y'see. Well, I said, if thass all yew can ring I hent coming up here no more. So we set about them and I reckon we got six good ringers at the finish.'

I never met Billy West. I only heard him talking on tape after his death. But each time I hear the bells pealing at Holt I can picture him telling these stories and they remind me of the simple inscription on one new bell: 'Praise God and Remember Billy West.'

The other name they remember at Holt is Sir John Gresham, who founded a grammar school there in 1555 which is now a public school administered by the Fishmongers Company. One of its Old Boys was Lord Reith, whose bust in Broadcasting House I used to pass each morning on the way to the studio. If the programme had not been a good one I always avoided his eye on the way back.

The village of Gresham, where Sir John's forebears lived, has been much developed of late and its only fragment of the distant past, Gresham Castle, was long ago reduced to its foundations. Baconsthorpe offers a much more splendid ruin, the extensive remains of a fifteenth-century fortified manor house and two gatehouses, one of which was still occupied until earlier this century. But this is a much-advertised tourist attraction. I prefer to pay my respects to another building in Baconsthorpe, the old Rectory, not only because it looks good but the man who built it was called the Revd Zurishaddai Girdlestone, and a name like that is worth remembering.

A village which does not appear in the holiday brochures, nor even on some maps, is nearby Metton, but it may acquire a few visitors now it is on the Weaver's Way. When I saw the signpost in the village I thought Weaver's Way must have as significant a history as the Peddars Way or even the Icknield Way. I pictured Flemish weavers from medieval Norwich, toiling up this path to the seaside for their annual vacation. Actually it is a modern creation for the benefit of tourists, a scenic path which crosses Broadland and takes in Blickling Hall as its main attraction. Part of it runs along the route of a disused railway, which should confuse future historians even more.

What is genuinely ancient about Metton is its church, which was built so close to the wall of the farm next door that an archway was made under the tower so processions could pass right round it.

In recent years a sad notice appeared on the church door. 'Will you of your charity remember in your prayers April Fabb, who disappeared from this parish in April 1969, of whom nothing has since been heard. Please remember also the parents and relatives who still wait and hope.' Twenty years after that teenager's disappearance the police held a news conference in the hope of stirring memories and uncovering new information. The operation proved fruitless. April is still missing, and the notice is still on the door.

That's the Way the Coast Road Goes

The Weaver's Way takes us back to the coast and its two holiday towns, Sheringham and Cromer. Pretty Corner, in the wooded hills behind Sheringham, lives up to its name, and Sheringham itself has always been our favourite seaside resort in Norfolk, ever since we took our firstborn there for his first encounter with the sea. I have to say he hated it. He hated the pebbles at high tide because they were too hard, and he hated the sand at low tide because it was too soft. He also hated the Norfolk breeze – some might call it a gale – that often comes in off the sea. He is in his thirties now and when we went back recently he wore gumboots, an anorak and three sweaters, his standard Sheringham wear. 'Nothing has changed,' he said.

But we used to enjoy the stroll along the narrow promenade to the lifeboat station, where the lifeboat has to be revolved on a turntable to point towards the sea. We used to play on the Krazy Golf course, and visit the model railway exhibition and peer through the telescope on the front at absolutely nothing. And back on the beach we enjoyed a pot of tea on a battered tin tray from the seafront café, wrapped up in our woollies and raincoats and protected by a couple of Mr Dumble's windbreaks.

Mr Dumble, undisputed ruler of Sheringham beach for so many years – woe betide you if you brought your own deckchair – has long since departed, though his windbreaks live on. The café, when I last saw it, was boarded up and derelict, the model railway exhibition was closed, the Krazy Golf course was flanked by an adventure playground. Only the telescope remained the same: I could still see absolutely nothing. There are many more facilities for holidaymakers now and in the summer the streets are as packed as Cromer next door. There is no way of recapturing the unsophisticated and idyllic holidays of the fifties.

Even so, there is still a Norfolk flavour about Sheringham, with its narrow main street running straight down to the sea, its fishing boats drawn up on the shingle, its narrow alleys and jumble of flintstone cottages. Cromer was a fishing village too, as its famous crabs still testify, but most of the town was custom-built as a holiday resort in the nineteenth century, and you will find similar towns all round the English coast. But I must say I bridled as much as any crab-boat fisherman when a young lady in the cast of the pier concert party commented on television that Cromer was 'the pits – the end of the world!' There's no accounting for these furriners.

The nearby villages have geared themselves to the holiday trade, with a helping hand if necessary from the National Trust. Felbrigg Hall is the star attraction, left to the Trust by the distinguished Norfolk writer R.W. Ketton-Cremer complete with a vast park with a church in it. But if you prefer stately horses to stately homes there is the Shire Horse Centre at West Runton, which unexpectedly features a pit pony called Larry. He qualifies, I suppose, because he too pulled a cart for

Seaside delights at Sheringham and Cromer: *top left*, a corner of The National Trust's Sheringham Park; *above* sunset over Sheringham beach; *left* the Sheringham lifeboat being launched from its turntable; and *below* Cromer Pier Pavilion and the lifeboat house beyond.

77

a living. He worked underground for fourteen years, in the company of other stallions and geldings. Then he came to the sunshine and sea air of West Runton, and met his first mare – in fact, a whole stable full. Every year he fathers two or three foals and at the age of twenty-two showed no signs of flagging. Happy as Larry? Every day is Christmas . . .

Some villages choose tourism, others have tourism thrust upon them. That is what happened to Overstrand and Sidestrand, which were just peaceful seaside hamlets until a journalist called Clement Scott discovered them in 1883, extolled their delights in the *Daily Telegraph*, wrote poems about them, and even invented a new catchy name for the area. Before you could say Poppyland the visitors poured in.

Those who could afford it built handsome country houses, those who couldn't lodged with the locals. Even the local bricklayer and roadmender were offering 'apartments with good sea view'. The railway company launched the Poppy Line from Cromer to Mundesley, new hotels were built, new shops were opened. The Metropolitan Drinking Fountain and Cattle Trough Association installed a trough at Overstrand and named it in Scott's honour.

Those heady days have long since gone, and so has a considerable chunk of Poppyland, including Sizeland Church and its graveyard, all washed away by the steady inroads of the sea. Most of the hotels closed during the last war and never reopened, the Poppy Line disappeared under the Beeching axe, and as the final blow the bungalow builders moved in. There was an attempt to revive the magic name in 1974 when new local authorities were created and someone suggested a Poppyland District Council. The magic no longer worked; it was called North Norfolk District Council instead.

But there are still reminders. A number of the side lanes off the new coast road come to an abrupt end on the cliff edge and you can

The Norfolk coastal area from King's Lynn to Yarmouth

At the turn of the century North Norfolk was known as Poppyland, and in spite of intensive farming and chemicals there are still quite a few around. These are at Keswick, near Norwich.

Some of Poppyland has disappeared into the sea, leaving roads leading to nowhere, like this one on the cliffs at Trimingham.

look down on the rubble-covered beach and see traces of the cottages that used to stand level with you. And in the fields on the clifftop, in spite of all the chemical sprays, the poppies still survive.

I find this a depressing stretch of coastline, though the residents obviously like it. At the end of it the expanding resort of Mundesley does nothing to cheer me up, but it must cheer others or it would not be expanding. I would turn inland from Trimingham (where the three-hundred-foot cliffs are reputed to be the highest point in Norfolk) and head for Gimingham and Trunch. The names are irresistible.

'Gimingham, Trimingham, Knapton and Trunch, Northrepps and Southrepps hang all in a bunch.' The old Norfolk chant is now out of date. There are now eleven parishes in the bunch, looked after by the Trunch team ministry, and no team could be blessed with a more striking set of churches in which to minister.

The only one lacking in character, predictably, is Mundesley, which was in ruins for over a century and one Rector used part of it to stable his horses. 'Walking into this church now,' says the church guidebook a little hopefully, 'the first feeling is of admiration.' Certainly it looks sprucer now, and the horses have gone.

Then you visit Trunch church and the feeling is not just of admiration but amazement, and at Knapton you can only marvel. The six-legged canopy over the font at Trunch is a quite astonishing structure; the double hammerbeam roof at Knapton, with about 150 assorted archangels, prophets, apostles and saints, all poised in mid-air as if about to take flight, is considered the finest in Norfolk. A rector called John Smith had it erected in 1503; if he wanted to immortalise an otherwise unmemorable name, he did it in style. If you can take your eyes off the roof you will find that this font cover too is unusual. It is inscribed with a Greek palindrome: ΝΙΘΟΝ ΑΝΟΜΗΜΑ ΜΗ ΜΟΝΑΝ ΟΘΙΝ, meaning, 'Wash my sins and not my face only.' The Greeks not only had a word for it, they had it backwards too.

Sir John Betjeman said of Norfolk's churches: 'Some are miracles of soaring lightness with wooden angels in their high-up roofs; some have painted screens, or Georgian box pews, or medieval carved bench ends, or ancient stained glass. Each is different from its neighbour, even if it is less than a mile off or in the same churchyard'. And so it is in this little group. Antingham does indeed have two churches in its churchyard. One is in ruins, the other has a brass to Richard Calthorpe, early member of a famous Norfolk family as old as the Lestranges, with a plate below it showing nineteen of his children; no wonder the line survived.

Southrepps has a splendid assortment of medieval corbels. Swafield has a crucifix found in pieces on a beach, presumably from a church submerged by the sea. Trimingham has buttresses not only outside the tower but inside the nave, to withstand the gales on this

The astonishing double hammerbeam roof in Knapton church, decorated with about 150 assorted angels, prophets, apostles and saints, all poised for take-off.

exposed coast. Bradfield has a medieval wall painting of Christ on a rainbow, Gimingham has a curious little room over the porch, Paston has so many monuments to the letterwriting Paston family they don't leave much room for anything else. The 400-year-old thatched barn next to the church is almost as well known in Norfolk as the Paston letters, and I suspect a lot more people have seen it.

81

That only adds up to ten parishes. The eleventh, Thorpe Market, has a church in a class of its own. In 1795 Lord Suffield of Gunton Park commissioned the building of 'a sensible, modern church'. The result has been described rather scornfully as 'churchwarden's Gothic', a simple rectangle with two south porches, hexagonal turrets at all four corners and windows patterned with orange and blue diamonds. It is not everybody's cup of communion wine but it does have its admirers. A 1958 guide to English churches says, 'It would be difficult to find a more attractive church of the "pasteboard scenery" type of Strawberry Hill Gothic.' I suppose that's a compliment . . .

A little pasteboard scenery might have been useful at Bacton, where the attempt to landscape the massive North Sea gas terminal has been called at best pathetic and at worst – I cannot repeat it. But there is more to Bacton than gas piping. For instance it was Norfolk's defence headquarters against Zeppelins in the First World War. The airships made several attacks on the county, not always for obvious reasons. They bombed the tiny village of Wellingham, about as isolated from wartime activity as anywhere in Britain, and killed a Mr Frederick Pile as he strolled down the village street – perhaps the unluckiest casualty of the war. There was some debate as to whether his name should go on the war memorial, as he had not died on active service, but the pro-Pile lobby argued that he had been killed by enemy action, and in the end his name was included. But it comes last, not in alphabetical order; a good Norfolk compromise.

Although there were scores of raids, only two Zeppelins were brought down. Bacton's defence system was about as adequate then as its landscaping is today. But in medieval times it did achieve one notable coup. Bromholm Priory acquired in the thirteenth century a holy relic from a travelling salesman – actually a chaplain who had fled from Constantinople with assorted ecclesiastical goodies and was hawking them round the English monasteries. At St Albans he managed to dispose of two of St Margaret's fingers, but they declined the little double crucifix which he claimed was a portion of the True Cross. Perhaps the idea of a double cross put them off. The monks of Bromholm had more faith – or were they just more gullible? – and agreed to take it. They could not have done themselves a greater favour. It is recorded that, thanks to their new acquisition, thirty-nine people were brought back to life, lepers were healed, the lame walked, the blind could see. Suddenly this rather hard-up and obscure little priory became famous. Chaucer helped by publicising it in *Canterbury Tales*: 'Help, Holy Cross of Bromholm!' you may recall the Miller's Wife exclaiming. Piers Plowman plugged it too. 'Bid the Rood of Bromholm bring me out of debt,' he pleaded.

Pilgrims poured in from all over Europe. So did the money, and the monks built themselves a smart new priory. Bromholm remained in Rood health for centuries, rivalling Walsingham in popularity, but while Walsingham still prospers Bromholm is in ruins. It had the ignominy of being used as a defence post in the last war, with bits of concrete stuffed into its ancient stonework. As for the Holy Rood, who knows? Perhaps Holyrood House in Edinburgh has the answer.

Now we head down the east coast into more bungalow and caravan country. I have heard it suggested that caravans should be painted green instead of white to merge better into the landscape, and perhaps in the new Green climate the idea will catch on. Meanwhile the only way not to see them is to make as wide a detour as possible, and happily the coast road does. It comes within sight of the sea, and the inevitable caravans alongside it, only two or three times between Bacton and the vast holiday complex that spreads out from Great Yarmouth.

Walcott's only claim to fame is it once had a parson christened Horatio Nelson Comyn. The unfortunate fellow was Nelson's godson and was inflicted with his names, a practice to be discouraged. Hasten on to Happisburgh; or, to match the pronunciation, do not hasten but happisen. Apart from its confusing name (more helpful maps sometimes spell it Haisbro) it has a splendid red-and-white lighthouse, just as picturesque in its own way as Cley's famous windmill and with a much more interesting story. It is not only the only lighthouse in Norfolk, it is the only privately operated lighthouse in the country. Trinity House decided it was superfluous; the locals claimed it was not. There was a petition, an appeal to the Duke of Edinburgh as Master of Trinity House, and a campaign that achieved national fame. It all worked – and so does the lighthouse.

The Norfolk coastal area from King's Lynn to Yarmouth

Happisburgh lighthouse is the only one on the Norfolk coast and has just become the only privately operated lighthouse in the country.

The road returns to the coast again at Sea Palling, but I am not sure why it bothers. The village was inundated by the 1953 floods, but as at Snettisham and Heacham the shacks and chalets have returned, unabashed. It has been unkindly labelled Sea Appalling, but the villagers (who I am sure lead very happy and fulfilled lives there) may like to know that even ruder things have been said about their neighbour, Waxham. A letter in the *Eastern Daily Press* observed:

> Waxham is one of the most desolate and inhospitable places imaginable. Apart from the beautiful beach which is usable for a very few weeks of the year, it is not a place in which to linger. There are no hedgerows or vegetation other than a few twisted and stunted trees which give an indication of the remorseless east wind from which there is no cover for man or beast. To live in Waxham is a survival test and no one who has left has ever returned.

The letter came from the sun-kissed Leeward Islands, so perhaps the writer was prejudiced, but this was certainly a great area for wreckers and smugglers, who thrived on these bleak conditions.

One parson records how his church suddenly emptied in the middle of his sermon, when news came of a shipwreck. The congregation were anxious not to miss the pickings. And the Revd Henry Ready, who was Rector for nearly sixty years, told his son that when he arrived he was advised by the retiring incumbent to make sure he looked outside the front door each morning. If he found a keg of brandy on the doorstep it meant his barn was being used by smugglers and strangers must be kept away. The all-clear came when another keg appeared. 'Brandy for the parson' was not just a poetic invention . . .

The Great Barn of Waxham has achieved notoriety in more recent years for a very different reason. This Grade I listed building, a splendid relic of agricultural grandeur, became so tumbledown that the repair bill was estimated at £300,000. The county council wanted to restore it, the district council wanted it demolished. The argument dragged on for so long that the Great Barn became something of a Great Bore, and the poor old place might well have fallen down anyway and ended the matter, but the preservationists triumphed and work got under way in time to help it survive the devastating gale of early 1990.

I have not taken you inland lately because we are in Broads country now, which has the next chapter to itself. At Horsey the Broads come within sight of the sea, and during flooding the two have met. Julian Tennyson, who wrote so lovingly about Suffolk, was rarely tempted across the border, but he did visit Horsey after the 1938 floods and was appalled by what he saw: ' . . . the finest fields in Norfolk pitifully wasted, cottages gutted and abandoned, great heaps of rotting fish, windmills peeping absurdly from some still aggravated portion of the flood, farms and their buildings doomed as surely as if the dreaded mark of the plague had been written on their doors . . . '
I wish I could have written as eloquently when I reported the similar floods of 1953.

Eight months later when the waters had receded Major Anthony Buxton, the local landowner, said it looked like 'a red-brown salt desert on the shores of the Dead Sea'. Nevertheless there is still a Buxton at Horsey, and other stalwart souls, trusting in the new sea defences across the notorious Horsey Gap. There are even the ubiquitous caravans where the red-brown salt desert used to be.

East Norfolk beaches are criss-crossed with sea defences in the hope – sometimes a vain one – that they can keep the North Sea at bay. Even when they succeed they hardly improve the scenery. These are at Happisburgh.

Somerton, which is sometimes called West Somerton but its eastern companion has long since disappeared, is a place you drive through on the way to somewhere else, but a tomb in the churchyard is a reminder that this was the home of the Norfolk Giant, Robert Hales, the son of a local farmer, who was seven feet eight inches tall and weighed thirty-two stone. Mr Hales made a useful living by touring fairs and showgrounds in Britain and America, but spare a thought for his sister Mary, who was also more than seven feet tall and could have been a star too if she had not been overshadowed, as it were, by her big brother.

Robert finished up as licensee of the Craven Head Tavern in London, where his formidable size not only attracted the customers but ensured their good behaviour. He died in 1863 and is buried in his native soil, beneath an imposing memorial, while Mary's grave, which must be nearly as big, languishes in obscurity.

Winterton is the last village along the coast that still looks like a Norfolk village, mainly because of its church, which was a navigation mark for passing mariners and a resting place for a good many of them. It has a Fisherman's Corner with nets and ropes and anchors, a ship's lamp and a cross made from ship's timbers. It was the idea of a rector who himself died from drowning in 1932, trying to rescue a choirboy who had gone for a swim and was swept away.

That's the Way the Coast Road Goes

Beyond Winterton you are in Hemsby and Caister and Great Yarmouth, and you have left rural Norfolk behind. What is there instead? The *Companion Guide to East Anglia* is in no doubt. 'At Hemsby Gap,' it says crisply, 'there is Bingo.' But if you continue past Scratby, which looks like it sounds, and California, which certainly doesn't, there is a little Norfolk history to be found at Caister-by-Yarmouth. This should not be confused with Caistor-by-Norwich, a very different kettle of Roman fish. There were indeed Romans at Caister, but Sir John Fastolf left a more permanent mark. The ruins of his castle still stand, embellished these days by a car museum. In the fifteenth century it was the scene of the last medieval battle fought in East Anglia, a most uneven contest involving three thousand men trying to capture it and thirty men trying to keep them out. The three thousand won, but only just.

Sir John, a slimline model for Shakespeare's Falstaff, came home from Agincourt and built the castle with the ransom money for a captured French knight. He left it to the Pastons, perhaps in recognition of all the letters they had written about him, but the Duke of Norfolk claimed it had been left to him. It was his three thousand men who eventually took it after a year's siege, but the whole operation was pretty pointless as it returned to the Pastons eight years later. The Pastons passed on but the ruins remain.

R.H. Mottram wrote of Great Yarmouth: 'That long front and much else might, except for the air, be at Blackpool or Brighton, and is no doubt well worthy of a book. But I am not qualified to write it, and stick to that part of Yarmouth which cannot be found elsewhere.' That is a good example to follow, and once you are away from Yarmouth's Golden Quarter-Mile there is much that a Norfolkman can be proud of. For instance, it has one of the largest market places, with the smallest alleys, in England. The alleys, called Rows, are so narrow that normal carts could not get along them, so Yarmouth invented the troll, a horse-drawn trolley with the wheels below the body to save space. There were more than a hundred Rows, and it is an indication of their width that when the buildings between two of them were demolished to make a roadway, the Rows on each side were just the right width for pavements.

The town also claims the biggest parish church in the country, covering twenty-three thousand square feet. It used to cover a lot more before it lost its side chapels in the Reformation, but it still has the widest aisles in Britain.

Yarmouth can claim only the second-highest Nelson's Column, just a foot shorter than the more famous one in Trafalgar Square. It bears a figure of Britannia instead of Nelson and she faces inland instead of out to sea, which looks a little odd, but at that time Yarmouth was primarily a fishing port and faced the harbour, before it developed as a holiday resort and turned round to face the beach.

For a couple of months in the summer of 1989 the Column had an unlikely competitor on the Yarmouth skyline. It was the town's answer to the Blackpool Tower, an oil rig nearly 350 feet high which was deposited a few hundred yards off the Wellington Pier. Local boatmen prospered taking trippers around the rig until duty called it back to the day job.

The Norfolk coastal area from King's Lynn to Yarmouth

Yarmouth's answer to the Blackpool Tower. A trip around the oil rig was quite an attraction until it returned to the oilfields.

Logically Norfolk should end at Yarmouth, since the River Waveney is the county boundary for most of its length and this is where it eventually reaches the sea via Breydon Water. However the authorities seem to regard Gorleston, on the other bank, as a suburb of Yarmouth, and have included it in Norfolk. Gorleston itself takes a very different view and has fretted for years about being the poor relation. It was there, after all, before Yarmouth. It formed a pressure group to get more money spent on its holiday amenities; I hope the pleasanter parts of Gorleston do not get submerged in the process.

Burgh Castle, three miles inland, also falls within this extra slice of Norfolk, but in Julian Tennyson's time it was still in Suffolk, and he reckoned he could see thirteen windmills from the ruins of the old Roman castle that commands the entrance to the Waveney. He could also see for many miles along the river and its border towns and villages – but that's another chapter too.

4 Putt-putt Go the Diesels
The Norfolk Broads and their rivers

In the summer months the most familiar sound in Broadland is
not the crying of the birds, or the rustling of the reeds, or the gentle
lapping of the water on the banks, but the constant putt-putting of
the engines as cavalcades of cruisers parade back and forth along the
waterways. You might call it the Lullaby of Broadland, which each
year thousands of holidaymakers 'come along and listen to'. At the
last count there were over eight thousand motor vessels chugging
around the Broads, and weaving between them were four thousand
sailing craft and rowing boats. Put that lot in a hundred miles of
waterways and you can work out the chances of 'getting away from
it all'.

Personally I get away from it altogether during the summer,
and I know few Norfolk people other than sailing fanatics who
voluntarily go anywhere near the Broads between May and September.
But at other times, as you can imagine, it is a very different place.
The villages are peaceful again, the rivers are deserted, the Broads are
left to the fishermen and the hardy all-weather sailors. The marshes
and watermeadows and reedbeds, particularly at dusk on an overcast
November evening or during a February gale, have a mystical eeriness
about them which is not to be found anywhere else in East Anglia. It
conjures up pictures of the medieval peat-diggers who lived and worked
in this watery wilderness and actually created the Broads in the first
place.

Most people say the best way of seeing Broadland is by boat –
particularly the people who hire them out. Certainly many parts of
the Broads are inaccessible by road. On the other hand many of the
most attractive areas are inaccessible by boat, and even in the places
where boats can go, you can often see little more than the reedbeds
on the banks and the rear of the boat in front. But that is the route
that most visitors take, to the delight of the boat companies, the

provision merchants and publicans in the riverside villages, and those of us who can leave them jostling for a mooring while we enjoy the unspoilt countryside out of their reach.

Filby Broad cannot be reached by boats on the main Broads network, so the rower can fish in peace.

People who have never been there may imagine the Broads as an interlocking network of waterways which offer a variety of touring routes so there is no need to pass the same spot twice. In fact there are three separate rivers with Broads strung out along them, and you would normally decide on one of them and sail up and down that. The Bure is the most popular because you can sail further up it, it has the most Broads, and there are a couple of tributaries, the Ant and the Thurne, to explore. If you choose the Yare however you can sail from Yarmouth to Norwich and moor within an easy stroll of the cathedral and the city centre.

The Waveney is the least frequented by the holiday trade. It offers the shortest distance upriver for boats and there are no Broads beyond Oulton. Indeed many Broads visitors may not regard it as Broadland at all. It has a greater significance for me as the county boundary between East Norfolk and Suffolk, with the Little Ouse performing the same function further west, so these two rivers will have the next chapter to themselves.

My plan for touring Broadland is first to follow the Bure upstream, with diversions into the surrounding countryside to see what the boating folk are missing, then do the same up the Yare. All this could take two or three days by car, two or three weeks by boat. If you actually attempt it you could combine the two, with a fair amount of walking thrown in.

Once the Bure has escaped from the environs of Yarmouth it wisely heads inland, away from the crowded coast. It runs parallel with the notorious Acle Straight on the A47 trunk road, a lethal stretch of single carriageway where frustrated drivers, temporarily free of the

Putt-putt Go the Diesels

usual Norfolk bends and corners, make desperate attempts to overtake long lines of lorries, only to find that drivers in the opposite direction are doing exactly the same. The Bure offers a much safer alternative.

Stokesby, the first village it touches, used to be called remote, but no village can stay remote on a holiday river and Stokesby has expanded and adapted like the rest. For real remoteness you need to leave the river and find Runham, a farming village deep among the cornfields which offers one of the saddest sights in Norfolk, a deserted, derelict church. From a distance across the meadows it looks like many others, a pinnacled square tower, arched windows in flint walls, a tiled nave and chancel. But closer you can see that one of the pinnacles has broken off and lies at the foot of the tower, all the windows are smashed, and pigeons are flying in and out of the roof. Even the board outside the crumbling porch, asking hopefully for donations to be left at the Post Office, is falling to pieces. Inside the pews and flooring have gone and the pulpit has been burned to ashes.

A deceptively solid-looking Runham church. But it is deserted, derelict, and seems doomed for demolition – if anyone can afford to knock it down.

The cost of reconstructing St Peter and St Paul's has been estimated at over a hundred thousand pounds and the figure goes up all the time. It will take many, many donations at the Post Office to achieve it. Set in the middle of an isolated field well away from the village it seems useless for any kind of conversion. The ancient church looks doomed for demolition – if anyone can find the money to demolish it.

This is gloomy stuff. Nearby Thrigby offers a more cheering sight. Its old church still stands, though it is covered in what Lady Harrod of the Norfolk Churches Trust generously calls 'atmospheric greenery'. There is even better news at Ormesby St Margaret, where the original fifteenth-century building is not only in excellent order but has a twentieth-century extension. The project was not without opposition, but the result has to be admired. The extension consists of meeting-rooms, kitchen and cloakrooms so the building can be used

90

seven days a week instead of just the seventh. The new flint walls have been matched so accurately with the old ones it is difficult to spot the join, and the ancient tombstones, now largely illegible, which were moved to make room for it have been used effectively to form a paved area outside. The project has brought new life and interest to the church; Lady Harrod must be delighted.

There is little else to get excited about in Ormesby St Margaret, which straddles a busy road to the coast. But close by it are the Trinity Broads, to me quite the most delightful in Broadland, because they are not linked with the river system and so cannot be reached by holiday craft, unless they are carried there.

The Trinity Broads – Filby, Ormesby and Rollesby – are easily spotted by motorists since the two main roads run between them, but they are not so easy to reach. The best vantage point on Ormesby Broad is the garden of the Eel's Foot pub in Ormesby St Michael, a delightful haven out of season with some of the best-cooked and least expensive bar meals in Broadland. You may hire a rowing boat if you wish, but I have been content to watch the ducks do the paddling, against the background of still waters and tree-covered banks. If you can imagine a Scottish loch without mountains, this could be it.

Filby Broad, still deserted, except for that fortunate fisherman – and the odd duck. . .

Unfortunately this area is too close to all the seaside holiday camps and caravan sites at Hemsby and Winterton, and if you attempt to find a quiet pub at Martham, for instance, you are likely to be invaded by a coachload of trippers even in late autumn. Martham must have been very secluded when there were oakwoods full of the pine martens which gave the village its name, but now the only seclusion is to be found in the quiet corner around the church, well away from the traffic that pours through the main street. I searched the church for a much-quoted inscription left by Christopher Burroway in memory of his wife Alice: 'In this life my sister, my mistress, my mother and my wife.'

Martham Green looks deserted too except for the trio on the village sign, but the trippers are not far away.

The Burroways found themselves in this confusing situation because Christopher's father had an incestuous relationship with his own daughter and baby Chris was the result. He grew up away from the village and returned to work for his mother-cum-sister. It was only after he married her that they found out their already complicated relationship. It must have been quite a shock, even in the days in remote Norfolk villages when everybody had the same surname, but Christopher seems to have thought of himself as no end of a dog, and left this message about his unlikely achievement for posterity.

Posterity unfortunately is no longer able to read it. The church guidebook observes tersely that the memorial to his mother-sister-mistress-wife is now under the organ. Presumably subsequent parishioners – Victorians, perhaps – did not regard his exploit so favourably.

They also probably disapproved of a curious entry in the parish register, but they could not put the organ on top of that. It records the burial in 1724 of Edward, 'base-born daughter of Mary Biggs'. This was not an early sex-change. Miss Biggs gave birth to illegitimate twins in 1723 and the midwives, after a cursory glance, decided they were both boys. They were duly baptised Robert and Edward. Robert died a few weeks later and Edward only survived for a year. Only at the baby's death was Edward's correct sex revealed, but since it was recorded as Edward on the baptisms page it had to stay Edward under burials. A note was added explaining how it had happened 'through the mistake of two or three good old women'. Unlike Alice Burroway's memorial stone, this unorthodox entry has been reproduced in the church's literature for all to see.

High time to return from these bizarre happenings to the calmer waters of the River Bure, which has now reached Acle and left the A47. Acle was one of the worst bottlenecks on the trunk road until a bypass was opened in 1989. Even without the through traffic it is still a busy bustling village of two thousand people. The parish is actually larger than it looks, because in 1862 an Act of Parliament enabled it to annex Nowhere.

Many Norfolk villages may seem on the road to Nowhere, but Acle literally is. A nineteenth-century map in the county record office shows Nowhere is an area of marshland by the Bure, on which the eleventh-century villagers of Acle had salt-pans in which they preserved their food. Nowhere was in fact miles from anywhere, but the 1862 Act formally incorporated it in Acle parish. It must be one of the few places where you can honestly reply, if you are asked where you are going, 'Nowhere!'

Upton is definitely somewhere, and has a village sign to emphasise it. Unlike most signs it is in the village pond, and there are further signs of eccentricity in the church; to be precise, a metal dragon and the bone of a whale.

The dragon turns out to be a weathervane which was taken down when the tower was repaired in 1982. It would be nice to think it has a fascinating history, but it was only erected in 1930 to replace an earlier one. It was not one of St George's conquests; the church is dedicated to St Margaret, who had an unpleasant encounter with a hungry dragon but emerged – and I mean emerged – unscathed.

The whalebone has a much odder tale to tell. It was carried into the church on Christmas Day 1612 by two local rapscallions, Wicked Will Enderton and Simon Bullock – 'the said William making a great and roring noyse all waie of his coming, and they went staggering and reeling too and fro in a scoffing and wild profane manner, the minister being reading divine service at the time'. The church authorities in due course reprimanded them and confiscated their whalebone. The one now on show may just possibly be it.

Thurne village used to be as isolated as Upton, but it is at the junction of the Bure and the Thurne, and once the developers found it, it stood no chance at all. It now incorporates a 'holiday village' and is not even remotely remote. There is more fun to be had up the Thurne at Potter Heigham bridge, where you can watch inexperienced sailors bang their heads as well as their boats. On the riverbank is the Helter-Skelter House, which was once the top of a helter-skelter at Yarmouth and is now a rather peculiar holiday cottage. Windows and doors have been inserted and extensions added, but it is still quite unmistakable.

Upton village sign is unexpectedly sited in the village pond, perhaps to discourage any vandals.

The low bridge at Potter Heigham, where inexperienced sailors bang their heads as well as their boats for the entertainment of spectators.

Although a lot of holiday homes have grown up around Potter Heigham Bridge this is not Potter Heigham. The village is a mile away, with some pleasant old houses near the church and plenty to see in the church itself. Unfortunately, like so many churches in Broadland it is kept locked, which perhaps is why the effigy of a wild man over the door looks so wild. It is a great sadness that vandalism and thefts have forced so many villages to lock up their most interesting building; a locked church is almost as depressing as a ruined one, and certainly more frustrating.

The Thurne leads on to Hickling Broad, and another disappointment. The main place of interest in Hickling, apart from the church, is the Royal Thatched Lodge, which an old guidebook was very enthusiastic about: 'It is built almost in the water and beautifully thatched with Norfolk reed and ridged with sedge grass. Inside are many paintings by local bird artists . . . The place has a marvellous period architecture.' I have to take their word for it because the lane to the lodge is now marked private and I was told firmly it is not open to the public.

Hickling can now offer one consolation, which was missing for half a century. The bells of St Mary's had to remain silent for that time because the vibration could have brought down the tower, but in 1989 the parish completed repairs costing fifty thousand pounds and made it safe. For the first six months the bells could only be pealed for half an hour at a time to make sure the repairs had worked, but now they go like the clappers to provide a regular feature of Sunday morning on Hickling Broad.

The Bure's other tributary, the Ant, also has a well-known bridge to negotiate, fortunately of more spacious proportions. Again, Ludham Bridge is well away from Ludham village, which is a lot more attractive. The painter Edward Seago certainly thought so and lived there for many years. Down on the marshes where the Ant joins the Bure are the ruins of St Benet's Abbey, with the remains of a mill emerging incongruously from its gateway. The Bishop of Norwich, who is also Abbot of St Benet's, makes an annual pilgrimage by boat, followed by a flotilla of small craft carrying his congregation. The scene is reminiscent of the Boat Race except that the Bishop always wins.

The Ant's other familiar landmark is How Hill educational centre, a large thatched house on one of the few real hills overlooking the Broads. It has a splendid view of the river winding through the reedbeds and the marshland, with a restored windpump in the foreground and on a clear day the spire of Norwich Cathedral on the horizon. Just below it on the riverbank is Toad Hole Cottage, a former eel-catcher's cottage which was used as a lifesize Wendy house by the family who owned How Hill and is now a little museum. The county council bought the property in 1966 and it is now a charitable trust running courses for adults as well as classes for schoolchildren. I have spent a weekend at How Hill myself and there is no better way of seeing the real Broadland, the areas beyond the reach of the holiday cruisers.

Popular Broadland land-marks: *top* the ruins of St Benet's Abbey with its intrusive mill-tower, and *below* a more happily sited mill near How Hill.

You travel in the Electric Eel, a shallow-draught boat powered by batteries, which moves quite silently through the narrow dykes that lead off the main channels. This is where the reedcutters work, scything the reeds and loading them into long narrow lighters, which they quant along the dykes with a long pole, rather like undergraduates on the Cam but with much less room for manoeuvre. The marshmen maintain that Norfolk reed is still the finest, in spite of pollution problems. When the church council at Woodbastwick, one of the Broads villages, talked about importing Romanian reed to thatch their church the outcry was louder than the putt-putting of a thousand Broads cruisers.

The How Hill excursion took me across Barton Broad, which every visitor knows, and into the Dilham Canal, which few people know at all. You may not associate Broadland with canals – there seems quite enough water about already – but the good burghers of North Walsham decided they were being left out of things and built the canal to connect with the Ant at Dilham, and thus to the Bure and Great Yarmouth. It has long since been abandoned, but if you can find the entrance you can get along it in a small boat for about a mile, as far as an old packhorse bridge. It is the most secluded and enchanting boat ride in Broadland, with water lilies brushing the sides of the boat, the branches meeting overhead and not another soul, one feels, for a hundred miles.

Dilham Canal has been disused as a canal for years but it still provides a secluded waterway for small craft at the Dilham end.

It is difficult to picture this idyllic little waterway as a working canal, but there is proof of it further upstream. If you drive over the bridge at Briggate you can see the remains of a lock, the wooden gates wedged permanently open and the water pouring down a steep drop between perpendicular walls into the bottom of the lock. It is a gloomy, uninviting spot, and not a place to lose your balance.

There are more old locks at Honing Common, but Honing is neither gloomy nor uninviting. It remains comparatively unspoilt, probably because the canal and the railway which used to serve it no longer function. It is a great contrast to its near-namesake Horning, which is one of the main holiday centres and completely overrun in the season.

North Walsham, at the far end of the canal, can also get very crowded and its one-way system is not user-friendly, but if you follow the signs to the middle of the maze you will find a little market place with a dozen parking places, a market cross which looks like a three-tiered tin hat, and the second largest parish church in Norfolk. Most of the tower fell down in 1724 but nothing else has collapsed since. Two impressive gargoyles, presumably from the roof, stand on each side of the tower door, but they now seem to be used as litterbins. Inside the church hangs a board bearing the arms of King Charles on one side and of the Commonwealth on the other. I suppose the Rector was hedging his bets.

Alas, there was no way a later Rector and his church council could avoid losing out on a more recent conflict involving the church.

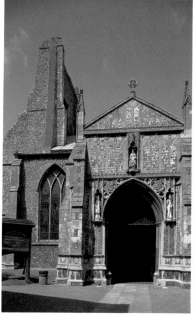

North Walsham's two focal points: *left* the Market Cross with its three-tiered roof and *right* the parish church, which lost most of its tower in 1724 but is still the second largest in Norfolk.

In 1988 they planned to move the medieval screen as part of a scheme to make the building more practicable. An opposition group led by a retired brigadier objected and the case came before a Consistory Court, a procedure which is not only very rare but very expensive. To most people's surprise the objectors won and the church had to pay legal costs of twenty thousand pounds. It took twelve months' hard work to meet the bill. The other alterations have now gone ahead but the screen remains where it was, the most expensive non-event in the church's history.

The River Ant meanwhile has meandered off to Stalham, a sprawling and congested village which is worth negotiating in order to reach Ingham, and the remains of a Trinitarian priory endowed by Sir Miles and Lady Stapleton. The Trinitarians were founded to raise money for ransoming knights captured in the Crusades. Once the Crusades were over the Order rather lost its point, and faded away, but Ingham church still has a reminder of Sir Miles and his wife, albeit at third hand. It is a drawing of a rubbing of a brass, no less. It depicts them hand in hand, a rare feature in fourteenth-century brasses, and at their feet is their pet dog Jakke. We know his name because it is recorded on the brass, which is rare too. From their composed expression the Stapletons could well be assuring him, 'We're all right, Jakke.'

Above Stalham the ant wanders northwards past North Walsham to the attractive but privately owned lake which is its source. This is well beyond the reach of any boats, quiet farming country where few strangers penetrate. Indeed when I pulled up at the little Post Office to examine what looked like a tiny pillarbox – it turned out to be a joke litter bin – a passing villager had to be reassured that I was not planning to raid it.

The tiny post office at Antingham has an even tinier 'pillarbox'. It is actually a joke litter-bin.

Back on the Bure, upstream from its junction with the Ant, there is a string of Broads to the south of the river stretching from South Walsham to Wroxham. This is where all the boats on the Bure eventually converge, and while South Walsham at one end has remained a fairly small village, Wroxham at the other has expanded to link up with Hoveton as well. If you stand on Wroxham bridge at the height of the season it is difficult to tell which has the longest queues, the road or the river.

The tourist brochures designate Wroxham as 'Capital of the Broads', but instead of a palace or a castle it has Roy's, which proudly claims to be the largest village store in the country. Roy's is to Wroxham what bookshops are to Hay-on-Wye, but not nearly as quaint. One has to search very hard in Wroxham to find any quaintness at all, but you might try the Barton House Railway, in a privately-owned garden on the riverside. It has a genuine signal box and station rescued from the extinct Midland and Great Northern Line, still lit by oil lamps, and a set of working signals including one on a 27-foot post. It issues old-fashioned cardboard tickets, bearing legends like 'Wroxham to Riverside, First Class, 15p', and there are cheap day returns and excursions, 'privilege tickets' for railway staff and 'furlough tickets' for members of the Forces. As the Wroxham to Riverside Line is just five hundred feet long, I think that qualifies as quaint.

The line had its silver jubilee in 1988 and celebrated by raising over five thousand pounds for charity. I was able to present its owner with a genuine British Rail green flag, which I had been given when

I waved away the first so-called Sprinter train from Norwich Thorpe station. I knew it would come in useful eventually.

My own choice for Capital of the Broads would be Ranworth, but I hesitate to suggest it lest it gets like Wroxham. It enjoys the best of both Broadland worlds, on land and water. It has one of the more attractive Broads, much enhanced by a conservation centre and a nature trail through the marshes around it, and the village itself has retained its character in spite of all its visitors. There is a fine old Hall, one of the best churches in Norfolk, and probably the finest rood screen in the country. It also has the Sarum Antiphoner, written and illustrated on sheepskin by the monks of Langley Abbey in the fifteenth century and still easily readable – if you understand Latin.

The church stands on another of Broadland's rare hills, and from the tower I am told you can see the course of the Bure from Acle to Wroxham, the spires of Norwich Cathedral and Yarmouth church, and a glimpse of the sea at Cromer. To achieve this you have to climb eighty-seven steps and a couple of ladders, and stand behind a very low parapet, often in a very high wind. I confess I have not checked it myself.

Nor have I risked checking the strange tale of Colonel the Hon. Thomas Sidney who once lived at the Old Hall. He was a noted lecher and drunkard, but managed a bit of hunting as well. He liked to boast he could ride like the devil, and it was said a figure in black could sometimes be seen riding alongside him. On New Year's Eve 1770 he challenged another hunt member to a race. His opponent foolishly drew ahead of him and the colonel promptly shot his horse, so the poor chap fell and broke his neck.

It must have been the last straw. At the hunt banquet in the Old Hall that night the door was flung open by a tall figure in a black robe who dragged the colonel outside. He mounted a black horse, with the terrified fellow kicking and screaming under his arm, and rode away across Ranworth Broad, the hooves raising clouds of steam from the water. The colonel was never seen alive again, but on 31 December you may catch a glimpse of him and his black-cloaked captor riding across the Broad in a cloud of steam and spray . . .

There are no Broads beyond Wroxham but many boats continue upstream to Coltishall, where the pleasant moorings are insulated from the heavy road traffic by a broad meadow. There is no escape though from the roar of aircraft engines; there is an RAF fighter station nearby. Anne Boleyn's father was reputed to ride over Coltishall bridge long after he died, but I doubt he could stand the noise now.

Between Coltishall and Aylsham the Bure flows past Little Hautbois, remarkable only for its name (pronounced Hobbies), and Buxton, which is not even remarkable for that. It was the home of Sir Thomas Cubitt, whose name appeared on building sites all over nineteenth-century London, but even this devoted developer might baulk at some of the new housing in his native village. It also has a signpost pointing to 'Alysham', which I am sure he would have made the county council repaint. I wonder how that slipped past them.

The river used to be navigable beyond the fine old mills at Oxnead and Burgh-next-Aylsham as far as Aylsham itself, but it is in a very different state today. The railway has stopped functioning too but the town has continued to grow and its streets are as congested as any market town in the county. The time to appreciate it is in the evening, when you can pause in safety to admire the old houses in the Market Place and share some of the peace that Humphrey Repton enjoys in the churchyard. Repton landscaped many of Norfolk's stately gardens, but never achieved the fame of Capability Brown. If Mr Brown had never been given a nickname and Humphrey had been called Reclamation Repton the story might have been different . . .

Two fine watermills on the upper reaches of the Bure, out of reach of holiday cruisers: this one is at Burgh-next-Aylsham. . .

Aylsham is the gateway to a particularly pleasant and unspoilt area of Norfolk. The upper reaches of the Bure and its tributaries flow gently through woods and parkland and peaceful villages. It is my favourite part of the Bure, because it seems a million miles from the crowds and the cruisers downstream. And although it may seem largely deserted, there is much to see. Grazing by the river at Ingworth, for example, is a famous flock of black sheep owned by the aunt of Richard 'the Virgin' Branson. And in the church at Saxthorpe is an altar rail which looks like two bedheads joined by a garden gate, and the round knobs on it have been confirmed by at least one short-sighted bishop.

Across the bridge from Saxthorpe the church at Corpusty tells a sadder story. It has a commanding position above the river but it has been disused for years, with corrugated iron blocking the windows, bars across the porch and only the remains of the chancel screen inside.

The most macabre church furnishing in this area is the Little Barningham skeleton. It was carved by a morbid fellow called Stephen

Crosbie in 1640 and stands on the end of a pew holding a scythe in one hand and an hourglass in the other, with a shroud hanging from its skull. Beneath it is the cheering inscription: 'As you are now, even so was I. Remember death for ye must dye.'

There is an Oulton in these parts but it has no connection with Oulton Broad unless you follow the Bure and then the Waveney for fifty-odd miles. It does have a connection with a courtroom drama which became a catastrophe. Sir Robert Bell, who lived at the Big House in Tudor times, was one of Elizabeth's judges. He was trying a case at Oxford Assizes in a courtroom filled with the stench of the prisoners, who must have been even scurvier knaves than usual. The fumes were so appalling, according to reports, that he and the entire jury and other officers of the court were taken ill and died within fifty days. The total death toll was said to be three hundred, so it must have been a very large courtroom and the prisoners must have been very smelly indeed. After this unpleasant experience judges were given a nosegay and prisoners, I hope, were given a bath.

... and this is at Oxnead, in the parkland which used to be owned by the letter-writing Pastons.

One of the Bure's nearby tributaries, Scarrow Beck, takes you to a village with a more fragrant memory. Aldborough also has a counterpart in Suffolk but it prefers football on the green to music in the maltings. One of its Rectors was the Revd J.G. Nelson, a notable Victorian bulb grower, and the east window of the church has panes of colourful spring flowers in his honour. As you might expect, the churchyard is full of flowers in the springtime, said to have been planted by Mr Nelson, and the Norfolk Naturalists Trust has wisely classified it as a conservation area.

Another village on Scarrow Beck is Erpingham, the home of Sir Thomas of that ilk who fought alongside Henry V at Agincourt and built the Erpingham Gate in Norwich as a thank-offering for surviving. The martial brass figure in the church is sometimes thought to be him, but it dates from about 1415 when he was still in France whooping it up with King Henry. It is actually in memory of his father, who must have died without knowing about his son's part

in this famous victory. Fortunately Shakespeare knew about it, even
down to the conversation he had with the king on the eve of battle.
'The Lord in heaven bless thee, noble Harry.' 'God-a-mercy, old heart,
thou speakest cheerfully . . . ' And so on.

Matlaske, 'the meeting place beneath the oak' – or is it ash? – is
tucked away in the heart of this quiet countryside, though on my last
visit I saw ominous signs that a development company had discovered
it and was about to move in. Up to then it seems to have changed very
little since a momentous Sunday in 1726 when the entire chancel
collapsed in the middle of communion. The pessimists attributed
this to the wrath of God, the optimists pointed out that by the grace of
God the walls fell outwards and nobody was hurt. The round Norman
tower and the nave look good for another few hundred years.

The thatched roof of Thurgarton church was in danger of
collapse a few years ago but the Norfolk Churches Trust and others
came to the rescue and the new thatch on the roof bears witness to
their efforts. Among the jolly carvings on the pew ends is an elephant
complete with howdah, an unlikely visitor to this corner of Norfolk.
Whoever carved it has a worthy successor now living and working in
the village, a woodworker and furniture maker whose dressers, chairs
and dining tables may well last as long as that elephant. I hope so; I
have a set of them, custom-made to fit into my cottage.

So these remote and placid villages have many surprises to offer,
but they are not the principal feature of this area. It is the profusion
of Big Houses which lurk out of sight in their parkland, still occupied
in many cases by the original families. Blickling is the one everybody
knows, partly because it is easily seen from the road and partly because
it is the Norfolk showpiece of the National Trust, but I am thinking of
places like Mannington Hall, a marvellous fifteenth-century moated
manor house, restored by the Walpoles and still occupied by them. I
was invited to plant an oak at the opening of a nature trail round the
estate and happily it survived the great gales of 1987 and should be
quite a picture a hundred years from now. Meanwhile Robin Walpole
has inherited his father's title and has had to face the pleasurable
dilemma of whether to remain at Mannington or move into the even
grander Wolterton Hall on the neighbouring estate. It is the kind of
housing problem only the Norfolk gentry encounter.

Other families like the Bulwers of Heydon and the Motts of
Barningham have not budged for many generations, and the villages
that sit outside their park gates, like many others in rural Norfolk, still
have a faintly feudal atmosphere. Nobody would dream of occupying
the squire's pew in church, and although nobody actually touches a
forelock one can sense the automatic impulse to do so. The Lord of
the Manor can no longer order a house to be demolished if it spoils
his view, but then none of the locals would be rash enough to build
it there in the first place.

Perhaps the most familiar
façade in Norfolk: Blickling
Hall, built by the Hobarts
in the 17th century, now
the Norfolk HQ of The
National Trust.

There is still a certain paternalism which is not a bad thing in
these materialistic times. An old retainer may still be allowed to stay
in his cottage rent-free, a hard-up family in the village may well get
a helping hand, and if the church tower is in danger of falling, there
may still be a handsome contribution from the Big House – if they
can still afford it.

This is not always the case. Death duties have often joined forces
with deathwatch beetle, and the Big House itself has to go. Gunton Hall
was badly damaged by fire a century ago and became almost derelict,
with only a few rooms still habitable. Happily the new owner has
managed to preserve the elegant façade overlooking the park, and
behind it there is now more manageable accommodation, and the
original kitchens and outbuildings have been turned into separate
apartments. The family chapel, thanks to the Redundant Churches
Trust, looks just as it did when Robert Adam built it as a change
from fireplaces in 1769, and there is still Gunton's unique feature down
by the ornamental lake.

This low timber building with its thatched roof might be a
summerhouse except it has no windows. It might be a boathouse
except it has no access for a boat. In fact it is one of the oldest sawmills
in the country, housing a water-powered frame saw with a vertical
blade, the type that was used long before circular saws were thought
of. Originally these pitsaws were worked by hand, with one man in a
pit under the log holding one end, and a second man standing on the
log holding the other. It may well have been the chap in the pit, fed
up with being smothered in shavings, who invented this mechanised
version. It can use more than one blade and cut four planks at a time,
thus inspiring a new compliment among rural communities. 'It is the
best thing,' they say, 'since sliced wood . . . '

Gunton lies just above the 'V' formed by the Ant and the
Bure, and is outside Broadland proper, but there is one other village
inside the 'V' I must not omit, because its name has passed into the
language. They were probably making cloth at Worstead before the
Flemish weavers came, but they then perfected the closely woven
worsted we know today. The weavers' houses with high ceilings to
take the looms stand beside the church and there are a dozen looms
in the church itself, operated by the recently revived Worstead Guild
of Spinners, Dyers and Weavers. When I was there they were weaving
a new altarcloth for the chapel. They had already produced a curtain
for the church entrance, made from the fleeces of the Norfolk Horn
sheep which graze in the churchyard.

The Flemish weavers made
Worstead a household
name, tailor-made for posterity, and the looms are
still in action in Worstead
church – a pleasant distrac-
tion, perhaps, during a boring sermon?

The church itself was indeed built on wool, which was all very
well when Worstead was a town and the money from worsted sales
was pouring in, but it became a great burden when it started to crumble
six hundred years later. The population was down to six hundred and
the worsted trade had long since departed. But this gallant six hundred
got weaving themselves, in various ways, and in eight years they raised
the £50,000 required.

A couple of miles away there is another church far too big for
the community around it, like so many Norfolk churches, but in this
case it is a Georgian Baptist chapel, built in 1829. Nonconformists were
not too popular in North Walsham, the nearest town, so they created
their own little settlement from scratch, with a minister's house and
just a few cottages plus a chapel big enough to accommodate all the
Baptists for many miles around. The little settlement has suffered the
usual bungaloid growth but the chapel still towers above them and the
village is still known as Meeting Hill.

I could happily linger in this area of Broadland and its environs, but there are those who prefer to take the southern Broads route up the Yare, and they have history on their side. This was the route taken by the early trading ships, followed by the Norfolk wherries, those magnificent sailing vessels which ferried goods between Norwich and the coast during the first half of this century. Only one trading wherry survives, the *Albion*, which was rescued by the Norfolk Wherry Trust forty-odd years ago and is now used for holiday charters.

There are one or two luxury wherries about, like the *Haytor*, which was designed for the Colman family complete with a butler's pantry at the rear, but the Wherry Trust says the *Albion* gives you a flavour of the real thing. 'It's the difference between staying at a farmhouse for bed and breakfast, and actually working on the farm.' Given the choice I would sooner have the butler, but the queue for the *Albion* speaks for itself.

One of the few surviving Norfolk wherries, the *Haytor*, a luxury version complete with butler's pantry. It is tied up by Pull's Ferry in Norwich.

A cruise up the Yare from Yarmouth involves a rather daunting first stage across the expanse of muddy estuary called Breydon Water. Then it continues through marshland for some miles, an unexciting area reclaimed from the sea and virtually uninhabited. The only lumps on the horizon are the occasional mill and the even more occasional train. The Berney Arms Mill stands isolated in the middle of the marshes, the highest windpump in the country. The river is the easiest way to reach it, though the occasional trains do occasionally stop there. Otherwise it means a long muddy trek across the marsh. It stands seven storeys high, a tarred tower with a white cap and sails and a blue fantail. As well as pumping water it used to grind cement clinker, which is where the railway must have come in handy. Now it

is a museum which welcomes the more intrepid holidaymaker during the summer months.

Even more welcoming is the next stop on the river, the Reedham Ferry. Apart from being the first human habitation after leaving the marshes it has good moorings, a pleasant riverside pub and as a cabaret act the chain ferry, the only means of getting a car across the river anywhere between Yarmouth and Norwich and a delightful reminder of a gentler age of public transport. It is only on a minor road and in November, when I last used it, there is very little traffic, but judging by the extensive areas set aside for cars waiting their turn to cross it must be a great attraction in the summer. At £1.50 a car plus tenpence a passenger it must be quite a goldmine too; the crossing only lasts about a minute and a half. But on that crisp winter morning it was a great delight to stand by the car and enjoy the views up and down the river as the twin chains rattled over the cogs and hauled us towards the jumbo sausages and local bitter at the Inn.

Reedham village is well away from the ferry, rescued from isolation by the railway, which actually has a junction here, one branch going to Yarmouth and the other to Lowestoft. Not far away, however, there are isolated communities where the roads peter out into the marshes and few strangers ever tread. Tunstall is one such village, a cluster of cottages around a ruined church at the end of a lane to nowhere. Wickhampton is another, a tiny community on the edge of the marshes where the church is intact but alas, kept locked – can there be vandals lurking even in the reedbeds?

Freethorpe is more accessible and its church provides a wonderful example of the way of life of the Norfolk squirearchy. In 1850 Richard Henry Vade Walpole – yes, one of *the* Walpoles – decided he wanted more privacy during services, so he built his own side chapel opening off the chancel, designed like a cottage parlour with a timbered ceiling and an open fireplace with a chimney sticking through the roof. He and his family were thus able to worship in comfort, out of sight of the congregation, though the parson was able to take an occasional sideways glance at them from the pulpit. More likely, he faced the Walpoles and took an occasional sideways glance at the congregation.

To do Mr Vade Walpole justice he also restored the church, enlarged the churchyard and built a little cottage opposite, perhaps for the sexton, which bears the quite enormous initials 'V.W.' Freethorpe is no doubt more democratic these days, and certainly the squire's chapel is used as a meeting room, but I suspect that, not far below the surface, the spirit of the Vade Walpoles lives on.

Between this isolated corner and the Norwich suburbs there is not a lot to see on the north bank of the Yare, except of course the Cantley sugar refinery, which looms over the landscape like the modern equivalent of a feudal castle. The squire in this case – presumably the chairman of the British Sugar Corporation –

Reedham Ferry is the only means of getting a car across the River Yare anywhere between Norwich and Yarmouth – and a very civilised way of doing it too.

has acquired not a personal chapel but a personal road, a broad and well-maintained carriageway for the beet lorries to drive right into the factory gates, where the road ends. It is a great contrast to the little bumpy lanes that run off it. Cantley has a sizeable community of about six hundred people, but judging by the age of the houses most of them have only been there about the same time as the refinery.

The Yare lies beyond it and is invisible from the road. Indeed by car you do not sight it again until Thorpe St Andrew, near the Norwich ring road. There is the occasional oddity en route. At Buckenham there is a semi-circular pulpit built into the garden wall of the Rectory, where a preacher renowned for his powerful sermons attracted crowds too large for the church; and on Strumpshaw Hill you should be able to see Norwich in one direction (which I can confirm) and the North Sea in the other (which I can't).

Otherwise the road is just another road, separated from the river by marsh and railway except at Postwick, a little rural pocket in the Norwich suburbs tucked between the railway and the river. Even here the river is not easy to reach, but Postwick comes into its own when the Norfolk Churches Trust holds its annual sponsored cycle ride and the local Sea Scouts operate an impromptu ferry for riders and their bikes.

Motorists have to go on into Norwich to cross the river and they should really have chosen the south side in the first place, which has a lot more to offer whether you are driving or sailing; and if you are a devoted beet factory buff you can still see the Cantley refinery.

Upriver from Reedham Ferry some quiet country lanes, or in a boat the even quieter River Chet, will lead you to Loddon, which is happily now bypassed by the main road from Norwich to Lowestoft. Not too long ago the little country town was considered so remote from the forces of law and order that the bank manager was provided with a revolver. The story goes that he once fired it to test local reaction and got no response at all. A member of the fire brigade, which might have offered assistance, was quoted as saying 'Yes I heard that, but I was just settin' down to my tea.'

Loddon now has at least two banks and neither of them, I believe, has an armed manager. The sailing fraternity makes it a busy place in summer, but it still preserves out of season much of the tranquillity which prompted R.H. Mottram to write, 'If I had my choice I would live at Loddon and grow old, playing bowls.' There has been one notable change since his day; the parish church is now shared by the Methodists, and the noticeboard of this 'Anglican Methodist Church' bears the address of the Manse as well as the Rectory. I would have been interested to see if this had caused any changes inside the church, but here again I found it locked, so Loddon too must have its quota of thieves and vandals. Perhaps the bank managers should be armed after all.

The villages around Loddon offer some more accessible attractions. Hardley has a cross beside the river marking the boundary of the City of Norwich's jurisdiction. Like the City of London, which has a similar boundary stone at Staines, Norwich extended its taxes far beyond the city walls. Langley has the ruins of a Premonstratensian Abbey, where the monks, having mastered their multisyllabled title, had no problem in writing the elaborate Sarum Antiphoner now in Ranworth Church. Raveningham Hall is the home of the Premier Baronet of England, Sir Nicholas Hickman Ponsonby Bacon, whose son, the future baronet, is endearingly called Hicky. And I must mention Seething, if only because of its evocative name. 'What's this village called?' 'It's Seething.' 'I dare say, but what's it called?' Morecambe and Wise would have loved it.

Rockland St Mary has its own channel from the Yare leading to Rockland Broad and the New Inn. The inn really does look quite new for a change, and so does much of the village, but the Broad itself looks a picture, well away from all the chalet bungalows and surrounded by trees and reeds.

The last port of call before the Norwich suburbs must be Surlingham, home of the much-loved naturalist Ted Ellis whose daily column in the *Eastern Daily Press* now has to be maintained by four writers, and who became a television star in his later years talking about the Broads he loved. After his death in 1986 a trust was set up to look after the marshes, carrs and woodlands at his home at Wheatfen, and with his widow as the guiding force it has been opened to the public on a limited scale, a *natural* nature reserve and one of the more magical backwaters of Broadland, only a few miles outside the city.

There is nothing very magical about the river's approach to the city itself, unless you are bewitched by factory chimneys, derelict warehouses and blank walls. The river divides here. The Yare heads

Relaxing between studies by the upper reaches of the Yare – the university is not far away.

off into the southern suburbs but the river traffic takes the right fork into the Wensum, just as the medieval merchant ships used to do. The boom towers on each side of the river, which formed part of the city's defences, are still there, but there is no longer a chain slung between them to prevent boats leaving or arriving without paying their tolls. These days the way is obstructed for larger boats by the Carrow Bridge, but it can be raised if the need ever arises. The thousands of drivers who pour across it rather hope it never does.

The river passes the factory site where Mr Colman built his first mustard mill, and the Boulton and Paul factory where they built the R101 airship. Woodrow's City Flour Mills, built in the 1830s for spinning mohair yarn, still looks part of the Industrial Revolution. At this stage you may wonder why you came. But take heart. Get beyond the Foundry Bridge (the foundry has long gone, only to be replaced by a hardly more picturesque hotel) and you are alongside green lawns and willow trees which lead to Pulls Ferry, arguably the most photogenic dried-up canal in Britain.

It was once used to transport Caen stone for Norwich Cathedral, but it is now a pathway leading from the river to Cathedral Close and people queue to photograph the old archway by the river with the cathedral spire beyond. A few yards upriver is the Bishop's Bridge, not a grim span of metal like the last two but three stone arches which have been there for seven hundred years. Beyond that is the Cow Tower, used variously as a stronghold, a toll house and a dungeon but never, so far as I know, by cows. The pole on the opposite bank is actually a wherry mast, marking the site of a former boatyard which used to build them.

Just upstream from Pull's Ferry, the 700-year-old Bishop's Bridge is the oldest in Norwich.

The head of navigation is a mile further on at New Mills, but there are five bridges to negotiate and nothing much to look at in the process. Most people tie up near Pulls Ferry and complete their exploration on foot. This is quite the most civilised way of entering the city, but unlike the Three Wise Men, you cannot return by another route. You must sail back down the Yare to Yarmouth, where if you wish you may re-embark for the Waveney Valley. As for me, I'll take the car . . .

opposite Any Norfolkman's favourite Christmas card: Pull's Ferry, the most photogenic dried-up canal in East Anglia, and Norwich Cathedral beyond.

5 Verging on the Border-line
The Waveney valley and the Little Ouse

The Waveney forms the county boundary between Norfolk and Suffolk for most of its length, but before it flows into Breydon Water there is a small slice on the Suffolk side, including Gorleston and Burgh Castle, which has been transferred into Norfolk. What makes it more confusing is that the Diocese of Norwich, which once included the whole of Suffolk, has still retained some of it in this area, and it extends further than the county boundary. East Anglia does like to du different.

For several miles the Waveney runs through featureless marshland and nobody is too bothered which side is which, but you might think that the matter would have been resolved by the time boats coming upstream reach civilisation, the road bridge that carries the A143. Logically the bridge would be a convenient place to cross from Norfolk into Suffolk, but logic still does not apply. After crossing it you will find that Fritton, with its famous decoy lake, is now in Norfolk too. Back in Julian Tennyson's day, before the last war, it was in his beloved Suffolk, and very proud of it he was too. Wild duck used to be decoyed into a funnel of netting on the lake by a dog running along the bank. These days it is a country park and lures tourists instead of wildfowl.

A reminder that Norfolk's jurisdiction extends across the Waveney at this point is St Olave's windpump, which stands just below the bridge on what looks like the Suffolk side, but it is a protégé of the Norfolk Windmills Trust. However the next one up the river, the Herringfleet smock mill, is in Suffolk. It is all very confusing, and life gets a lot simpler when the boundary links up with the Waveney all the way from Herringfleet to its source.

Nearby is Suffolk's local showpiece, Somerleyton Hall, and the unreal little village that goes with it. Sir Samuel Peto was a Victorian railway tycoon with an eccentric taste in architecture. The hall he built

One bank is Norfolk, the other is Suffolk; the River Waveney provides a photogenic boundary between the two counties. This is near Bungay.

on the site of an Elizabethan mansion is a mixture of Jacobean, Italian, Palladian and Peto. Enthusiasts call it 'a daring marriage of brickwork and stone'. George Borrow called it 'pandemonium in red brick', but Peto had built a railway across Borrow's land at Oulton, so he may have been prejudiced.

Peto's village is unashamed mock-Tudor, with black timbers and thatched roofs, all much too good to be true. It is quite a relief to find that behind it is a straightforward estate of modern houses in unpretentious red brick.

Back at St Olave's bridge there is a very different example of nineteenth-century ingenuity. A second bridge spans the Haddiscoe Cut, a canal which links the Waveney with the Yare and forms a triangular no-man's-land between them. It was built in 1827 by the cunning burghers of Lowestoft in the hope of tempting shipping to use their port instead of Yarmouth en route to Norwich. These days it mainly serves as a shortcut for holiday cruisers from one river to the other without having to venture into Breydon Water, where the two rivers meet.

In contrast to the flat marshland around it, Haddiscoe Church stands on quite a substantial hill, and the chequered parapet of its round tower is a landmark for miles around. In the nave floor is a slab with a Dutch inscription referring to Peter the Dykegraaf, who died in 1525. The church guidebook comments guardedly: 'There is some connection with a scheme for land reclamation by draining the marshes.' Bolder commentators say there is no doubt this was Jan Piers, 'master of the dykes' when all this marshland was reclaimed.

On the churchyard wall is a rather dashing inscription to William Salter, a stagecoach driver. It goes in for verses like:

His uphill work is chiefly done,
His stage is ended, race is run.
One journey is remaining still,
To climb up Zion's holy hill.

Let us hope his many years of climbing Haddiscoe Hill stood
him in good stead.

Aldeby was called Aldeburgh in the Domesday Book, but thank
goodness somebody changed it before it became invaded by confused
music-lovers looking for Billy Budd. It lies in a remote little Norfolk
peninsula formed by a wide loop of the Waveney, and I expected Aldeby
to be remote too, but unfortunately it has a major mineral workings
coupled with a waste disposal site just beside the village, and, like
Cantley, it has an access road out of all proportion to the neighbouring
lanes. Incidentally one illustrious guidebook credits Aldeby Church
with the Willliam Salter poem, calling him William Slater, but who
am I to cast a stone from the pages of this glass house?

Apparently more remote, at the tip of the peninsula, is Burgh St
Peter church, with quite the weirdest tower in Norfolk. It looks like
a pile of enormous toy bricks, getting smaller as they get higher, made
out of a hotchpotch of materials. It stands alone down a muddy lane,
with the emptiness of the marshes stretching out below it, but just
out of sight around the corner is a modern marina and hotel beside
the river.

On the far side of the Waveney is Oulton Broad, a Mecca for
small-boat sailors and these days for speedboats too, which would
not have pleased the squire of Oulton in the 1850s, George Borrow. He
was wont to leap into the Broad fully clothed, 'staying under water
for a minute or more, and spluttering and shouting when at last his
great white head bobbed dripping on the surface'. These days his great
white head would probably have been taken off by a propeller. He was
also inclined to startle passing craft by crying out to his Arab servant:
'Bring lights hither, Hayim Ben Attar, son of the miracle.' But although
he made a fair amount of noise himself he abhorred it in others, and
when he lost his battle with Peto over the railway line he left Oulton
and went off on his travels. No doubt powerboats would have had much
the same effect.

Beyond Oulton Broad is Lowestoft and the Suffolk coast, the
subject of a later chapter. From Burgh St Peter there is no way of
getting there anyway, except by boat. The next bridge is five miles
upstream, at Beccles.

In my early days in Norfolk I always linked Beccles with
Bungay, just as Dereham went with Fakenham and Thetford went
with Watton. There were the names of the local papers. I worked
on the *Dereham & Fakenham Times*, the adjoining area took the

Two aspects of Oulton
Broad: *above* sailing squibs
making the most of a good
breeze. . .

. . . and *below* 'Lavengro',
once the home of – guess
which author.

Thetford & Watton Journal, and somewhere beyond that, on the edge
of the Norfolk News Company's empire, was the *Beccles & Bungay
Journal*. All I knew about these two towns was that they shared the
same initial, the same paper and the same river.

On the face of it they do have similarities. They both suffered
major fires in the seventeenth century, so their buildings mostly date
from Georgian times, but their origins were quite different and they have
developed quite differently since.

Beccles was a Saxon seaport. Herring catches were brought into
the Old Market along the Scores, the equivalent of Yarmouth's Rows,
linking the river with the town. Now the Old Market is a bus station
and the New Market, which only goes back to medieval times, has been
carved up by the developers. The quay where the Norfolk wherries and
the little Yorkshire coasters were still tying up in the 1920s is now
given over to holiday craft.

Verging on the Border-line

You can find reminders of earlier days if you can extract yourself from the one-way system. There is a 600-year-old wall behind the church and the church itself has a separate tower which was bought by the town council in 1972 for a Beccles penny. The coin is still embedded in a plaque on the wall to recall this bargain deal, though in fact it was not such a snip since the council had to raise £68,000 to restore it. Other oddities around the town are a crinkle-crankle wall in Hungate, a good example of this eccentric but quite common style of Suffolk wall construction, and a milestone outside the town hall which looks like a relic of the coaching days but actually dates back all the way to 1984.

Beccles church and the tower which the town council bought for a Beccles penny – then spent £68,000 restoring it. The penny is in the plaque.

Nearby Worlingham Hall has been called 'perhaps the most beautiful house of manageable size in Suffolk', but I am sure that owners of other manageable Suffolk houses would not agree. In spite of its proximity to Beccles it still has a fine sweep of parkland going down to the river. Gillingham too has a hall and a park, but it has acquired a new main road and a mass of new housing around it. There has been much change since the parishioners provided their ageing Rector, the Revd John Lewis, with a device like a saddle in the pulpit when he became too infirm to stand, 'because he had always been an ardent horseman and hunter, and was never so happy as in the saddle.' It has long since gone, along with the epitaph to Thomas Jackson, Comedian, which every old pro must envy. 'The season being ended, his benefit over, the charges all paid and his account cleared, he made his exit in the tragedy of Death . . . '

Geldeston, the next village on the Norfolk bank, has probably the most inaccessible pub in East Anglia. Originally the only form of transport that could reach it was a boat. All its supplies and most of its customers came that way. Now you can drive across the watermeadows and marshland on a very bumpy track to what used to be a cosy riverside inn but has now been extended into a major entertainment venue. But it still has in the garden the venerable lock which was in use until 1934 to allow wherries upriver to Bungay.

No boat of any size passes that way now, and the next glimpse a motorist has of the Waveney is at Ellingham Mill. It is a glimpse to treasure. This in my view is the most attractive spot on the river, a delightful combination of old buildings, immaculate gardens, quaint little sluices and waterfalls and a series of narrow bridges crossing the divided waters of the river. There are other Ellinghams in Norfolk and I would not be too put out if you went there by mistake instead, because this little haven on the Waveney was quite deserted while I was there and it would be nice to keep it that way, but if you have stayed with me this far you deserve a breather in idyllic surroundings, and Ellingham on the Waveney is the place to enjoy it.

Ellingham Mill, one of the most attractive and least frequented spots on the Waveney, mercifully undiscovered by Munnings or Constable.

On the Suffolk side, soon after leaving the river, you emerge on the main Beccles–Bungay road, preferably with great care. It is not a road for dawdlers or sightseers. Nevertheless there are sights worth seeing if you can find a turn-off or a lay-by to take shelter. There is, for instance, a striking contrast between the churches of Barsham and Shipmeadow, only a mile or so apart but in other respects they could be in different worlds.

Julian Tennyson, who knew every church in Suffolk, really fancied Barsham Church, with its round tower, its thatched roof, and the diagonal ribs of the east window extending down to the ground on the outside wall. He reckoned it was 'the most perfect to the eye' in Suffolk. Happily it is still immaculately kept. Lord Nelson, whose mother was born in the Rectory, would find it entirely shipshape. But Tennyson and Nelson would both have winced to see the sorry state of Shipmeadow church as I saw it in 1989. It was declared redundant some years earlier and sold to a developer for conversion, but the conversion has been a long time coming and meanwhile the church fell into decay. The lychgate, a memorial to the six Shipmeadow men who died in the First World War, was leaning at a crazy angle, its roof slats loose or missing, its crucifix broken off. It stands, though only just, right alongside the main road, a sad sight which you could not fail to notice as you drive past. I hope by now the developer has noticed it too.

Barsham's unique east wall, with the diagonals from the window continuing in the stonework. Julian Tennyson considered this church was 'the most perfect to the eye' in Suffolk.

Incidentally Nelson might have had another jolt if he visited nearby Ringsfield, which has the tomb of Princess Caroline Letitia Murat. She was the great-niece of his old enemy Napoleon.

Bungay is just down the road, and if you want to cross the river you have to brave a bleak industrial area which could not be less like the crossing at Ellngham Mill. But Bungay itself is a pleasant little town, set in a loop of the Waveney, which was never as important for trade as Beccles but was much more significant historically as a stronghold of the Bigods, arguably the most devious and double-dealing family in East Anglia's history. Throughout the Middle Ages they were involved in every plot against successive sovereigns. It was a Bigod who helped put Stephen on the throne, then turned against him and supported Matilda, then made friends with Henry II, then turned against him too. It was this same Bigod who is said to have cried when under attack at Framlingham, 'Would I was in my castle of Bungay, upon the river of Waveney, I would not care for the King of Cockney.'

It was another Bigod who helped to lead the barons against King John, another who defied Henry III, and yet another who refused to serve in Edward I's army and coined another treasured

Suffolk quotation. 'By God,' cried the king (or did he mean Bigod?), 'you shall either march or be hanged.' 'By God,' cried Bigod (no doubt Who he meant), 'I will neither march nor be hanged.' Edward took a look at Bigods forces, made an excuse and left.

Bungay from the tower of St Mary's church; Bungay Castle is top left, the Goddess of Justice on the Butter Cross on the right. Spot anything odd about her?

The Bigods' castle at Framlingham is still one of the great showpieces of Suffolk, but Bungay Castle has been in ruins for five centuries, and it is not easy to locate behind all the modern buildings. However there is a prominent reminder of Bungay's other famous character. In the centre of town is probably the only lamppost in the country which has a dog on top of it instead of at its foot. This is the Black Dog of Bungay, a terrifying hound which rampaged through the church during a thunderstorm, to the great discomfiture of the congregation.

The story is recorded by the Revd Abraham Fleming, a sixteenth-century cleric with such vivid descriptive powers one might not realise that he was not actually present at the time. Old Shuck, as the dog came to be known, 'ran down the body of the church with incredible haste and great swiftness, in a visible form and shape. It passed between two persons as they were kneeling on their knees occupied in prayer, and as it seemed wrung the necks of them both at one instant clean backward, in so much that even at a moment, where they kneeled, they strangely died.'

According to Mr Fleming his fellow cleric the Rector was on the roof at the time cleaning the gutter. This seems a curious occupation during morning service, but it was obviously by Divine guidance since he escaped the attentions of Old Shuck and was able to rejoin the congregation afterwards 'to partake of the people's perplexity and lead them in prayer'.

119

Near Old Shuck's lamppost is the butter cross with its whipping post and the figure of the Goddess of Justice holding her scales and sword, but surprisingly without the usual blindfold. Perhaps she wanted to keep an eye on her ferocious neighbour.

Bungay has other distinctions. It is the only town in Britain with a town reeve, a much older office than mayor, and in 1938 the reeve was a woman for the first time in history. It has two parish churches almost alongside each other, one of which was made redundant in 1977 and is now used for flower festivals and the like – a happier fate than befell Shipmeadow. There is a flat-topped circular stone in St Mary's churchyard which is said to be two thousand years old and have Druidic connections, and a lane called Cork Bricks, which must be connected with something but I failed to discover what. It also has one of Britain's first public baths, a building by the river just outside the town. A local apothecary, John King, built it about 1730, not merely as a public amenity but as a source of research. His 'Essay on hot and cold bathing' must have afforded him many happy hours of observation.

The bath-house is actually in the parish of Ditchingham, better known as the home of the Rider Haggards – Sir Henry, whose books about Egypt are commemorated by the pyramid-shaped village sign, and Lilias, who wrote so stylishly about Norfolk. After Lilias's death Ditchingham House was said to be haunted. Part of the story is quite inexplicable: a man in a red coat is supposed to appear at 1.30 a.m., do nothing in particular, then disappear. But the other part has a touch of authenticity about it. A guest awoke to find a woman with a kind face and grey hair at her bedside, stroking her hair on the pillow. In spite of the kind face the guest was understandably apprehensive and gave a loud scream. The figure retreated across the bedroom and sat down almost on the floor before disappearing.

This happened in what was Lilias's bedroom, and what lends the tale a certain veracity is that her writing desk was where the figure sat down. Since her death the floor has been raised, so was that why the figure sat so low, to be level with where the desk used to be? I would not care to say – but wouldn't her grandfather have made it into a great story?

If you continue upstream on the Norfolk bank you will find Earsham, which was once unknown to the world until otter-lovers poured through it to find Philip Wayre's Otter Trust, where there is one of the largest colonies of this endangered animal in the world. There is not much else on this side of the river and I would suggest heading for the Saints' Country, across Homersfield Bridge.

Pause for a moment on the bridge itself, because next to it is the original one, not particularly picturesque and limited to pedestrians these days, but nonetheless a piece of bridgebuilding history. It was built in 1870, in the very early days of concrete, and the experts say it is the oldest surviving concrete bridge in Britain. The new one was

Now you can see – and so can she! Bungay's Goddess of Justice has dispensed with the traditional blindfold.

built a century later and it is flat instead of arched, but the concrete
seems much the same.

The Homersfield Swan, next to the old bridge, once had a
landlord called Pum Borrett, a name still remembered with affection
by the locals. He acquired the nickname because of his fondness for
bands and processions. As a boy he joined in the marching, singing
happily, 'Pum tiddly-pum, tiddly-pum-pum-pum.' The habit stayed
with him all his life, and when his marching days were over he still
pum-tiddly-pummed behind the bar; it is said he even snored to the
same rhythm.

A variegated row of Bungay
houses; the one this end
used to be the London and
Provincial Bank.

Properly refreshed, you are now ready for the Saints' Country, a
magical area which is the nearest Suffolk can offer to my own corner
of High Norfolk. Successive writers have been captivated by it, and
by the folk who inhabit it, not because of the breathtaking beauty of
either, but because they still preserve the essence and the character
of East Anglia, before the incomers came.

Fifty years ago Julian Tennyson described it as the wildest and
most desolate country in Suffolk, 'a stretch of land dipping down into
tiny valleys, of insubordinate hedges and narrow aimless lanes. Here
the signposts point as they please, here you may walk for hours and
meet nothing more civilised than a couple of horny labourers and a
few derelict farms.'

R.H. Mottram, about the same time, records some typical
reactions to a stranger's request for directions. 'What d'yew wanter
knaow that for?' replies one. 'D'yew go back the way yew come,'
replies another. And most discouraging of all: 'The way yor goin'
thass about twelve thousand miles, boy.' It meant you were going
in the opposite direction.

As recently as the 1960s the Saints' Country was still being
described as the backwoods of East Anglia, 'a real hillbilly land into

which nobody penetrates unless he has good business, and that is always connected with agriculture.' It sounded to me irresistible. But could it still be the same in these days of tourism and development and relentless expansion?

Happily it can. Not many farms are left derelict these days and the 'labourers' though still probably horny, spend their time operating complicated farm machinery instead of ambling round the lanes. But the atmosphere of remoteness remains unchanged. The signposts are still quite baffling; most of them merely say, 'To Farm'. The villages, once you find them, seem to have been spared the usual rash of redbrick chalet-bungalows. In one of them I pulled up and waited patiently while the drivers of a van and a tractor continued their leisurely conversation, their vehicles completely blocking the road. I did not have the temerity to toot, and I was rewarded, when the conversation ended, by an almost imperceptible nod. Had I actually tooted, I could be waiting there still.

There are two groups of saints in Saints' Country, the South Elmhams and the Ilketshalls, and the saints on offer are St Cross, Mary, two Margarets, Nicholas, James, Michael, Peter, John, Andrew and Lawrence, plus two All Saints. To a stranger there is little to choose between them. They all cherish their obscurity, and I suspect they are rather embarrassed by the presence in their midst of South Elmham Minster, the only excuse a tourist has for invading their privacy.

What makes it more exasperating for them is that the tourists have probably got the wrong Minster and the wrong Elmham. Both North and South Elmham have claims to be the centre of the original diocese of East Anglia, but the experts now agree that North Elmham in Norfolk has the remains of the genuine Saxon cathedral. It is now thoroughly excavated, the ruins preserved, and explanatory notices erected. There are signposts for miles around North Elmham and no doubt in due course there will be an ice-cream van in the car park and a picnic area covered in crisp packets. I do not view this prospect with enthusiasm, since North Elmham was my home in the nineteen-fifties and I much preferred it when the cathedral was a neglected ruin and we were left in peace.

South Elmham Minster however has none of these refinements. It is on private land, well away from any roads, and its remains are still crumbling and overgrown. It is surrounded by trees and a ditch, and 'Minster' seems a very grand title for what was quite a modest chapel – not seventh-century as originally thought, but some four hundred years later. I am purposely playing down its significance and emphasising its inaccessibility lest I encourage more visitors to invade Saints' Country, and those two chaps in the van and the tractor find themselves deafened by tooting horns . . .

If you manage to find your way back to the Waveney and follow it upriver you will see Redenhall church on the Norfolk

Verging on the Border-line

bank. The historian Blomefield said it has 'the finest tower of any rural parish church in the country'. One loses count of church towers which are the finest, or the handsomest, or the most dramatic, or even the ugliest, but Redenhall's tower is certainly impressive, and it has one distinction which few others can claim. On one of its pinnacles is a carved rebus, a pictorial pun of a former Rector's name: a shell and a tun for Shelton. Bishop Goldwell left his own rebus on some of the bosses in Norwich Cathedral, but one rarely finds a village parson indulging in such a conceit. Incidentally Redenhall was the home of Samuel Fuller, who was physician and surgeon on the *Mayflower*. If the tun had been depicted overflowing it could have commemorated Dr Fuller too.

A pleasant lane links the Saints' Country with Mendham, birthplace of A.J. Munnings, and it is argued that if he had stayed put he could have done for the Waveney valley what Constable did for the Stour. Those of us who have become entangled with Constable coach parties will be much relieved that he did not. But if you seek more activity you can cross the river into Harleston. Although the river road now bypasses it the streets are still busy and there is the inevitable one-way system to whisk you into the town and out of it again. You may catch a glimpse of the wrought-iron inn signs along the main street and the eastern-style minaret on top of the Midland Bank, calling the faithful to greater overdrafts; then the signs usher you on. Harleston seems quite strong on signs. Even when you reach some pleasant wooded lakes just outside the town you are confronted by the stern and forbidding warning: 'No bottles or cans. No dogs. No picnics. Anyone leaving litter will be expelled.' And don't forget to wipe your feet.

The Pulhams, north of Harleston, had an Airship Festival in 1989, an unlikely celebration for such an obscure corner of Norfolk, but it was here seventy years earlier that the airship R34 landed after its historic two-way flight across the Atlantic, starting from Scotland, flying to New York and circling Long Island before returning to Britain, adding the extra few hundred miles to Pulham for good measure. The feat is commemorated on the village sign, but these days the name of Pulham is linked more with drinking than dirigibles. It has one of East Anglia's increasingly successful vineyards.

St Margaret's church in Tivetshall contains a massive coat of arms for the first Elizabeth, 'said to be the finest in existence' – there we go again. But we are getting too close to the main A140 road from Norwich to Ipswich and it would be wise to retreat back across the river at Brockdish. The Big House is said to be where the bride so ill-advisedly hid in the chest in the legend of the Mistletoe Bough. But there are almost as many places claiming the legend as there are finest coats of arms and handsomest church towers. You may take your pick.

Pulham's sign commemorates the R33, but its sister airship the R34 made the historic two-way flight across the Atlantic. They were both based at Pulham.

Fressingfield is not content with one claim to fame, it has two right next to each other. The Fox and Goose is very ostentatious about itself – the inn sign does not just say Fox and Goose but 'The Famous Fox and Goose'. I am afraid a sign like that would send me away again; I would sooner eat and drink in more modest surroundings. But I am assured the food is excellent, and although the front of the pub looks plain enough, the rear wall backing on to the churchyard is splendid timber and brick dating back to its days as a guildhall.

This was once the back of the guildhall at Fressingfield, but if you go round the front you will find it is now the Fox and Goose – and not quite so handsome.

The church itself is the other claimant, via a Dr Cox, author of *Bench Ends in English Churches*. 'This church is better fitted throughout with excellent fifteenth-century benches than any other church in the kingdom,' he announces. And here we go yet again, you may murmur, but Dr Cox is obviously a bench-buff and ought to know. I am not a carpet-buff but I would say that Fressingfield has the most striking carpet in the kingdom too, with the possible exception of Axminster, which is understandable. It is quite a knock-out, royal blue and wall-to-wall. And judging by the visitor's book it is the most contentious development involving the church since Archbishop Sancroft, whose portrait hangs on the wall, refused to take the oath to William and Mary and was sent back here to oblivion.

The entries start quietly. 'I think the blue carpet takes away the church's character', 'I certainly do not agree with this wall-to-wall carpet in this beautiful fourteenth-century church.' Then they warm up. 'I am disgusted that William Browse's brass has been covered up.' And more strongly, from a Swansea visitor: 'It seems a shame that this church which survived the onslaught of Cromwell's Roundheads now looks set to be desecrated by those in whose care it temporarily rests.'

Verging on the Border-line

The pro-carpet lobby hit back. Fressingfield Girl Guides wrote defiantly: 'We like the New Carpet.' Another visitor wrote: 'I certainly don't agree with the Welsh person from Swansea. Typical of the Welsh to find fault with everything British!'

That was a false move. 'The Welsh person from Swansea,' it is forcefully pointed out in the next entry, was born and bred in the village and her great-grandfather presented one of the stained-glass windows. The onslaught on the carpet was resumed. 'Hope it doesn't last as long as the pews,' says a later visitor. 'Such a pity.'

The argument may still be going on, though I cannot imagine the embattled church council ripping up this very expensive expanse of carpeting and putting it in the next jumble sale. Perhaps Catherine de la Pole foresaw an attack by enraged parishioners when she built the fortress-like porch with its battlemented flat roof, where the carpet could be defended to the last churchwarden.

The battlemented church porch at Fressingfield, apparently designed to repel attackers rather than welcome worshippers.

The de la Poles, Earls of Suffolk, were very much in evidence in this part of the county. Alice de la Pole, whose initials AP are carved on one of those famous benches, was a granddaughter of Chaucer. There was a de la Pole at Harfleur, another at Agincourt, and yet another led the siege of Orléans against Joan of Arc. The first earl built Wingfield Castle, a few miles from Fressingfield, and the walls still loom majestically over Wingfield Green. The de la Poles, however, have long since departed and in 1981 a Mr Fairhurst bought it for an apparently modest £250,000. There was talk of it then being bought by a Mr Johnny Rotten, described as a 'singer' with the Sex Pistols, but Mr Rotten failed to materialise, though for a time the medieval gatehouse did resound to assorted pop groups, allegedly practising. In 1987 Mr Fairhurst sold the castle for a reputed million pounds, which shows just how modest that original figure was. Two years later it was reported that yet another pop star, perhaps impressed by the gatehouse acoustics, had bought it for even more. This was Roland Gift of the Fine Young Cannibals, no less. The de la Poles, heroes of Harfleur, Agincourt and Orléans, will be interested to know that the old homestead is again echoing to the beat of heavy metal.

Long before the de la Poles there was fighting much closer to hand, when the Danes invaded East Anglia. Not far away at Hoxne (it rhymes with oxen) is Goldbrook Bridge where the young Saxon King Edmund was discovered and killed on the spot. Sceptics argue that this may not be the right place, but there is a plaque on the bridge, a fresco depicting it on the wall of nearby St Edmund's Hall, and an aged Hoxne resident who told the story to Julian Tennyson had no doubts at all. He retells it in *Suffolk Scene* using the original Suffolk dialect. It goes on for several pages, but here is a flavour of it, the discovery of Edmund by a courting couple.

> By'nby there come a chap an a gal, orf to be marrerd they was, they come 'long ower the bridge, they was a scroogin and a noodlin one nuther like willy-oh, silly young fules, so they stopped on the Goldbrook a bit cos they din't think there was nobuddy about. Time they was a noodlin together yew woulden ha thot as they'd ha noticed much would yew, but dret if she din't then goo and sing out, 'Whoi, John boy,' she say, 'stop tittlin me will yew, whativer's that down there, there's suthen a glistin in the watter d'yew see?' 'Whoi thass roight, Meery,' he say, 'there's suthen down under th'ould bridge, that look like a cupple o' sparrs [spurs] on't yew think so? Theres ony one chap has gowld sparrs like that,' he say, 'an thass King Edmund, the Deens is arter im,' he say, 'less goo an tell em.' Now I dew think that was the wustest trick of all, pore young faller, he niver ad na luck, did he?

This same Suffolk sage, when asked for proof of the story, recalled that an ancient tree which stood nearby was found to have an arrowhead embedded in it, evidence that Edmund had been tied to it and killed. Mr Tennyson did not argue with him, and nor would I. Even the strange end to the story, the discovery of Edmund's severed head being guarded by a wolf and shouting 'Here! Here! Here!' was good enough for Tennyson and it is good enough for me.

Before returning to the Waveney you must not miss Eye, one of the most charming little towns in Suffolk but not too frequented by tourists. I last visited it in the early evening when the traffic had died down and one could cross the main street in safety. I was able to amble round the town and admire the old Guildhall by the churchyard, the almshouses, the chemist's shop with its sloping timbers, the twenty-one curves in the crinkle-crankle wall, and in the centre the quite astonishing Victorian town hall with its domed clock tower and a bell tower on top of that.

The venerable chemist's shop in Eye; the main beam seems to have a touch of the bends.

There is a castle too, or the remains of one, but it has not been kindly treated over the years. Once there was a windmill on the castle mound, but in 1845 General Sir Edward Kerrison knocked it down and built a house for his batman instead, as a reward for saving his life at Waterloo. The locals did not seem too put out by this, and a few years later they made him their MP – the General, that is. They even put up a monument to him opposite the White Lion Hotel. The batman's house no longer survives, but in 1980 the borough council elaborated on the General's idea and built twenty houses on the castle's bailey, thus virtually eliminating it. No matter. You can still climb the castle motte if you respect the Danger signs, and gain a commanding view of the Suffolk countryside, just as Stephen de Blois did when he held the castle, before becoming King Stephen.

Eye does not rely entirely on ancient history. The car park of the Queen's Head has become the regular venue for the World Ferret Racing Championships, an event which has featured on Australian television and was reported in the *Daily Mail* under the headline: 'You've got to hie to Eye to see the real drain brains.' Ferrets, as everyone knows, spend most of their time down rabbit holes or up trouserlegs, so it comes as second nature to race along a twenty-foot drainpipe, the standard championship course. One year a ferret tried to turn round, got jammed, and bit the finger that freed it, but such bloodletting is rare. Competition however is keen. The owner of the

The dramatic rood screen in Eye church; the panels feature fifteen assorted saints and kings.

1989 winner, a three-year-old female ferret called Petal, was quoted as saying: 'She was brilliant. All her special training up and down my trouserlegs has paid off.' Not many trainers of sporting champs can say that.

The road from Eye to Diss takes you into a no-man's-land where major roads join and form bleak little triangles of industrial activity, but it is worth finding Billingford to see its restored windmill, and it is worth driving through Scole to see the oldest coaching inn between Ipswich and Norwich, though its famous sign no longer spans the road. It cost over a thousand pounds when the inn was built in 1655, which gives an idea of its size and splendour.

The Mere is Diss's central feature but most of the buildings seem to have turned their backs on it – except the church.

'Diss' means standing water, and in 1989 the town found that water can stand too long. Its six-acre mere became covered in a gruesome green slime, so the ducks acquired green legs and, if they had been feeding, green bills. It was something to do with the long hot summer. However Diss still managed to win the Norfolk Civic Amenity Award for the best-kept small market town, which says a lot for its other charms.

Betjeman said it was his favourite Norfolk town, but I am not sure he would say so now. On British Rail's good days it is only ninety minutes from the City and it is becoming a commuter town. The station which was once on the outskirts has now become part of it. Fortunately the town centre has not been affected, except for the inevitable one-way system, and it is worth a stroll up the hill to the much truncated market place to see the timbered Dolphin House and the parish church where Henry VIII's tutor, the poet John Skelton, was Rector. Skelton wrote of his own poetry: 'Though my rime be ragged, tattered and jagged, it hath in it some pith.' He should know.

The public gardens by the Mere are pleasant enough, but all the buildings on the hill opposite seem to have their backs to it, so one gets an uninspiring view of backyards and blank walls. For once I cannot blame modern developers; these were mostly built a

129

few centuries ago. But what a chance was lost to give both residents and visitors something pleasant to look at.

The man with the best view in town is Robert Manning, who lives in the only remaining windmill; there used to be eleven. Mr Manning was not born to the mill, nor did he achieve it; the mill was thrust upon him. He really wanted the miller's cottage next door, but the derelict mill had to be part of the deal. Having acquired it he converted it, and from five flights up he can now see the whole town and the countryside beyond. What a splendid opening line for a thriller: 'Mr Manning went to the window – and Diss appeared.'

Within a few miles of the town – they may even be within Mr Manning's range – are villages with fascinating tales to tell. The most famous must be Burston, scene of the longest strike in British history. The village schoolteachers, Tom and Annie Higdon, were dismissed for helping farmworkers to form a union. The children went on strike, the Higdons set up a rival school, and it flourished for twenty-five years, from the start of the First World War to the start of the Second. The Burston School Strike Rally is still held by trades unionists in the village each year, and the school building is preserved as a reminder of how Norfolk folk like to 'du different'.

Cut-out figures relive the Burston School strike, when pupils walked out in support of their teachers and stayed out for twenty-five years.

These days Bressingham is probably better known than Burston, thanks to Adrian Bloom and his steam engines and gardens. If you prefer less publicised attractions there is a stained-glass window in the church at Winfarthing commemorating a miraculous sword which had the dual powers of locating lost horses and disposing of unwanted husbands. The latter was a long process. According to the instruction book 'it helped to the shortening of a married man's life, if that the wife who was weary of her husband would set a candle before that sword every Sunday for the space of a whole year, no Sunday excepted.' For wives in a hurry to dispose of their loved one, perhaps the sword itself offered a swifter solution.

There is little else to observe at Winfarthing. It used to have a thousand-acre deer park, and there was reputed to be an ancient oak more than thirty feet in circumference, but there is not much left of either, and indeed it is difficult to visualise this area as a wooded deer park. It is far more reminiscent of the fens, vast flat fields with deep dykes along the side, and only the occasional tree. You are not even likely to win any farthings at Winfarthing. The name has nothing to do with coins. 'Farthing' is derived from 'fourth' and the village is the quarter-share which Wina acquired from his Saxon father. Shelfanger, down the road, is doubly confusing. There is no connection, say the experts, with wardrobes. 'Shelf' comes from scylf, meaning a hill, and 'hangra' is Old English for slope. But there are no hills and precious few slopes in Shelfanger. Maybe the experts are wrong, and a Saxon tailor chose the name to publicise his shop.

All in all I should leave Winfarthing and Shelfanger to brood over their origins and go south of the river again into more scenic Suffolk. You will find Wortham, which according to Julian Tennyson has 'the most gaunt and uncouth church in Suffolk'. That seems a bit hard, since the top of the tower fell down in 1780 and nowhere looks its best after that. But what the church lacks in masonry it makes up for in the fame of its Rectors. You have the choice of William Cratfield, who became a highwayman on Newmarket Heath and died in Newgate Prison, or Richard Cobbold, a very different character who immortalised the story of Margaret Catchpole, East Anglia's famous smuggler's moll. He wrote the story as a novel but she did operate on the Suffolk coast, and I shall come to her in that chapter.

Richard Cobbold was a member of the wealthy Ipswich brewing family, but as the twentieth child of his father's two marriages his share of the business would have been minuscule, so he went into the church instead. His younger brother – yes, number twenty-one – did the same, but he lacked Richard's literary skills and there is little trace of him left. The Cobbolds may have been responsible for another notable character in Wortham's history, 'Tumbledown Dick'. This was the name of a pub, probably owned by the Cobbold brewery, now a private house on Wortham Ling. Its sign used to show a man tumbling off a chair, but it was actually named after Richard Cromwell, Oliver's less talented successor. 'Now the far-famed Diogenes is dead, the Tumbledown Dick is come in his stead.'

A more tangible piece of history exists at Botesdale, a few miles away. A medieval chapel of ease became a famous grammar school for three hundred years, then in the last century it was restored to its original use, but with a house firmly attached. The bell which calls parishioners to church on a Sunday summoned pupils to school

Julian Tennyson called Wortham church 'the most gaunt and uncouth church in Suffolk'. Seems a little strong. . .

four centuries ago, at five a.m. during the summer and seven a.m. in the winter. Lessons continued until five p.m. except on Saturdays and half-holidays, when they ended at three. No wonder they produced some very brilliant scholars for the universities.

The Waveney valley and the Little Ouse

opposite Tennyson could hardly complain about Wortham's splendid pew-ends. This one illustrates Psalm 104: 'Man goeth forth to his work. . .'

left Botesdale church has a house firmly attached to it, legacy of its years as a grammar school.

Nearby is Thelnetham windmill, the oldest and in my view the most attractive tower mill in Suffolk, restored by the Suffolk Mills Group. Its fantail is painted a cheerful red, white and blue, visible for miles around. But the real significance of this area lies in Lopham and Redgrave Fen, seventy acres of shoulder-high reeds and sedge pitted with sinister black pools, where you may find either the Great Raft Spider or David Bellamy; I am not sure which would startle me most. This is where the Waveney rises and heads off to the east, while a little way away the Little Ouse rises and heads off to the west. They are so close together that on some maps they look like the same river, impossibly flowing in opposite directions. So far as the county boundary is concerned, the Little Ouse picks up where the Waveney leaves off. In theory you could cross the gap between them dry-shod, but in reality you would probably finish up ankle-deep in bog.

Thelnetham windmill *far left* is the oldest tower mill in Suffolk, and perhaps the most attractive. Certainly *near left* the Thelnetham countryside could hardly be bettered.

One or two lanes cross the Ouse in its early stages but there
is not much to see until you reach Rushford, which has the remains
of a fourteenth-century college on one side of the river and Rushford
Hall on the other. The star turn between Lopham Fen and Thetford is
Euston Hall, a vast mansion set in a vast park which was made even
vaster to cover the area where the village once stood. The village was
moved outside the gates and only the church was left behind. There
are many tales attached to the Hall and its occupants. They ranged
from Lord Arlington, who paid the King ten thousand pounds to be
made Lord Chamberlain, to Henry FitzRoy, one of Charles II's assorted
offspring, who pushed a bill through Parliament to have Westminster
Bridge built so he could reach his other house in Croydon without
having to use a ferry. But whatever these gentlemen reveal of political
skulduggery among Top People, one gets a more down-to-earth picture
of them from the French traveller de la Rochefoucauld, who was a dinner guest at Euston in 1784. He recorded with understandable distaste:
'The sideboard is furnished with a number of chamberpots and it is
common practice to relieve oneself whilst the rest are drinking. One
has no kind of concealment and the practice strikes me as indecent.'

Just down the road is Fakenham Magna, which is actually
smaller than its namesake in Norfolk and would seem to be
unrelated. Honington was the home of Robert Bloomfield, whose poem
'The Farmer's Boy' was condemned by Charles Lamb – 'he makes me
sick' – but nonetheless was translated into Latin, Italian and French.
One wonders what they made of rural life in Suffolk when they read
it in Paris or Rome; it must have seemed a different planet.

R.H. Mottram might feel the same way if he could return to
modern Thetford. 'This flint-built town of the Brecks,' he wrote,
only fifty-odd years ago, 'is one of the quietest old-world places
you can want, unless you live right on its main street or facing
the station.' The postwar London overspill plan put an end to all
that. The population quadrupled in twenty years, and Mr Mottram
would need to negotiate a sea of red brick to locate the remaining
flint buildings. The new bypass has reduced the traffic, but even
Thetford's most fanatical supporters would hardly call it quiet and
old-world. Ironically the main street he found noisy, presumably Old
Market Street, is now one of the quietest, in a backwater of the new
town. Some original buildings have survived, but in different guise.
The market hall is an office furniture warehouse, the old gaol has
been turned into flats (the top floor windows do still have bars, but
only to stop small children falling out), and the brewery opposite is
occupied by an upholstery firm.

Pit Mill, which marked the limit of navigation on the Ouse
and was once Twining's coffee mill, is now a Masonic Hall. The old
'cage' lock-up and stocks have been moved to make way for a modern
assembly hall, the remains of Thetford Priory are mixed up with the

edge of an industrial estate, and Castle Mound, once the largest motte in England, is largely obscured by housing.

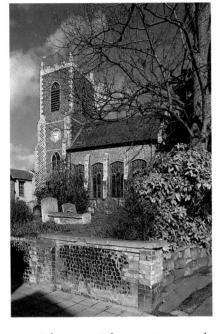

far left Thetford has three medieval churches, but this one, St Peter's, is now used as a church hall. *left* The statue of Thomas Paine, author of *The Rights of Man*, is a much more recent arrival; it is the work of Sir Charles Wheeler, notable President of the Royal Academy.

I do not wish to paint too gloomy a picture. There is a pleasant riverside walk near the new shopping precinct, and Tom Paine, Thetford's most famous son, still stands defiantly on his pedestal brandishing his *Rights of Man*, which played its part in the American and French Revolutions. But apart from a street called Icknield Way and a firm called Iceni Heating and Plumbing I could find few reminders that this was a major Roman centre on the main route into Norfolk, and the seat of a Saxon bishopric, before Norwich Cathedral was built. In Georgian times it was planned to make it East Anglia's answer to Cheltenham. Instead it has become East Anglia's answer to Hemel Hempstead. Its greatest attribute is that it makes a good centre for exploring the countryside around it. Let us lose no more time in doing so.

If you seek open heathland Knettishall Country Park has 360 acres of it. It is also the southern end of Peddars Way, which you can follow to the Norfolk coast ninety miles away, and the western end of the new Angles Way, which runs for seventy miles along the Waveney Valley to Lowestoft and Yarmouth. It is also planned to recreate the Icknield Way, down to the south-west. However this long-distance trekking is not compulsory. A quiet stroll along the nature trails with the chance of seeing a hen harrier or a White Admiral is probably quite enough.

Since the arrival of the Forestry Commission in 1922 much of the heathland has disappeared and there is now the largest area of

lowland wood in England, fifty thousand acres stretching westwards
to Brandon, with the Little Ouse running through the middle. There
was a time when the Commission's only interest in Thetford Forest
was producing more and more timber, but recently it has become
tourism-conscious. It appointed the first forest park development
manager, whose primary aim is to encourage more people to make
use of it. There are bird trails, forest walks, conservation areas, and
the inevitable picnic sites.

It all centres on Santon Downham, a modern-looking community
yet its history goes back to the days when there was hardly a tree
between Thetford and the Fens. As late as 1872 a traveller wrote:
'So barren is this land that one is often reminded of the deserts of
Africa. Hardly a drop of surface water, and for miles neither pitch,
pond nor spring. Little cultivation is possible but the loose sandy soil is
occasionally tilled.' This loose sandy soil was too much for the original
Santon Downham. In 1669 it was blotted out by a sand blow-out, and
it remained a dead village until the Forestry Commission revived it as
its headquarters.

In another part of the forest you will find the confusingly named
Grimes Graves, which are not graves and do not belong to a Mr Grimes.
Four thousand years ago these were flint mines, where Mesolithic
man, one step away from the cavemen, hacked away at the chalk
with deer antlers to dig up flints for tools and weapons. You can go
down one of these mineshafts to a depth of thirty feet and see how
they dug out the galleries by the light of animal-fat candles, and in
their tea-break drew the odd elk on the walls.

The art of flintknapping is nearly dead in Norfolk, but not
quite. Just one full-time flintknapper still builds flushwork flint
walls for those who want a very special piece of decoration and are
not in too much of a hurry for it. He sits on an old kitchen chair
with a pad strapped to his knee. On it he rests each flint and taps
it with a hammer at just the right spot to make it split. How does
he know where to hit, I asked him. It's a matter of angles, he said.
What he meant was, he just knows.

He chips the smooth face of the flint into a rectangle, and this
is the face which is exposed on the wall. The back of the flint is left
rough to bind into the mortar. When he gets into full production he
can knap two flints a minute. I met him one January when he was
working on the front wall of a moderate-sized house. He had started it
the previous September and expected to finish about May. When he is
not caught knapping he is touring local schools with the antler picks
and flint tools his predecessors used in 2000 BC, a happy wanderer
roaming the same Norfolk countryside that they did, reviving their
ancient skills. And yes, that must be a knapsack on his back.

Grimes Graves has been called by romantics the Sheffield of the
Stone Age, which would make Weeting, its nearest neighbour, a sort

of Neolithic Rotherham, but you would never guess it. Weeting must have been an attractive little village in medieval times and it still has the remains of a twelfth-century fortified hall set in pleasant parkland, where Hereward the Wake is said to have taken refuge on his forays out of the fens. It also has a fine row of thatched cottages beside the green. But a main road now carves the green in two and the chalet-bungalows have marched within a hundred yards of the Hall.

It is partly a dormitory for Brandon, a couple of miles away, which in turn is a dormitory for the American air base at Lakenheath. Brandon was once the centre of the flintknapping industry and there are flintstone houses in the older part of town, but its main street now straggles for a mile or more towards the airfield, flanked by petrol stations and industrial estates and redbrick cul-de-sacs. I am afraid it provides an unlovely southern approach to the Norfolk border.

I have a love-hate relationship with Brandon. That long street is invariably clogged with parked cars, so the lines of traffic have to crawl through, but I know that once I am over the bridge and across the railway I am back home in Norfolk again, so it is worth enduring the frustration. Unfortunately there is always the chance of being stopped at the level crossing. It amazes me that a line which is reputed to have such an inadequate service can always produce a train just when I come in sight of that crossing.

The area around the air base is the traditional sandy heath of Breckland, the way Thetford Forest looked before it was a forest. The base was built on Lakenheath Warren, probably the largest and oldest warren in Britain, owned for six hundred years by the Bishops of Ely, who relied on it for a steady supply of rabbit pies. Inside the perimeter fence, apart from the actual runways, the heathland has been tamed into a golf course, but there must still be a few rabbits around, if those long ears can stand the roar of the aircraft engines. Far more obvious are the planespotters who camp by the roadside at the end of the runway, noting all the landings and departures. They cannot all be spies, and the Americans seem to ignore them unless they distract them from their golf, but it seems a very uncomfortable hobby, doing nothing for ninety per cent of the time and getting deafened for the other ten. And what do they do with their information? Do they swap plane numbers with Greenham Common, or provide arrival times to pilots' wives? I often feel like asking them, but they always seem deeply engrossed in nothing in particular.

The only other sign of human presence around this perimeter fence is Wangford church, now marooned on the edge of the airfield. A new road bypasses it, built across the peaty ground on a low causeway to link the main road with the village that gave the airfield its name. It would be nice to report that Lakenheath still preserves its Suffolk character in spite of all the activity on its doorstep. Alas, that is too much to expect. It could be a commuter village in the Home Counties,

or in the Black Country, or indeed around Sheffield. It is more of a
small nondescript town than a large nondescript village. If I called it
a miniature Haverhill I don't know which could take offence.

The Little Ouse wisely avoids Lakenheath. A few miles north
at Wilton Bridge it passes from Breckland into Fenland and heads off
to the west across a sparsely populated plain of isolated villages and
flat hedgeless fields. It could not be a greater contrast to the Waveney
Valley where the county boundary began. It seems to become bored
with this flat expanse, and who can blame it. Instead of meandering
along like the Waveney in curves and loops between woods and hills,
it takes a straight route across the open countryside, less of a river now
and more of a channel, integrated into the Fenland drainage system.

Twenty-odd miles from Brandon it may be disheartened to find
it is only at Brandon Bank, a little clump of cottages alongside the
river, and even when it reaches the A10 trunk road between King's
Lynn and Ely it cannot escape the name because this is Brandon
Creek. But the end is in sight. The Great Ouse is just beyond the main
road, and perhaps with a certain relief the Little Ouse relinquishes
its separate existence and joins its big brother. Its mundane task as a
drainage channel is over; its weightier duties as the county boundary
are complete.

6 No Real Need to Hurtle

Beside the A45 from Newmarket to Ipswich

You may regard it as a concrete scar across the fair face of Suffolk, or a vital artery bringing the life-blood of trade and tourism. Some villages along its route are grateful to it for relieving their traffic problem, others regret that it has brought them developers and commuters. Love it or hate it, the A45 trunk road which links the Midlands with Bury St Edmunds, Ipswich and Felixstowe is the only uninterrupted dual carriageway road in East Anglia.

The A12 from London to the East Anglian coast is still quite sizeable when it crosses the border from Essex, but in its later stages it is reduced to a winding single carriageway. The other trunk roads, the A11 from London to Norwich and the A47 from the Midlands and North to Great Yarmouth, are notorious for their dangerous inadequacy. They only occasionally burgeon into two carriageways on the new bypasses, though the Attleborough bypass remains unaccountably single-carriageway and the Thetford bypass was intended to be also until the contractors pointed out the falseness of this economy.

Only the A45 offers a clear run right across the heart of East Anglia, and as a result drivers hurtle past some of the finest countryside in Suffolk seeing little more than a vague green blur. Let me urge you to change down a few gears, mechanically and mentally, and turn off the road into the byways on either side.

Between Newmarket and Bury St Edmunds you have the choice of flat breckland and forest to the north, or rolling hills and valleys to the south. The south is prettier, the north is more historic, to the extent that there is still an Anglo-Saxon village at West Stow and you reach it via the ancient Icknield Way. It looks like any country lane at this point, and you can only tell its significance when your map shows its name in Olde English type. It is of course much older than that, you are probably treading the same path as Boadicea trod in the first century AD.

139

No Real Need to Hurtle

The village, I have to admit, is just a reconstruction and looks rather like a collection of thatched garden sheds, but it is built on the foundations of the original Saxon houses and down by the River Lark, now devoted to unlovely gravel workings, there was once a Roman pottery. The whole area is now a country park, well geared up for tourists with nature trails and picnic areas, and it will not surprise me if in due course they sell Anglo-Saxon curios in the village and Roman pottery by the river, all shipped in from Birmingham courtesy of the A45.

The genuine treasures in this area were discovered on a farm at Icklingham, one of the many villages whose names are linked with Boadicea's Iceni and the Icknield Way. There were priceless Romano-British bronzes dating back to the second century and the star exhibit was a bronze cheetah studded with silver. The Icklingham Treasure, as it came to be known, has had a chequered history. It was allegedly removed from Weatherill Farm by people using metal-detectors in the early 1980s, and some years later it reappeared in the United States; it is not clear what happened in between. The farmer, who seems to spend much of his time camping out in the hedgerows on the watch for more marauders, has been understandably irked by the loss of the Treasure and has conducted a lively campaign to retrieve it.

Life is more placid in the nearby village of Flempton, where thatched cottages sit picturesquely round the village green, mercifully just off the through road so few strangers spot it, let alone stop. It was here, while browsing through the list of Rectors in the parish church, that I came upon the memorable name of the incumbent in 1682. Sandwiched between the fairly average John Thurston and the even less remarkable William Richards is the Reverend Blastus Godly, a name surely unique in ecclesiastical history.

A fine line-up of hassocks in Flempton church; the Revd Blastus Godly would have been proud of them.

His parishioners may have found it difficult to accept, because the memorial to him and his devoted wife Deborah (it takes a certain devotion to say, 'I take thee, Blastus . . . ') is concealed behind the organ. I would emblazon such a name on the church tower, possibly in coloured lights, with perhaps an honourable mention for the Rector's parents for devising it. One likes to picture the scene round the font when the parson said, 'Name this child,' and got the response, 'Blastus!' He must have thought they'd forgotten . . .

Flempton Church also features a more familiar name, but in an unfamiliar setting. A stained glass window depicts a surprisingly youthful Queen Victoria being favourably received at the Throne of Judgement. A benign Deity is welcoming her, with assorted angels applauding from nearby clouds. Her orb, sceptre and crown lie beside her, and the artist, perhaps worried that you may not recognise her, has written 'VICTORIA' round the edge of the crown. It gives the impression that she used to mislay it in the changing rooms.

You can cross the A45 in reasonable safety either at Risby or Kentford. Risby's main street opens straight on to the dual carriageway and is more accessible to strangers than most. Perhaps that is why it has a 'Country Style Shopping Centre', to give them their first taste of the rural life. The profusion of new houses suggests that Risby itself now qualifies as a 'Country Style Village'.

Kentford has grown greatly too, but it does have a legend to take one's mind off the surroundings. In fact no guidebook I have read can find anything else to say about Kentford except the gipsy boy's grave. The story goes that he was accused of sheepstealing and hanged himself rather than face transportation. As a suicide he was buried by the crossroads at Kentford, and somehow there are always fresh flowers on his grave. Certainly when I last saw the sad little cross with the inscription: 'Joseph, the Unknown Gipsy Boy, RIP', there were a few tattered flowers beside it.

Beside the A45 from Newmarket to Ipswich

A youthful Queen Victoria arrives in Heaven with her name-tagged crown; one of the windows in Flempton church.

There are always flowers on the Gipsy Boy's grave at Kentford Crossroads. In Epsom Week they may forecast the Derby winner.

No Real Need to Hurtle

Since then I have heard a sequel to the story which gives it an added flavour. During Epsom Week, so it is said, the flowers on the grave are the colours of the jockey who will win the Derby. I am not sure what flowers one would find if the colours include black, but the grave might be worth a visit next race day.

Kentford and its neighbour Kennett are too near the A45 to preserve their charm, but the River Kennett which flows through them fares rather better. If you follow it upstream into the Suffolk hills to the south it will lead you to Moulton, where a four-arched packhorse bridge straddles it, with cottages to match. It is no longer in use, but there is a ford alongside and the stream is rarely more than a trickle. At Dalham, however, bridges are far more important, because the Kennett has created a deep dyke alongside the main street, cutting off the cottages on that side. This provides an attractive vista of little white bridges, and also a maintenance problem for the residents, I imagine, unless the bridges rate as part of the highway.

Moulton's packhorse bridge across the Kennett, no longer in use now that packhorse traffic has fallen away.

If we continue too far up the Kennett we are straying into the Suffolk hinterland, which rates a chapter of its own, but there is one more village in the river valley which we might treat ourselves to. It could just as easily be in Dorset or Sussex, but from the hills above Ousden you can see across the county boundary to the flat plains of Cambridgeshire. The world and most of the tourist guides seem to have passed Ousden by, and its scattered cottages are well hidden at the foot of the valley, reached only by a narrow lane. Overlooking them is St Peter's Church, from the outside a delightful jumble of architectural styles which the church guidebook describes over-modestly as 'humble and unprepossessing'. On the contrary, I think it is rather jolly.

It has a twelfth-century flint rubble tower, an eighteenth-century chancel covered with grey rendering, a nave which is thirteenth-century at one end and nineteenth-century at the other, a redbrick chapel jutting out of it and a twentieth-century mock Tudor porch. The gem of this happy hotchpotch is the doorway inside the porch, which could not make up its mind whether to be Norman or Early English. One side has a wavy design with a Norman capital, the other has a moulded capital on top of a circular Early English pillar. The arch is pointed, which means it is Early English, but the decorative moulding on it is Norman. Maybe the chap who built it was neither Norman nor Early English, just a medieval mason with a sense of humour. In centuries to come the experts may be just as baffled by that mock-Tudor porch.

Next to the church is a small stretch of parkland on which sprouts a fifty-foot clock tower and a dovecote. They are part of the original Big House, demolished only in the 1950s. Its coach-house and outbuildings were converted into a Not-So-Big House which is still quite big enough to have horses stabled in one wing. It makes a rather quaint setting for a most unusual church, and I hope that mention of it will not cause its tranquillity to be too disturbed.

Ousden is just a flavour of that little-known area of West Suffolk I call the hinterland, and you pass through more of it to return to the A45. In a maze of little lanes you may come upon Great and Little Saxham, Hargrave, Chevington and Dunstall Green, each one more peaceful than the last. You may also come across Barrow, with streets more broad than narrow, because there is a large experimental station to study the esoteric qualities of sugar beet, and a larger housing estate which holds the dubious distinction of being built in fifteen weeks. It goes in for tile-hung walls, which provokes the wrath of the *Companion Guide to East Anglia*. 'Tile-hung walls,' it storms, 'are a south-of-the-Thames expedient and have nothing whatever to do with East Anglia, except where introduced by people who ought to know better.' The builders actually came from Doncaster, but I am sure that is no excuse.

If you too are alarmed by tile-hung walls you are in for much more serious palpitations at nearby Horringer. The Horringer Horror, as not even the *Companion Guide* has yet called it, is Ickworth Hall. What the Guide does call it is 'the eighteenth-century equivalent of one of the Pyramids of Egypt, a vast monumental edifice put up by a very rich man for his self-glorification'.

The rich man did not come from Doncaster this time, nor did he come from the West Country or Northern Ireland, even though he was called Earl of Bristol and Bishop of Derry. These were titles that Frederick Augustus Hervey picked up along the way, as rich folk did in the eighteenth century. The French traveller de la Rochefoucauld reckoned that all the Herveys were a little mad, and quoted Voltaire as saying that in England he met three kinds of people – men, women and Herveys. Such views from two Frenchmen put me on the side of the Herveys; you can't beat a little English eccentricity. But I must say Frederick Augustus did go over the top with Ickworth Hall.

No Real Need to Hurtle

He started with a massive rotunda and added two curving corridors leading out to the east and west wings, so the effect is like an octopus with two legs, except the body of the octopus is six hundred feet high. That is the mental picture which puts the horror into Horringer, and perhaps succeeding Herveys felt the same way.

The massive rotunda and two wings of Ickworth House – a two-legged octopus with a 'body' six hundred feet high.

Frederick Augustus died long before it was finished, and his son was stuck with a half-built white elephant – or perhaps, white octopus. He and later generations did their best to turn it into something approaching a home, but I imagine they were not too inconsolable when the government took it over in 1956 in lieu of death duties and dropped it in the lap of the National Trust.

When you emerge from Ickworth Park, either dazzled or appalled, you find yourself on the outskirts of Bury St Edmunds. Do not be put off by these outskirts, nor by all those history lessons you are bound to get from enthusiastic locals. The body of King Edmund was brought here thirty years after he was killed by the Danes (Bury St Edmund's could hardly be better named). King Canute founded the monastery and Edward the Confessor financed it, the barons met here to plan how they would force King John to sign the Magna Carta, and so on. But it is an attractive town even without the history – which is just as well, because the scene of all these goings-on, the abbey itself, has long since been reduced to ruins. The west wall, the largest piece still standing, has had houses built into it during the last three hundred years so chimneys now emerge incongruously from the ruins, making the abbey even more difficult to picture, while the present cathedral, which started off as a parish church, was upgraded in 1914 and has been growing by bits and pieces ever since, seems to be set in a permanent building site.

The ancient abbey in fact is little more than a public park, with a few piles of rubble where children's swings would normally be. You may think from this that I come to Bury St Edmunds not to praise it. But elsewhere there is much to admire, and even the park has a unique feature, a garden seat constructed from the metal framework of a Flying Fortress, one of the most famous bombers of the Second World War. It commemorates soldiers and airmen who were stationed in the area. The Rose Garden also has an American connection. It was paid for out of the royalties of a book of Suffolk memories by one of those airmen. And in the new cathedral the painted shields bearing the arms of the Magna Carta barons were donated by the Dames of Magna Carta – who could only be American.

One of the remaining walls of the Abbey at Bury St Edmunds, with anachronistic chimneys and windows.

Outside the Abbey Gardens is Angel Hill, the old Saxon market place, with an assortment of old buildings unconnected with the Abbey or the Americans. The Athenaeum, once the centre of Bury's social life, was built by the architect responsible for Ickworth Hall, but mercifully in one of his quieter moods. Angel Corner is a Queen Anne house whose master was handily placed to stroll across to the Athenaeum and ogle the ladies. Today it is a clock and watch museum, more concerned with ticking than clicking.

The most prominent building on Angel Hill is the Angel Hotel, very proud of its Dickens connections and with so much foliage on its front wall one wonders which holds up which. If you think the Angel looks likely to be costly, do not be tempted by the oddly-named One Bull Inn round the corner, where I bought surely the most expensive pint of Ruddles bitter in East Anglia, about twenty pence above normal prices. Perhaps I was being fined for drinking Ruddles in the home town of Greene King ales.

The One Bull looks picturesque outside, and in the big archway are the door hinges from its old coaching days, but the arch no longer leads into a courtyard but straight into the main bar, where the walls

No Real Need to Hurtle

Contrasting hostelries in Bury St Edmunds; *left* the Angel Hotel, patronised by Dickens and a host of other Victorian worthies, and *right* the Nutshell, smallest pub in Britain, patronised only by a handful at a time.

are alive with the sound of fruit-machines. For a more modest drinking house, head for the Nutshell near the Market Place. It claims to be the smallest pub in Britain, and you cannot get more modest than that. Actually the claim is contested by the Smith's Arms at Godmanstone in Dorset, which bears on its front wall the unequivocal statement 'England's Smallest Inn'. Someone has finally got around to checking these claims with a tape measure, and I am glad to report that while the Smith's Arms measures nineteen-and-a-half feet by ten, the Nutshell is a mere sixteen feet by seven-and-a-half. East Anglia, not for the first time, is ahead of the field.

opposite Bury St Edmunds' oddest item of street furniture, a copper vat outside the Greene King Brewery.

The Nutshell has happily retained its original function, though you may not be able to take advantage of it. In the tiny bar, three's really a crowd. Elsewhere around the Market Place area the Corn Exchange and the old Fire Station have been converted into shops and the Market Cross, originally a theatre, is now an art gallery. Moyses Hall in Cornhill has seen even greater variety. It started in 1180 as a private house, became an inn, was said to have been converted (in more senses than one) into a synagogue, and is currently a museum. Opposite the Greene King brewery, still very much a brewery, is the Regency Theatre Royal, which acted as a beer store for nearly forty years before being restored to its former glory in 1962.

For many years it has been the proud boast of the city fathers of Bury that one could walk from Angel Hill into open country via the Abbey Gardens and the River Lark, without passing a house or crossing

No Real Need to Hurtle

a road. As this now brings you merely a close-up view of the biggest sugar refinery in England I suggest you are better off staying on Angel Hill. Alternatively, just keep going.

It must add to the prosperity of Bury St Edmunds, if not its beauty; this is the biggest sugar refinery in Britain.

Once you have got clear of the refinery, the A45 and the railway you may find yourself in Ixworth, which must not be confused with Ickworth though they both owe their origins to the Icknield Way. A bypass has taken away Ixworth's through traffic, but as in so many bypassed towns enough new traffic has somehow been created to fill the available space. Could I have discovered a new Parkinson's Law? Most of it seems to be permanently parked at the kerbside, so negotiating the main street is as difficult as before.

Walsham le Willows is worth a visit, if only to check that the willows are still there. They were at my last visit, along the bank of the river, and so were some fine lime trees by the church. Presumably the willows were there first, or we might be talking about Walsham le Limes.

The church's main claim to fame is the medallion, or crant, in memory of a young lady who died a virgin in 1685. The idea was to garland it with flowers on the anniversary of her death. The crant is regarded locally as something of a rarity, but I recall that at Abbotts Ann in Hampshire there are about forty of them hanging in the church. Does this mean the young ladies of Hampshire led purer lives than in Suffolk, or did they just marry earlier or die younger? Actually it is not a fair comparison because they were still hanging up their medallions at Abbotts Ann until thirty years ago, whereas in Walsham le Willows they seem to have given up the practice, perhaps wisely, in the seventeenth century.

In the tourist season the village's mellifluous name must be its own worst enemy, since it attracts a lot of people who just spot it on the map. One local hostelry, the Blue Boar, has geared up to cope with this and offers plenty of food and seating, and a big garden for the children. On the other hand the Six Bells, a delightful old pub which takes its name from the peal in the church tower, could not even offer me a sandwich. This doubtless pleases the locals, who can enjoy their drinks and gossip without interruption, and I am not sure whether to commend the Six Bells for its independence or carp at it for its lack of initiative. By now it may well have fallen into line and be selling overpriced ploughman's lunches with the rest of them – while the real ploughmen go elsewhere.

Heading back towards the A45, Stowlangtoft church has some old Flemish panels, which have been authenticated, and a memorial inscription which may be more dubious. It commemorates a lady called Lettice: 'Grim death, to please his liquorish palate, has taken my Lettice to put in his sallat.' It could be the work of the same doleful humorist who wrote on a tombstone in Bury St Edmunds: 'Here lies Jonathan Yeast. Forgive him for not rising.'

Sadly I could not locate Mr Yeast in Bury, and at Stowlangtoft I could not verify Lettice's epitaph or the panels, since the church was locked with no clue to the keyholder.

Pakenham may be unique in Britain in having a windmill and a watermill which both still work. Indeed the sign at the entrance to the village, which would normally say 'Please Drive Slowly', announces proudly, 'Village of Two Mills'. There was a watermill functioning on this site when the Normans arrived. It was replaced in Tudor times and again in the late eighteenth century. The present one stopped functioning in the 1970s until the Suffolk Preservation Society bought it and started the wheel turning again. Now you can acquire stoneground flour from the site where the Saxons ground it, nine hundred years ago.

Pakenham is proud to call itself 'The Village of Two Mills', and here they are to prove it, one powered by water, the other by wind, and both still working.

Rex Whistler was stationed in Pakenham during the war with the Scots Guards before going abroad, and painted a bewigged eighteenth-century parson on the dummy upper window of the Vicarage, some say as payment for hospitality, others as a merry

149

jape. The story goes that some of the work was done in the rain, with fellow officers taking it in turns to hold an umbrella over him on the ladder. These days the painting is protected by glass, which makes it look all the more realistic. But don't go looking for it on the present Vicarage, which is the chalet-bungalow next door. The old Vicarage is now called Mulberry House and a hedge of conifers has grown so high the painting is invisible from the road. If you want to see it, do please be civil and ask the lady of the house before wandering about in her garden.

This corner of Suffolk has two curious links with Henry VIII, though I doubt he ever passed this way. When he built Nonsuch Palace in Surrey he did not exercise his usual compulsory purchase procedure and just help himself to the land, he paid the landowners compensation. It took the form of Ixworth Priory, which he had just acquired by his standard methods from the Augustinians during the dissolution of the monasteries. This meant that the Codrington family of Surrey suddenly found themselves the Codringtons of Suffolk, and Richard Codrington has a very grand tomb in Ixworth church to establish their presence.

Henry's other link is with the village of Norton, where he was persuaded there was gold to be found. 'Drawn by a credulous kind of avarice,' as one chronicler put it, he transferred miners from Cornwall in 1538, and instead of giving them a priory like the Codringtons he gave them some shovels and told them to start digging. Norton, to nobody's surprise except Henry's, turned out to be extremely low on gold, and one can only hope the miners did not suffer as a result. The workings were still visible near the village until fairly recent times.

Just before you reach the A45 again you may come upon Thurston, which manages to preserve a rural flavour even though a railway viaduct passes over the centre of the village. It has a fine gabled mansion on the outskirts called La Planche, marred only by an assortment of aerials and an incongruous satellite dish. Nestling by the entrance is a tiny Primitive Methodist chapel, so small it might double for a gamekeeper's cottage or a large garden shed. Happily it has not yet been converted to either and still functions as a chapel.

Under the lee of the A45 but without direct access to it is Beyton, which used to have the trunk road pass through the centre of it and must be heartily thankful it has gone. The church has one of the few round towers in Suffolk with buttresses. They were probably added about five hundred years ago, and although the rest of the building has altered quite a bit since then, the buttresses still stand – which of course is what buttresses are supposed to do.

The real fascination of this little church for me, however – and yes, I *could* get in – is the mosaic reredos depicting the Last Supper. There are only eleven disciples around the table. Presumably the artist decided that Judas had already left.

Beyton church has one of the few round towers to be held up by buttresses. They were put there 500 years ago and they seem to have done a good job.

It might have been an obelisk or a small factory chimney, but it finished up as a very substantial pillar for a pub sign, the Five Bells at Hessett.

Within sight of Beyton is Hessett Church, with another example of artistic licence. A wall painting shows the Seven Deadly Sins, and underneath is 'Christ of the Trades', showing Him surrounded by medieval tools and implements. And among them is a playing card, the six of diamonds. The painting is very faded but the diamonds stand out very clearly on the card. There are various theories. One is that the card represents an eighth deadly sin, another suggests it was an emblem of the card-manufacturing trade. My own view is that the artist had just won the jackpot at pontoon and decided to celebrate.

On the other side of the road, next to the angular modern dwelling called 'Clock Piece' – a name as inexplicable as the decision to allow such a development opposite a handsome medieval church – there is a brick obelisk some fifteen feet high which might have been designed as a memorial or a clock tower. It does indeed bear an inscription, but it merely says 'Pub Lunches, Evening Meals', and it is surmounted, not by a clock but by the sign of the Five Bells Inn. Somebody was determined it should be well out of reach of revellers.

Woolpit is on another loop off the new A45. Although the wool towns of Suffolk are not far away, the village got its name from the pit in which Saxons used to trap wolves. There were other pits too, where the clay was extracted for Woolpit bricks some centuries ago. But the ground around Woolpit was not only rich in brick clay and shortsighted wolves. It is recorded that in the twelfth century two green children emerged from a hole, attracted, they said, by the sound of church bells. They lived underground in St Martin's Land, which presumably was bell-less.

They were taken to the squire's house, where they would eat only green food. The boy died but the girl got married and went to live in King's Lynn, no doubt maintaining her green principles. It would be nice to think that this was the founding mother of the Green Party, and Woolpit may become a place for political pilgrimage.

No Real Need to Hurtle

Meanwhile pilgrims must be content with the church, where the eagle lectern was cunningly designed to take coins through the beak. These could subsequently be extracted, as one might expect, under the tail.

We are coming within range of Stowmarket now and one has to move further away from the A45 to find villages which have evaded the developers. As for Stowmarket itself, it is a busy modern shopping centre and anything with a rural flavour has been consigned to its open-air museum. Once out of the town centre you are plunged into a network of crowded main roads alongside the A45 which all seem to lead to Needham Market. It is not a bad idea to follow them. In spite of the heavy traffic that pours through its main street Needham has retained much more character than Stowmarket.

There are almshouses here which were put up so long ago nobody can remember who was responsible: ' . . . built and endowed by some benevolent individual whose name is now unknown,' says the inscription apologetically. There are nice old timbered cottages down side alleys as well as handsome old buildings in the main street, and a grocer's shop which has been in the same family since 1580. But its outstanding attraction for me is its extraordinary church, built right on to the pavement and surely the noisiest place of worship in East Anglia.

As you follow the traffic queue down the long main street, the first you see of it is the large clock perched on top of the porch. When the rest of the building becomes visible the effect is like a stunted clock tower with a church attached to it. The church booklet admits that its exterior is 'disappointing', but there is ample compensation inside. This must be the only church guide which invites you to lie on your back on a pew; in the tourist season the place must look like a dosshouse. But the reason soon becomes apparent. This mundane-looking church with its embarrassing clock contains the most remarkable wooden roof in Suffolk.

If you do indeed lie down, by far the most comfortable way of studying it, you get the impression you are looking into the hull of a ship. Imagine a Spanish galleon turned upside down, with angels sticking out all along it like spare figureheads. Nobody is quite sure how the whole thing stays up. One expert described it as 'the culminating achievement of the carpenter's art', but a lot of faith must have gone into it too.

I have a sneaking affection for Needham Market, perhaps because others have been so rude about it. 'The road to Needham is the road to poverty,' observed an early critic, who probably came from Stowmarket. John Burke, a great Suffolk enthusiast, describes it merely as 'a double file of houses down the main road with only the briefest vestiges of side streets'. Regarding the church he comments on the 'tiny mockery of the clock tower', which is reasonable, but considers the roof 'grandiosely out of place above this bare chapel',

The church guide at Needham Market advises visitors to lie down on the pews – it's the best way of viewing its remarkable roof.

**No Real Need
to Hurtle**

which seems a bit hard. Even Professor M.R. James, expert on East Anglian church architecture, just says, 'The church has a good roof and a pierced buttress,' and leaves it at that.

But I reckon that for a community which has to tolerate such appalling traffic Needham has done well to preserve its old buildings, its village atmosphere, and that terrific roof. Judging by the street decorations at Christmas-time, each one sponsored by a local shop or organisation, it has preserved its community spirit too. One day perhaps there will be a bypass that really works and Needham Market will look like an old-fashioned market town again, instead of just feeling like one.

At present the best way to escape that traffic is to drive under the railway bridge, which is so low the big lorries cannot get through. Cross the River Gipping which once carried barges from Stowmarket to Ipswich docks, get the other side of the A45, and take to the hills. Tucked away amongst them you will find Coddenham, its old cottages scattered along a steep narrow street, and side lanes running along the hillside with pleasant views across the valley. There is a fair amount of traffic but compared with Needham it is deserted. There are splendid old pubs, past and present, and lots of thatch and exposed timbers. Mr Burke called it a fairy-tale village, and this time I agree with him.

Coddenham is just the start of a peaceful backwoods which is a different world from the hurly-burly on the other side of the trunk road. Villages like Crowfield and Gosbeck are hidden well away from any main road, with vast views across open country. Beyond them is the Diss–Ipswich road and the strange little village of Helmingham.

This is in Tollemache territory. The family has been there since the fifteenth century, landed gentry living in a moated Tudor mansion where even in the 1960s the two drawbridges were raised every night.

Helmingham Hall, stately home of the Tollemache family, complete with drawbridge and moat. . .

154

A visitor recalls how the butler's farewell words were always 'Careful how you cross the drawbridge, sir,' and for all I know, he says it still. But the Tollemaches were not above going into the brewery business, along with another famous Suffolk family the Cobbolds, and each time I drink a pint of Tolly Original I hope it helps to oil the chains on that drawbridge.

Helmingham village is a Tollemache creation. Lord John Tollemache built the cottages to his own design in the last century, and they have remained unchanged and immaculate ever since. They have steep pointed gables and dormer windows and handsome painted doors with black wrought-iron hinges. Each has half an acre of land intended for growing corn or rearing pigs, though there is not much of either today. John Burke called them 'bright little doll's houses' or 'semi-detached almshouses'. I think they look just like the station-master's house that went with my Hornby train set. Either way they are very distinctive, and rather fun.

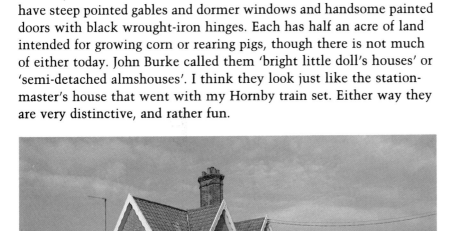

. . . and the mini-stately homes built by Lord John Tollemache for the villagers, perhaps anticipating the Hornby train-set school of architecture but with ironwork on the front doors.

But that is the last bit of fun you are likely to find this side of Ipswich. From here on the villages by the A45 and indeed over a much wider area have felt the developer's hand as the demand for housing around Ipswich has grown. The A45 continues beyond Ipswich to Felixstowe, and on that stretch it is a different story because the estuaries of the Orwell and the Deben are close by, and where there is water there is generally something worth seeing. But that is part of the Suffolk coastline and I will keep it in that chapter where it belongs. The place to end the story of the A45 is Ipswich itself, so take a deep breath and let's plunge in.

I always find it difficult not to compare Ipswich with Norwich – and always unfavourably. Perhaps the signs on the approach roads sum up the difference. The Norwich signs say quietly but firmly, 'NORWICH: A FINE CITY.' The Ipswich signs announce, as if it were the

No Real Need to Hurtle

most important factor to commend it, 'LATE NIGHT SHOPPING THURSDAYS UNTIL 8 P.M.'

Ipswich takes its name from the River Gipping, which unaccountably changes its identity at one of the bridges in the town and becomes the Orwell. This is a curious trait of Suffolk rivers. The Yox reaches Yoxford and turns into the Min, while upriver from Aldeburgh, Alde acquaintance is forgot and the upper reaches of the Alde are called the Ore. If Ipswich had been named after the Orwell instead of the Gipping and called Orwich, it might have come within an Nth of being a fine city too.

Ipswich thrives as a modern port but it still has reminders of its maritime past, moored at the Wherry Quay *above* and *below* the sailing ship *Maria Asumpta* outside the Customs House.

It is not Ipswich's fault that it has no great castle or cathedral, that much of the town was rebuilt in Victorian neo-Italianate Gothic, and that its main source of prosperity is the docks, which do not have the same peaceful charm as the moorings on the Wensum by Pulls Ferry. But it was somebody's fault that what remained of medieval Ipswich was largely obliterated by characterless buildings which can be found in any big town from Basingstoke to Blackburn. The only exception I can think of is the Willis, Faber and Dumas building in Friar Street, and you really need a helicopter to appreciate its most distinctive feature. The flat roof of this massive black glass building is covered with grass, and instead of a parapet there is a neatly cut hedge. There is a touch of whimsy about putting a meadow on an office block which I find quite disarming.

A meadow in the sky; the Willis, Faber and Dumas building in Ipswich has glass on the walls – the grass on the roof.

As for other modern offerings the *Companion Guide* selects for special mention the new boiler house and cooler tower at Ipswich Hospital and the underground spiral car park, 'a gigantic affair which should be visited by all car park lovers.' If a town has to rely for its architectural excitement on a roof garden, a hospital boiler house and an underground car park, there must be something lacking somewhere.

Julian Tennyson, in spite of his great enthusiasm for almost everywhere in Suffolk, could only muster a couple of pages about its county town. He mentions just two buildings, the Elizabethan Ancient House, which is now a bookshop, and Wolsey's Gateway, all that remains of the Cardinal's uncompleted college, which is now surrounded by unlovely dockland warehouses and factories. Julian was too early of course for the delights of aerial meadows and subterranean spirals.

It seems impertinent to try to better his list, but to be absolutely fair I must consult the official 'Town Trail', which should cover all

No Real Need to Hurtle

the goodies on offer. It starts you off in the Cornhill, which it calls 'the ancient market place of the town' – then adds very honestly, 'It now has a predominantly Victorian character.' In Westgate Street we are advised to note the stone façade of the former Crown and Anchor Hotel, designed in 'Venetian Gothic'. In Museum Street there is 'a particularly attractive building with an Ionic-styled door-case'. On a corner of Arcade Street there are 'huge and imposing Tuscan columns' on a building now used as a dancing school.

The Ancient House, about the only building left in Ipswich which still merits the name. Below all the elegant plasterwork is a thriving bookshop.

From here there is 'an interesting view' of the former Victorian Corn Exchange, now an entertainments centre. Behind St Mary Elms church the Trail discovers 'one of the oldest inhabited buildings in Ipswich, a cottage dated 1467'. Here at last perhaps is a corner the Victorians missed. But hang on. 'It forms part of an attractive row of buildings in the vernacular style.' Oh well.

It continues for another couple of miles around the town in much the same strain. It does locate some old churches, an early Nonconformist chapel and a scattering of timber-framed houses, some of which are actually genuine. There is also the Great White Horse Hotel, which was about the only reason that Dickens came to Ipswich. But I did get the impression that the compiler of the Trail had quite a struggle.

He finishes up in the pedestrian precinct called The Walk 'built in the Tudor style in the 1930s'. So he has brought us from Victorian Venetian-Gothic to nineteen-thirties Tudor, which perhaps is not the most uplifting of architectural experiences. Nevertheless, he is unrepentant. 'The warmth, human scale and attention to detail embodied in this reproduction craftsmanship,' he concludes defiantly, 'make an important and attractive contribution to the town's fabric.'

I think Mr Tennyson was right. Two pages is enough.

7 Rivers and Sand
The coast and rivers of East Suffolk

I left you marooned in Ipswich, and if you have failed to master the one-way system you are probably there still. Watch out for the signs to Manningtree, and when you have followed them through some of the more dismal corners of the Ipswich dock area you will emerge, with luck, on a roundabout that sends you off along the south bank of the Orwell estuary into the Shotley peninsula.

This part of the Suffolk coast is totally different from Norfolk's smooth unbroken curve. It has a succession of broad deepwater estuaries which can take sea-going yachts and cruisers, fishing boats and trawlers, and even cargo ships and ocean-going ferries. Perhaps this was how the North Norfolk coast used to look in medieval days, when ships set sail from Blakeney and Cley to sink Spanish galleons or explore new worlds, before the rivers silted up and the saltmarshes took over. Personally I would sooner have the saltmarshes, but I can see the attractions of these Suffolk estuaries, at one time for wool-traders and smugglers, now for container-shippers and sailors.

Of all the sights to be seen on the Shotley peninsula, none compares with the view as you enter it of the new Orwell bridge. The road takes you between its massive legs, and you can look up at the concrete bow curving high above you and get the full impact of its size and elegance. On the whole I am not too excited about modern bridges; they are too often just functional, unimaginative and very boring. It is only the suspension bridges, with all that fancy cablework and the great towers to hold them up, which have any pretensions to beauty. But the Orwell bridge is in a class of its own, and if the man who designed it had lent a hand with the redevelopment of Ipswich then Suffolk might feel a little prouder of its county town.

A mile or so down the bank of the Orwell estuary, still within sight of this marvel of modern building techniques, there is a structure which was something of a marvel itself in its own time,

Rivers
and Sand

One of the most spectacu-
lar engineering feats in East
Anglia since Vermuyden
built the Denver Sluice –
the soaring concrete arch of
the Orwell Bridge.

though it looks sadly neglected now. The sixteenth-century Freston
Tower stands six storeys high with a parapet and lantern on top, all
on its own on the river bank. Some say it was a watch tower, others
that it was a rich man's folly, but I prefer the story that Lord Freston
built it as a one-pupil training college for his daughter Ellen. Each floor
was designed to develop a different skill or virtue on each day of the
week.

She started off on the ground floor on Monday, practising charity.
If this involved distributing largesse to the passers-by it could not have
been too arduous, since the tower is in the middle of a private park, but
it gave her plenty of time for thinking about it. Tuesday involved a bit
more effort, with weaving on the first floor, then she worked her way
up through music lessons, classical and English literature, painting,
and finally astronomy. It was a strange form of vertical education,
and I have sometimes wondered whether the poor girl finished up as
a genius or a lighthouse keeper.

There is a more orthodox teaching establishment a couple
of miles away at Woolverstone Hall, a school established in the
eighteenth-century home of the Berners family. Even this has an
eccentric feature, the Cat House, from which the nearby boat marina
takes its name. In the western United States a cat house would have
quite a different meaning, but in this one there were no ladies of ill
repute, just a stuffed cat which was put in the window as a signal to
smugglers.

The contraband may well have come ashore at Pin Mill, the
showpiece of the Shotley peninsula and a scene which might have
been borrowed from the Hampshire or Dorset coast. The lane from
the main road runs straight into the estuary, and beside it is the
Butt and Oyster Inn, so close to the water that customers can buy a
drink through the bar window without leaving their boats. Even on a

weekday in December the pub was packed out at lunchtime, and in the sailing season I imagine the woolly sweaters are jammed wall-to-wall. There are few concessions to the tourist trade like concealed lighting or padded chairs; in fact the bar has very few chairs at all. This is an enthusiasts' pub, where sailing folk gather to talk about sailing, and if you wish to join them you must share the discomforts which sailing folk seem to relish. It may be Howard's Way, but it is not mine.

Let me put in a word instead for another pub which does not have the nautical ambience of the Butt and Oyster, but it does have excellent views across the water – and a certain amount of upholstery. This is the Bristol Arms in unfashionable Shotley, a modern collection of houses – I would hardly rate it a village – which grew up around the naval establishment, HMS Ganges. I recall visiting Ganges in the nineteen-sixties to report the annual display by the naval cadets, when they manned that famous mast with the button-boy perched precariously on top. It is a police training college now but the mast is still there, and you can just see the slender metal rod projecting from the top of it, just knee-high, which was the button-boy's only support.

I am sure my duties prevented me from visiting the Bristol Arms, but I have been there since. As at Pin Mill, it stands at the foot of the road where it meets the water, but here there is a car park on the water's edge and a strip of grass under the trees with tables, where you can watch the activity across the Stour estuary in the Harwich docks. I find this panorama just as interesting as Pin Mill's view across the Orwell on the other side of the peninsula, and there is room to enjoy it in comfort. The beer incidentally comes from the same brewer and the staff are just as civil. True, you cannot moor a boat outside the window, but you can park a car outside the door.

There is only one main road on the peninsula, the one that finishes up in Shotley, and I was surprised to find so much traffic on it in December, for what is just a long cul-de-sac. Fortunately there are quiet lanes that run off it, and one of them leads to isolated Shotley church, on the opposite side from the non-village. It looks across the marshes and the Orwell estuary to Felixstowe docks. Quite unexpectedly in this lonely corner there is a little war cemetery, row upon row of identical white tombstones all bearing the insignias of the Royal or Merchant Navies, and all commemorating sailors who died in these waters during the war. Men of the *Worcester*, the *Tunisia*, the *Whitshed* and the *Cape Finistere*, the entire ship's company of the *Gypsy*, and many more.

They lie in an extension of the churchyard, beside the plain walls of the little church, with just a handful of cottages clustered around. The view has changed across the estuary since they were buried there; the Felixstowe skyline has become a mass of huge dock cranes. It has changed closer at hand too. The *Companion Guide* says this little haven is 'undiscovered', but a builder has discovered it and erected a modern redbrick house by the churchyard with a roof which cannot be corrugated iron but certainly looks like it. It has a balcony to view the estuary and black and orange canopies over the windows. It fits into this peaceful little haven like a gold tooth.

Happily I found another redbrick house which offers the ultimate contrast. The mellow bricks of Erwarton Hall have been there for four hundred years. At one time the captains of HMS Ganges had the good fortune to occupy it, with working parties of cadets from Shotley to do the gardening. There are a number of halls in Suffolk like Erwarton, but none has a gatehouse to match it, an astonishing structure also built in Tudor brick but with nine chimney-like protuberances on the roof. They could almost be legs sticking up in the air, so that if you turned the whole thing over you would have an enormous hollowed-out sideboard.

This is not the only architectural oddity the peninsula has to offer. The Tattingstone Wonder was built as a folly, but at least it serves a useful purpose as well as improving – or marring – the view. From the Big House on the opposite hill it looks like a church; from the other side it looks like a house. An eighteenth-century squire decided he wanted to see a church from his window,, and as the real thing was out of sight in the village he built the Wonder; but very sensibly he made it habitable so that he could draw rent from it as well. From the 'church' side the only giveaway is the chimney that projects from the 'nave'.

Now you see it, now you don't; the Tattingstone Wonder, half-church half-house, built by an 18th-century squire to improve his view, if nobody else's.

The peninsula's most impressive set of buildings must be the Royal Hospital School for Sailors' Sons, with its tall pointed tower dominating the surrounding countryside. It has its ambiguous name perhaps because it looks as much like a hospital as a school, and the *Companion Guide* comments that 'whatever else one sees about the vast buildings, in term-time or vacation, one never sees a boy'. I drove through it during term-time and did not see an adult either. Is it possible that, like HMS Ganges, the sailors' sons have moved out and gone to school elsewhere – and nobody has yet noticed?

The Royal Hospital School for Sailors' Sons, founded in Greenwich in 1715 and transferred to its present neo-Wren grandeur at Holbrook in 1933.

As you complete the circuit of Shotley Peninsula you pass through Wherstead, once the home of Sir Robert Hall, who built the Big House in 1792. He is memorable only for his comment to the Rector when he sold the estate in 1848 for £111,000. 'I intend to spend the whole of it,' he told him. 'If when I am dead and buried there is half-a-crown over, it will be enough.' I doubt that he achieved his target – he died within the year.

The Felixstowe Peninsula, on the other side of the Orwell, has a very different character since it was split down the middle by the dual carriageways of the new A45. Heavy lorries pound up and down it day and night to serve the Felixstowe docks. Other roads have been diverted or renumbered or completely reconstructed to accommodate it; if you have an out-of-date map you can get hopelessly lost in the labyrinth that has been created east of Ipswich. It can be most disconcerting, as I know all too well, to be aiming for Woodbridge in the north and find yourself approaching the Orwell Bridge heading south, with no hope of turning round. There is not even the consolation of admiring the view from the top of the bridge; rather unkindly the architect has put high concrete parapets on both sides.

The best bet when entering the peninsula, if you want to avoid finishing up in the cargo hold of a German ferry, is to detach yourself from the main roads altogether and wend your way along the unaltered lanes which run parallel with the Orwell estuary. They take you through smugglers' country to Levington and the Ship Inn, one of the many hostelries on this coast which claim a link with the redoubtable Margaret Catchpole.

I am surprised Margaret Lockwood never starred as Miss Catchpole in one of those postwar bodice-rippers, with perhaps Stewart Granger as her smuggler lover Will Laud, and James Mason as the Excise officer who eventually captured her and shot Will dead. It would have been a combination of *Jamaica Inn* and *The Wicked Lady*, and I would have queued to see it. There is still a chance to fill the gap. Margaret Catchpole was transported to Australia for life; why not send for Miss Kylie Minogue to bring the story into the 1990s?

I fantasise, but the story of Margaret Catchpole is at least based on fact. She worked for the Cobbold family in Ipswich until she fell in love with Will Laud, ferryman by day and smuggler by night. She acted as his lookout and decoy, and the Ship Inn was one of their rendezvous, half a mile from the creek where he landed. It was in the mistaken hope of meeting Will in London that she stole a horse, was traced and arrested, and finished up in Ipswich Gaol. But this did not end the story. The enterprising Miss Catchpole escaped from the prison and the two lovers prepared to sail to Holland and safety. As they waited on the beach near Orford they were discovered by the Excisemen, led by one Edward Barry, who killed Laud and took her prisoner again, to be sentenced to transportation. That was the bad news; the good news was that Margaret earned her freedom in Australia, got married, and lived fairly happily ever after. So perhaps there is a part for Jason Donovan as well . . .

The Ship Inn still looks the part, a little thatched pub with ship's timbers among its beams, and you can sit outside and look down the hill to the marshes where Laud and his friends played hide-and-seek with the Excisemen. But make the most of the peace and quiet because Levington is the last haven on this shore before you run into the suburbs of Felixstowe. The Big House that dominates this part of the peninsula is Orwell Park, which is very big indeed and no doubt much impresses the parents of the boys who go to school there. It was the home of Admiral Vernon, who was cashiered for writing rude letters to the Admiralty and found a more effective way of castigating his former colleagues by becoming an MP. In the Navy his most lasting achievement was to dilute the rum ration, which then became known as 'grog' after the old grogram cloak he wore. Grogram itself was a heavy fabric named after the French *gros grain*, so next time you feel groggy you may like to know that the term is linked with the French cloth trade via a Suffolk admiral. Thus by such strange progressions the English language has evolved.

We must linger in Levington no longer. We have to traverse Trimley St Martin and Trimley St Mary, which have long since lost their trimness. They straggle all the way into Felixstowe, postwar housing estates linking up with Victorian terraces to create one amorphous suburb. In the middle of it all the two churches of St Martin and St Mary share the same churchyard, surveying each other glumly across the gravestones. But all is not lost. There is a mock-Tudor bus shelter down the road.

I am being unfair again. The Trimleys did produce a notable mariner, Thomas Cavendish, who was born at Grimston Hall and was the second Englishman to sail around the world. This exploit coincided with the arrival of the Armada off the English coast, so perhaps Thomas was well out of it, but Elizabeth apparently bore him no grudge. She is reported to have 'graciously waved' as he sailed up the Thames, though her graciousness did not extend to the customary knighthood. As it turned out, there was no need – the poor chap was lost on his next voyage, aged only thirty.

Felixstowe itself comes as a pleasant surprise. You may have pictured it as just a big container terminal, but it actually comprises four different sections. Next to the docks is the seaside resort which the Edwardians developed and the funfair tycoons took over. Beyond the shopping centre is an exclusive stretch of expensive retirement homes with sea-view balconies (the balconies wisely glassed in to keep the east wind from those ageing bones), a golf course for the more mobile and even a row of beach-huts for the positively lively. Beyond that again is the most attractive corner of Felixstowe, called Felixstowe Ferry, a little cluster of shanties, fishermen's cottages and boatsheds where time seems to have stopped still since about 1890. If old Peggotty came back and wandered down the coast from Yarmouth he would feel very much at home in Felixstowe Ferry today.

Two views of Felixstowe's lesser-known ferry terminal – not the international container docks but the isolated boatyard and landing stage on the other side of town, looking across the Deben estuary.

There is a primitive car park and a venerable snack bar but few other tourist facilities, and if you want to enjoy the view across the Deben estuary you must keep out of the way of the boatmen who are working around you. But the view is worth seeing nonetheless. The estuary offers a peaceful anchorage for sailing craft, and on the far bank are the neat if unwelcoming cottages owned by the Ministry of Defence. I discovered just how unwelcoming when I drove round there, but from a distance they provide a pleasant backcloth to the yachts moored in the river and the fishing boats pulled up on the shore. There could not be a greater contrast to that other ferry terminal on the far side of town.

Incidentally, Felixstowe is generally assumed to be named after St Felix, who founded a priory nearby, but some experts argue that this was a later development and the original name was Filthstow. This merely means a place of felled trees, but it sounds so uncomplimentary that the townsfolk prefer the Felix version, and who can blame them?

There is no road alongside the Deben from Felixstowe Ferry so you must go back into town and brave the A45 or the Trimleys; the former is marginally more picturesque. You can escape again at Kirton and head for the much quieter villages of Brightwell and Newbourn.

Brightwell is a small scattering of cottages on either side of a pleasant valley, and it would not add up to a village at all except for the church. It is quite a modest one, originally a chapel for the folk at the Big House, but brick obelisks grow out of the roof at each corner with a few more on the tower, making it look rather grander than it is. On the door is the original iron boss and closing ring which fugitives grasped to obtain sanctuary; it is not recorded if Will Laud ever tried to make use of it.

I went to Newbourn to see the grave of George Page, the Suffolk Giant, who was seven feet seven inches tall and could have eaten an Exciseman for breakfast. 'The deceased was exhibited in most towns in England, but his best exhibition was with his Blessed Redeemer,' says the inscription, but it has been obliterated by wind and rain. So was the east wall of the church when the great gales hit it in 1987. At that time most of the news stories about storm damage came from the Home Counties, probably because that is where most national newspapermen live, and it is a handy distance for the television camera crews. But East Anglia suffered greatly too, particularly here along the coast, and it must have been quite horrific for the villagers as they watched the gale demolish the exposed east wall – particularly as they had managed to put a new roof on the chancel only a few years before. Undaunted, they repaired the chancel and rebuilt the wall. When I was there it looked as good as new – or rather, as good as old.

Newbourn Church is also notable for the medieval graffiti artist who scratched on the porch a picture of a three-masted ship. It was done about 1500, probably by a sailor based at Gosford, which used to be a major port on the Deben but no longer exists. Wind and rain have failed to damage the little drawing, but modern graffiti now surround it, and some bright spark has scratched a clumsy imitation of it to confuse future experts.

Newbourn is much larger than Brightwell, partly because of an influx of unemployed Durham miners in 1937 who were moved into attractive new houses, well spaced out to provide each with a smallholding. I wish that other overspill schemes had been carried out as tastefully. There has been much in-filling since but the original houses are easy to distinguish, and the Durham expatriates must have marvelled at their luck.

Both these villages lie inland and there are only a couple of places between Felixstowe and Woodbridge where you can actually reach the river. There are none at all on the opposite bank, so this is a very quiet corner to go sailing. But Martlesham has a reminder of earlier days when much larger ships sailed and fought along these shores. The inn sign of the Red Lion is a figurehead from a Dutch ship which was defeated in the Battle of Sole Bay. The ferocious animal is painted so distinctively that if you blush in this vicinity you are 'as red as the Martlesham Lion'.

The sign of the Red Lion at Martlesham is a figurehead from a Dutch ship sunk during the Battle of Sole Bay, just up the coast.

Martlesham is in the midst of the new road network and you are likely to be redder still by the time you find the right road out. If by a fluke you find your way to Kesgrave keep an eye open for the grave of Shepherd Dobbs. Kesgrave is a suburb of Ipswich these days but the two stones marking the grave are still on the grass verge in a sidestreet next to an electricity sub-station, and helpfully it is still called Dobbs Lane. Dobbs hanged himself about 250 years ago and was buried in a suicide's grave beside the road. The story goes that many years later some roisterers at the Bell Inn decided to dig up the grave to see if he was still there. Sure enough they found a corpse, and it is said that one ghoulish member of the party removed a tooth from the skull and wore it on his watchchain. The corpse was re-interred and has not been disturbed since, but the tooth may still be dangling on a Kesgrave waistcoat.

Rivers and Sand

Before heading for Woodbridge, at the head of the Deben estuary, it is worth a diversion into the countryside just outside Kesgrave to find some villages that have not been swept up in the new road network. There is a rather ugly obelisk in the otherwise pretty churchyard at Playford, in memory of Thomas Clarkson, 'The Friend of Slaves', who lived and died at Playford Hall. Mr Clarkson was a colleague of William Wilberforce but his name never achieved the same place in history. His friends in Playford decided that at least he would not be forgotten in his own village, a commendable sentiment but rather clumsily put into practice. Personally I prefer the discreet little wooden memorial to a cat called Frodo which someone has attached to a tree outside the lychgate. It seems to fit in much better.

Playford and the other villages tucked away in these hills now have up-market houses with large well-kept gardens and coachlamps by the door. Just outside Great Bealing is the most up-market of them all, Seckford Hall, a grand Tudor mansion with six assorted gables and a dozen lofty chimneys, and any coachlamps you find are probably genuine. Much money has been spent on converting it into a superior hotel, but I was sad to find that the two splendid fireplaces in the public rooms contain imitation red-glow fires on which are perched, with great optimism, a saucepan and a kettle. Maybe I was wrong about the coachlamps.

The Hall is now separated from Woodbridge by the twin carriageways of the A12, but the name of Seckford lives on in the town. Thomas Seckford built the Shire Hall, the almshouses, a school and a public dispensary when Woodbridge was a busy port. Then ships got bigger, the channel got shallower, and the quay is now devoted to holiday craft. It is not easy to spot them because the road called Quayside is separated from it by the railway and assorted warehouses.

Survivals from Woodbridge's busier days: *left* the Shire Hall, built in the town's heyday as a port, and *right* the famous tide mill, which was the last in the country to work by tide power.

The famous tide mill, which was the last in the country to work by tide-power, has to be reached via a level crossing and a lane lined with office blocks, and you are banned from parking anywhere near it. You can see the masts bobbing about beyond the railway station, but it is quite an achievement to reach them. The best place to view the boats, in fact, is from a boat.

Similarly, the best way to view the town is on foot, or you will only catch a brief glimpse of the Bell and Steelyard pub, for instance, where the steelyard jutting over the road used to weigh complete waggonloads of corn. If a waggon stopped beneath it today the entire one-way traffic system of Woodbridge would come to a halt.

A plaque in Market Hill marks the home in his later years of Edward Fitzgerald, who is remembered by most of us for just one line: 'The moving finger writes, and having writ moves on.' Having writ his translation of the Rubaiyat he found no publisher was much impressed, so he printed it at his own expense, gave away copies to his friends and dumped the rest on a bookseller, who failed to sell them for a shilling and finally knocked them down to a penny.

His literary friends may have appreciated his efforts, but locally he was better known as an eccentric, and I cherish this vision of him, created by a contemporary description: 'A tall dreamy-looking man . . .with straggling hair and slovenly in dress, wearing an ancient, battered, black-banded, shiny-edged tall hat, round which he would in windy weather tie a handkerchief to keep it in its place; his clothes of baggy blue cloth, as though he were a seafarer, his trousers short and his shoes low, exhibiting a length of white or grey stockings. With an unstarched white shirtfront, tight crumpled stand-up collar, a big black silk tie in a careless bow, in cold weather trailing a green and black or grey plaid shawl, in hot weather even walking barefoot, with his boots slung to a stick . . . ' If you can get away with looking like that, who cares about the poetry?

On the outskirts of Woodbridge is Melton and its mobile Methodist chapel. It looks static enough these days, but when it was built in 1860 a neighbour complained that it encroached on his rights of ancient lights, and an order was made to demolish it. The Nonconformists decided not to conform, and moved it bodily instead. They detached it from its foundations, lifted it with jacks and rolled it on pine trunks for eighteen feet down the road until the neighbour's light was no longer obscured. I am told that one man stood in the pulpit throughout the operation, like a captain on his bridge, perhaps interspersing prayers for a safe passage with cries of 'Slow Astern!'

Melton has the only stretch of the Deben which is said to be haunted. In 1822 young Robert Manly was engaged to a Melton girl, Mary King, who fell fatally ill. She was terrified that bodysnatchers might desecrate her grave, so Robert promised to guard it. She died

that winter and he stayed by the grave every night, sleeping for a few hours during the day. When he eventually ended his vigil after many months, he gave away his few possessions, went down to the river and rowed away, never to be seen again, though his boat was found empty next day. Fishermen claim to have seen his sad ghostly figure, wandering disconsolately through the reeds, seeking Heaven via the Deben.

A couple of miles upstream is Ufford, an ordinary sort of name derived from an extraordinary dynasty, the Uffingas, sometimes known more endearingly as the Wuffingas. Were their unruly followers, I wonder, known as Wuffians? These were the first kings of all East Anglia back in the seventh century, and it was a Wuffinga, though nobody is quite sure which, whose burial ship was unearthed at nearby Sutton Hoo, still packed with priceless treasures. It dated – Wuffly speaking, I suppose – AD 654, about the time that Ufford was founded.

The village itself is famed for a later heirloom. The *Companion Guide* calls it quite simply, 'the finest font cover in England'. I prefer the one at Worlingworth, which may not be so finely carved but is more elegantly decorated and set in better surroundings, but Ufford's is certainly impressive, soaring upwards to the church roof like the elaborate turret of a fairy castle. Full marks to the parishioners of Ufford for keeping the church open so that visitors can enjoy it.

What looks very like an enormous font cover at Rendlesham, the next village up the Deben, is actually a gatehouse, an elaborate spiky affair with a high arch and a turret. It is a sorry sight now, only to be viewed through a padlocked gateway at the start of a neglected drive. Rendlesham House, which it used to guard, has long since gone. Instead there is an airfield, and indeed there are so many in this area that a wallhanging in Eyke Church includes in its illustrations of local activities an American Air Force Phantom. The Americans may wonder if the church key was designed in honour of General Eisenhower, since the tongue is in the form of the letters IKE, but this was the original spelling of the village, perpetuated by an ingenious fifteenth-century locksmith.

The Deben flows under an old mill at Wickham Market, offering another photo opportunity. The town is much more peaceful now than when John Burke was there in the 1960s and found 'a diffident cluster of houses and shops apologetically compressing the A12 into a tricky defile which can be widened for the benefit of rattling, reeking lorries only at the expense of some romantically subfusc houses'. Happily the civil engineers very civilly devised another solution. They built a bypass round the town instead, where the lorries can rattle and reek to their heart's content, and the centre of Wickham has become much quieter. Unfortunately the lorries now use the lower road of the town as a handy shortcut between the A45 and the fast new A12; really the planners can't win.

171

Rivers and Sand

From here the Deben turns into the Suffolk countryside, past isolated villages which rarely see a visitor and are all the better for it. It passes near Framsden, which does have a much-photographed postmill but it is privately owned and the owner makes it clear he likes to keep it that way. You will get a warmer welcome at the Dobermann Inn, which I thought might be a tribute to the *Sergeant Bilko* TV series (remember fat little Private Dobermann?) but it was renamed by a Dobermann breeder who became licensee and disliked its previous name, the Greyhound. In spite of its German name it could not be more English. It started as three sixteenth-century cottages, underwent a conversion job in 1785 and has been an inn ever since.

Back on the tourist route is Debenham, a picture-book little town where even the imposing Foresters' Hall has been converted into an antiques emporium. Beyond here, among the upper reaches of the Deben, I was drawn to a village called Kenton, because this is the place of birth recorded in my passport. I was actually born in Kenton, Middlesex; it was gratifying to find a place in East Anglia which shares the name. Approached from Debenham it is an attractive group of thatched cottages around a nice old church. Approached from any other direction it is a mass of modern farm buildings which are about as picturesque as the London Borough of Brent, in which my own Kenton now languishes.

The picture postcard town of Debenham, much geared to the tourist trade; even the imposing Foresters' Hall is now an antiques emporium.

Indeed farm architecture is so depressing in this area that a corn mill at Bedingfield, which adjoins Kenton, was described by a local councillor at a planning inquiry as one of the worst-looking buildings in the country, and other critics called it a hideous monolith, a monstrosity and an eyesore. They prevented it being extended but the mill itself still stands by the medieval parish church. Perhaps Prince Charles should add it to his portfolio.

I had another disappointment in this remote area between the headwaters of the Deben and the Waveney valley. This used to be the smugglers' route from the coast to Eye and Diss, and old records note that one hiding-place for the contraband was under the pulpit in Rishangles church. Alas, the parishioners of Rishangles have given up the struggle to retain their place of worship. It is now the Old Church Studios, privately owned and occupied, and although I was able to wander in the churchyard I have no idea whether the pulpit now conceals anything more sinister than a Hoover, if indeed it exists at all.

There is no trace of the Deben beyond here and we can return to the estuary and follow it down its other bank to the sea. At the end is Bawdsey, whose cottages were visible from Felixstowe Ferry, but this is not a place to linger. The coastal area has been occupied almost entirely by the Ministry of Defence since Robert Watson-Watt and his team established the first air defence radar station at Bawdsey Manor. They have set aside a picnic spot a hundred yards from the river, but elsewhere you are confronted on all sides by perimeter fences and warning notices. Even the quay is a security area.

Along the coast at Hollesley you can feel much freer – unless you happen to be sent to the open prison just outside the village. You can drive across the marshes to Shingle Street, one of the most windswept and isolated little communities in East Anglia. It is not much of a community these days, because most of the fishermen's cottages are only used as holiday homes, but on a bitter January afternoon, with the east wind biting through me and the sea crashing viciously on the shingle, I still came across hardy anglers crouched by their rods on the beach, and the inevitable dog-exerciser tramping doggedly – that must be the word for it – across the stones. This is the east coast at its wildest and bleakest, and the old Martello tower adds to the general grimness. If you are more energetic than I am you can walk along the shingle to the mouth of the Ore and see in the distance a more recent defence structure, the establishment on Orford Ness where the first radar research work was instigated and all manner of secret operations have been carried out since.

There is nothing secret or sinister about Orford itself. Generations of holidaymakers have wandered through its little square and bought smoked fish at the famous little smokery. They have explored the harbour, one of the snuggest on the coast and very different from the inhospitable beach at Shingle Street; and they have climbed the keep of Orford Castle, so well preserved it looks as though it were built by the Department of the Environment instead of Henry II. I wonder if they notice, incidentally, that the tower is polygonal outside but circular inside; perhaps the master mason wanted to show his versatility.

The Ore becomes the Alde after this and wanders parallel to the sea with just a narrow spit of shingle in between, then turns

Rivers and Sand

That's Orford in the distance, with the castle keep and the church on the skyline.

inland and widens out to form a kind of false estuary. Aldeburgh lies on the far side but on this bank there is hardly a habitation until you come to Iken and look for its church overlooking the river. You get no encouragment. The lane which leads to it bears the stern warning 'No Turning Space', and there are whitewashed rocks all along the verges to emphasise the point. But I advise you to ignore this sign and keep going, because there is indeed a turning space, quite big enough for three or four cars, just outside the church gate.

Inside there are more discouraging notices. The path apparently lies across a metre or so of private land, and you are warned not to deviate to right or left. Happily the church itself is more welcoming, and for a very good reason. The handful of parishioners have been trying to raise £70,000 to restore it, and the notice by the door says 'Please, please help'. I did, and I am sure you will, but those other notices do not help at all.

Julian Tennyson would have been delighted to know about the restoration work. 'There is no church in England,' he wrote, 'which gives you in quite the same way such a feeling of security and changelessness . . . When I was a child I decided that here was the place for me to be buried. I have not altered my mind.' Sadly he was killed in the war and lies, not in Iken churchyard but in the Burmese jungle.

A mile up the Alde there is an indication that you are coming into tourist country again, a huge picnic area and car park overlooking the river complete with nature trail. Sure enough, just around a few more corners you find yourself in Snape, outside the best-known maltings in the musical world.

There is little left to say about Snape Maltings and the Aldeburgh Festival, even if you enjoy Benjamin Britten's music. Full details, as they say, are available from the Festival Office. I would sooner

Dusk falls over Snape – and yes, there's more to it than just those Maltings. Sailing folk go there too.

continue up the Alde into the peaceful valley where George Crabbe was curate of Great Glemham and Sweffling and lived at Rendham. All these villages are tucked away in the hills alongside the river; Rendham actually boasts a bridge across it with a rather grand stone balustrade. Crabbe, a Suffolk poet of some renown, if only in Suffolk, had earlier been curate at Aldeburgh but failed to get on with his parishioners. Safely out of their range he wrote a very rude poem about them – a temptation which other parsons must surely have felt but were wise enough to resist.

He described his erstwhile flock, for instance, as 'a wild amphibious race, with sullen woe displayed on every face, who far from civil arts and social fly, and scowl at strangers with suspicious eye'. I bet they loved that on the parochial church council.

One branch of the Alde continues up the valley to Bruisyard, a delightful little village well away from the popular vineyard which bears its name. It has a venerable farmhouse which started life as a monastery in 1354. The monks were ejected 'owing to certayne complaints' and replaced by the nuns of the Order of St Clare. They presumably behaved themselves rather better because they stayed for a couple of centuries. At the Dissolution it was mostly demolished and rebuilt as a Tudor manor house, then became a farmhouse with the larger rooms used as dormitories by the farm workers.

Tennyson was delighted with it. 'It is solid and strong enough, and will no doubt continue to house a farmer and his men long after many of the ruined Saxon abbeys have been wholly absorbed by the earth.' He was nearly proved wrong. The building fell into a sorry state in the nineteen-eighties and could well have been 'absorbed by the earth', if English Heritage had not lent a hand. When I saw it early in 1990 the interior was still gutted, the windows were empty and there were holes in the walls, but it has since been made weatherproof and in due course I hope it will live up to Tennyson's forecast and again house a farmer, if not his men.

The other branch of the Alde forks off to Parham, a much busier village, and Framlingham, which is busier still. The little town with its triangular market place on the side of a steep hill is quaint enough in itself, but there are some less obvious features which take my fancy. Double Street, for instance, got its name because it was the first to have houses and shops on both sides of the road; the locals thought they were seeing double.

The tombs of Thomas Howard, third Duke of Norfolk, and his son Henry illustrate a remarkable good-news bad-news story from Tudor times. Both men were condemned to death by Henry VIII. Young Henry was beheaded just one day before the king died; that was the bad news. The good news was that his father was due to be beheaded just one day after, and the sentence was never carried out. On the tombs Henry is depicted with his coronet removed and placed beside him – the mason was not tasteless enough to remove his actual head. The reprieved Duke is depicted wearing a collar inscribed gratefully, 'By the Grace of God I am what I am.'

But the main attraction at Framlingham of course is the castle, where the Howards lived when they were not in the Tower. It would look a real story-book castle were it not for the incongruous brick chimneys which stick out of the ancient battlements like small red candles in oversized holders. They were put there by some Tudor joker for no logical reason, since most of them are dummies anyway.

Framlingham Castle was the medieval stronghold of the rebellious Bigods, and the walls are still imposing – but what Tudor joker stuck dummy chimneys in the battlements?

The early history of the castle was dramatic enough: stronghold of the Bigods, scene of great sieges as they kept on changing sides, confiscated by Henry VII, restored to the Howards, refuge of Mary Tudor before she was proclaimed Queen. But about the time those chimneys appeared the castle's fortunes changed. It became a prison for dissident priests, then a poorhouse and a school. It is now an Ancient Monument, complete with car park, teashop and picture postcards – cynics might say the most ignominious fate of all.

Just outside Framlingham is Saxtead Green, dominated by a white postmill with a bright blue fantail – I doubt the original miller would have thought of that. A few miles away, on the other branch of the Alde, is Dennington, where the church contains the only medieval carving in the country of a sciapod, an ingenious little half-human with one enormous foot which it held over its head while lying on its back to protect it from the sun. It may have been put there by the same imaginative carver who put the woodwose in Peasenhall Church, another half-human creature who lived in the forest instead of the desert but had equally engaging habits.

The 18th-century postmill at Saxtead Green, elegantly restored, and not a dummy chimney in sight.

Even the devoted Tennyson found fault with Dennington Church. 'It has no grace, no delicacy, no outstanding beauty of line or form. Beside Long Melford and Blythburgh it is like a bulldog to a borzoi.' Professor M.R. James added that 'the old glass windows are decorative only, without pictures, and the modern glazing is absolutely vile.' Later the church fell into disrepair and looked even less enticing, but much work has been done upon it and it is now in such good shape that the door is kept locked to preserve, I suppose, its newfound beauty – or to stop someone scarpering with the sciapod.

My last call in this area, and I urge you to visit it too, is Worlingworth Church, which is left unlocked for all its delights to be enjoyed. There is not only its spectacular font cover, which I rate the best in East Anglia, there is the enormous spit on which an ox was roasted to celebrate the jubilee of George III, and a more recent relic, a log from the cedar tree which was planted to mark Queen Victoria's funeral and blew down in the 1987 gales. The embroidered altar frontal is a work of art in itself, and I was greatly taken by the

wallhanging made at the village school in 1988. Appliqué pictures on
an embroidered background illustrate a little poem, which sums up
East Anglia for me just as expressively as Fitzgerald or Crabbe, and a
lot more simply.

Over the earth is a mat of green,
Over the green a dew,
Over the dew are the arching trees,
Over the trees, the blue.
Across the blue the scudding clouds,
Over the clouds the sun.
Over it all is the love of God,
Blessing us every one.

Back now to the best known stretch of the River Alde, down by
the sea, a different world from these remote little villages near its
source. Aldeburgh is so associated in the public mind with Benjamin
Britten's music festival that it is difficult to realise it is quite a normal
little seaside town. Not everybody goes round singing choruses from
Billy Budd. The festival has affected the town's growth, of course,
and what the sea has taken away over the centuries, the developers
have replaced further inland during the last few decades. But it was
changing with the times long before the first bass-baritone thundered
forth in the Snape Maltings. Back in the 1930s Julian Tennyson was
deploring its growth.

'I must confess that Aldeburgh to my mind was a much more
pleasant place fifteen years ago than it is today,' he wrote. 'A good
beach, beautiful country, a romantic river designed by providence for
sailing, fishing and shooting – these things may bring prosperity, but
more often than not that prosperity is exploited in a cheap careless
manner which relegates aestheticism to the ash-can.'

The same cry goes up throughout East Anglia even today. But
he went on to admit, 'I have met many people who have visited
Aldeburgh lately, and all have thought it one of the most delightful
places they have ever seen.' Even after another fifty years of prosperity
and exploitation, with the music festival thrown in, many visitors get
the same impression.

It still has its Moot Hall with its lofty 'drainpipe' chimneys, and
there are two lookout towers on the beach which were manned by
rival wreckers, the Up-Towners and the Down-Towners. They raced
each other to loot any wreck, and if they arrived simultaneously they
could well have had the original Up-and-Downer. A more recent
memento of the past, also on the seafront, is a statue of a terrier,
which commemorates not the dog but its master, Dr Robin Acheson,
who practised in the town for nearly thirty years. I hope the terrier's
friends and descendants treat the statue with respect.

A statue of a dog may seem unusual, but for eccentricity on a large scale you need only drive along the coast road to Thorpeness. The opening sentence in a publicity brochure in the 1960s sums it up: 'The first reaction of many visitors is to wonder – why?'

The answer was in the mind of Mr Stuart Ogilvie when he created perhaps the earliest and certainly the oddest of Britain's holiday camps back in 1922. Very sensibly he laid out a golf course and dug an artificial boating lake. Not so sensibly, perhaps, he built a mock-Tudor complex of which the central feature is a water tower disguised as an Elizabethan gatehouse. Another water tower, on a hill outside the village, was made to look like a very tall cottage, encased in wooden walls with a gable roof and a chimney. There is living accommodation under the water tank and Mr Ogilvie named it 'The House of Peter Pan', giving quite a new significance to the merry merry pipes. He actually found somebody game enough to live under thirty thousand gallons of water, a romantic lady who rechristened it 'The House in the Clouds', and the name has stuck. A mains water supply has made both water towers redundant, but they still loom over Thorpeness in their bizarre disguises.

The postmill opposite the House in the Clouds is one of Thorpeness's few genuine features, but it started life a few miles away at Aldringham. Mr Ogilvie spotted it and transferred it to his holiday village to amuse the guests. If he were about today, he would surely love to get his hands on its modern successor just up the coast, which generates its power very differently. Its critics – and there are many – would probably say that in its own way it is just as bizarre as Mr Ogilvie's creations. It is the atomic power station at Sizewell.

If you stand on Sizewell beach with your back to this massive concrete mausoleum and its fast-growing neighbour Sizewell 'B', you can just about picture the scene when this was still a favourite haunt of smugglers. The picture would be inaccurate because in those days there were cliffs to hide under and the goods were brought ashore through a cleft in them called Sizewell Gap. The sea has encroached over all this, but there are fishing boats pulled up on the shore, and even a beach shelter where you can sit and watch the sea, out of sight of that huge building further along the shore.

The Central Electricity Generating Board is doing its best to turn the place into a tourist attraction, with landscaping and guided tours and lots of commercials on television, and no doubt it has brought much money and employment into the area, but Sizewell hardly offers the peace and tranquillity which most people look for on the Suffolk coast. Similarly Leiston, just inland, is not a typical Suffolk town. Perhaps it is that mass of cables overhead, extending from Sizewell away to the Midlands, or perhaps it is just the knowledge of that awesome structure down by the beach, but I found little urge to linger in Leiston. As for Saxmundham, its near neighbour, John Burke merely

commented that it has an enticing name but little else, and he seems to have a point.

But one does not come to this part of Suffolk for its urban attractions, but for the vast stretches of empty countryside along the coast and the quiet little villages tucked behind it. Isolated places like Eastbridge, where the Revenue men used to make their headquarters at the Eel's Foot Inn. There were plenty of ambushes and chases along the tracks that lead from here to Sizewell Gap, and at least one confrontation at the inn itself. In December 1747 a party of smugglers rode into the yard while a detachment of Welch Fusiliers, there to assist the Revenue men, were having lunch inside. The lieutenant in charge ordered his men to down tankards, led them outside and called on the smugglers to surrender. The smugglers declined, and opened fire. Most of them escaped but two were captured and sent to London by sea – a safer route than taking them through the Suffolk countryside. When the Fusiliers moved on, however, the smugglers were soon occupying their seats again and quaffing from the same tankards.

The Eel's Foot got its name from a poorly painted inn sign which was supposed to depict the devil being put in a boot, a popular local legend. The visible part of the devil was mistaken for an eel, and the name has been accepted as official. The current sign unmistakably shows an eel.

Theberton was another favourite smugglers' haunt, and they were said to hide their contraband in the church, either under the pulpit or behind the altar, depending on who tells you the story. The church does contain concrete evidence however of the shooting-down of a Zeppelin over the village in the First World War. There is a piece of the airship in a glass case by the font, though the bodies of the crew, once buried in the churchyard, are now in a war cemetery.

Yoxford and Westleton are both on busy main roads and so have fewer smuggling connections. The church at Westleton, however, can offer a more bizarre tale than brandy under the pulpit or a chunk of Zeppelin by the font. There is reputed to be a witch's stone by the priest's door, and if you place a kerchief over the nearby grating and run round the church anticlockwise you will find the kerchief gone and the devil clanking his chains behind the grating. Although the story is quoted by Julian Tennyson and repeated by other reputable chroniclers, the church guidebook discreetly makes no mention of it, and I confess I could find nothing that looked like a witch's stone. The only grating nearby was a modern one for ventilating the church. Nevertheless I left a kerchief in the general vicinity and took a brisk stroll round the church. It was obviously not brisk enough. The kerchief did not move, and the grating remained boringly silent.

Yoxford on the A12 is much busier, and as you dodge the lorries heading north for Lowestoft and Yarmouth it is difficult to understand how it came by the restful title of 'The Garden of Suffolk'. It is more

Stuart Ogilvie's little joke when he created a bizarre holiday village at Thorpeness – 'The House in the Clouds', a heavily disguised water tower with living quarters below.

accurate to call it the Parkland of Suffolk, because in Tudor times the village had three Big Houses instead of the usual one, and each had a great stretch of park. Only Cockfield Hall survives, where Lady Jane Grey's sister Catherine ended her days after an unpleasant few years in the Tower with her husband. The incarceration must have had its lighter moments, though; they managed to produce two sons.

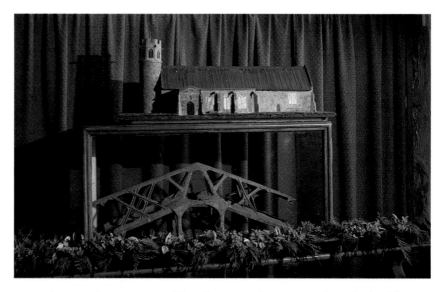

An unlikely exhibit inside (and under a model of) Theberton church; a piece of the Zeppelin which was shot down over the village during the First World War.

Close to the main road but fortunately equipped with double glazing is Satis House, a curious name which might apply more aptly to a manufacturing works. Who could complain about goods from Satis Factory? The name is not as odd, however, as one of the house's past owners, Mrs Clarissa Ricketts, who lost a fortune at Monte Carlo and died soon after her return, leaving cryptic instructions about her funeral. It took place after dark, conducted by an out-of-town undertaker who promptly disappeared. There were rumours that the coffin actually contained Mrs Ricketts's two dogs, or some other substitute cadaver. 'Mrs Ricketts is not dead, two fat pigs were buried instead,' suggested one anonymous graffiti-writer. Various sightings reported Mrs Ricketts boarding a train disguised as a man, Mrs Ricketts hiding out in Egypt, and Mrs Ricketts almost anywhere but in her Yoxford grave. The mystery, if indeed there is one, has never been resolved.

As you continue up the little river you encounter more tales of mystery and not a little imagination. Sibton, an innocent-looking village with a pleasant green, was the scene of a gruesome fight to the death between two gypsies, and subsequent spectral appearances which have never been explained; Peasenhall, just as innocent-looking, was the scene of a murder as notorious in its time as Polstead's Murder in the Red Barn. A maid was found dead with neck wounds and her body partially burned. She was pregnant, and a local carpenter was accused of being the father and killing her. He came before the magistrates sitting at the Swan Inn and was sent for trial, but there was no firm evidence against him and he was acquitted. The murderer was never caught, and I am assured that the customers in the Swan still argue about whether the carpenter was guilty after all.

Further upstream at Laxfield they really do still argue about the guilt of William Dowsing. There is no dispute that a William Dowsing toured Suffolk's churches on behalf of Oliver Cromwell, destroying paintings, ornaments, screens, murals, anything he considered 'superstitious'. There is also no dispute that a William Dowsing is commemorated on the wall of Laxfield Church, having died in the 1660s 'being of about ye age of 88 years'. What is disputed is whether these are one and the same. Most of the reference books say they are, but the good folk of Laxfield, understandably anxious to dissociate themselves from the unsavoury Dowsing, have suggested that, even if he were buried there, he was not a Laxfield man. The church guidebook observes pointedly, 'The iconoclast may or may not have been the Laxfield William Dowsing. *Scholars argue.*'

Whoever is right, Mr Dowsing did not have much to do at Laxfield, which was a Puritan parish anyway (so it is quite likely he was a local Puritan – but let's not start that again). He did, however, order two angels to be removed from the tower and a cross to be broken on the porch. The porch now bears two angels and a cross without a shaft; presumably the parishioners put them up again after he left.

I may have left another minor mystery behind me at Laxfield. I arrived late one winter's afternoon as the light was fading, and I was wandering around the church in semi-darkness when a cloaked figure appeared in the doorway and came towards me. I had a sudden vision of William Dowsing returning to finish off those angels, and as the cloaked figure came abreast of me I could not even gulp a greeting. It passed me without speaking and disappeared into the vestry while I disappeared out of the door. It was only then I realised it must have been the Rector, who was probably just as startled as I. If he is still wondering about that silent encounter in the darkened church, it was only me, sir, and I do apologise.

The name of nearby Stradbroke village has become well known throughout East Anglia, thanks to the sixth Earl of Stradbroke, an extrovert Australian who divides his time between the ancestral estates and his own seven thousand acres in New South Wales, and likes to be addressed as Keith. He lists his favourite recreation as 'making babies', and with the help of two successive wives he has pursued this pastime to considerable effect, with a total to date of ten. Stradbroke itself shows no obvious signs of excessive marital activity and is still described by the *Companion Guide*, perhaps to its relief, as 'drowsy'. To the casual visitor its most striking feature is the splendid mural of an old-fashioned fire engine which graces the village fire station, created by a local potter called Robin Welch.

Heading back towards the coast you may catch a glimpse of Heveningham Hall, reckoned to be the grandest Georgian mansion in Suffolk. It did not look too grand when I last saw it, festooned with scaffolding and canvas. It was once owned by the Vanneck family who opened it to visitors, and the National Trust did the same, but the government resold it to a private owner and it remained empty for years. A serious fire did not help. In its National Trust days John Burke wrote: 'The visitors include many inhabitants of the surrounding countryside who would feel a keen sense of deprivation if they could no longer make their regular refreshing pilgrimage to this treasure-house.' He was absolutely right, and the row between the villagers, the government and the absentee owner went on for years. I hope by now it is satisfactorily sorted out.

Nearby Bramfield was famous for the thousand-year-old Bramfield Oak, now reduced to a stump, but it still has a 700-year-old round tower next to the parish church with walls up to five feet thick. Many round towers like this were built as a defensive stronghold and that is why you sometimes find an entrance halfway up, which could only be reached by ladders. I am much more taken with the remarkable theory that these towers were originally wells, when the land level was far higher. As the land subsided and the walls were exposed, the astute well-owner put a door at ground level and a roof on top and used it as an early form of silo. As the subsidence continued the door was left well above ground level and the floor became an upper storey. Hang a few bells in it, tack on a nave and a chancel, and you've got your round-towered church.

All right, so you may detect a distant ho-ho, but that seems no more far-fetched or fanciful than a town being washed into the sea, four hundred houses and three churches all engulfed in one great flood, and the remainder lost piece by piece over the years as the sea ate into the cliff, until the last of its nine churches toppled over the edge earlier this century. Yet that is what really happened at Dunwich, once a major seaport and the centre of Christianity in East Anglia. All it consists of now is a handful of houses built in more recent times, well away from the cliff edge. Julian Tennyson wrote sadly: 'I know of no other place in England which has been reduced so completely from splendour into nothingness ... It is a place without industry, without hope, without support.'

But that was before the tourist industry saw the potential of such a story: a lost city, human bones sometimes washed up on the foreshore, the sound of a submerged church bell tolling away out to sea on a wild winter's night ... Add a few picturesque fishing boats on the beach, heath and woodlands to explore, and nature reserves on both sides, and the crowds start pouring in. These days there is a caravan park and camping facilities, a restaurant in the beach car park and a pub which does a roaring trade in bar lunches even in

December. I am not sure if Mr Tennyson would approve, but at least it is no longer without hope or support.

There is no coast road at Dunwich. If there were, the sea would probably not allow it to stay there very long. You have to return inland, and the next water you see is the River Blyth, which once flowed to the coast at Dunwich until man took away from the crumbling town what the sea could not reach, and dug a new channel for it from Blythburgh to Walberswick and Southwold. This cunning ploy to divert trade from Dunwich was soon foiled when the channel silted up, but Blythburgh had its spell of prosperity. It also has one of the biggest churches in Suffolk, a cavernous building in which Cromwell's men really did stable their horses. The church is quite close to the A12, and like the sound of bagpipes it is best enjoyed from a distance.

Blythburgh church, where Cromwell's men really did stable their horses, and it still looks rather barn-like, a vast building with a too-small tower. The horses may even have drunk out of the stoup *above* in the south porch.

Holton, further up the Blyth, is a pretty village with a postmill in the middle, but it lies within the junction of two busy main roads. Wenhaston, on the other hand, is not a pretty village but does escape the traffic, and it is worth a visit for the 'Doom' in the parish church, which illustrates various uncomfortable happenings on the Day of Judgement. The wooden panel was covered with whitewash and stood over the chancel arch, until it was left outside in the rain during repairs and the whitewash was washed away.

There is another wall decoration at Wenhaston as impressive in its own way as the Doom, but it is in a private farmhouse and not on public view. Over the chimneybreast in Watermill Farm is half the old waterwheel, looking, as somebody once described it,

like a toothed Norman arch. Above it is the windclock from the
mill, operated by a weathervane on the roof, so one can check on
the wind direction without budging from the fireside.

The 'Doom' at Wenhaston,
once concealed under
whitewash until it was left
outside during repairs and
the rain washed it off.

Wenhaston also had a railway station but that disappeared long
before the era of Dr Beeching's axe. A narrow-gauge line ran between
Halesworth and Southwold, but the route was more picturesque than
profitable and it closed in 1929. It was argued at the time that if the
gauge had been the same as the Great Eastern line at Halesworth and
the two had been connected it would have survived, but undoubtedly
Dr Beeching would have lopped off the branch line, and even the old
Great Eastern, now the Ipswich–Lowestoft line, has had its nervous
moments.

I visited Halesworth when it was still having a good stretch and
flexing its muscles after being set free from the heavy traffic which
had burdened it for decades. A bypass was built at the end of 1989,
and there had not been time for the local traffic to build up and take
its place, as it nearly always does. The town council hoped to thwart
it by designating the middle of Halesworth a pedestrian precinct. The
celebratory carnival floats which were the first to use the bypass were
also the last to pass through the town centre. Even without traffic there
is not too much to see – John Burke merely refers to 'a few pleasant but
undistinguished corners' – but I am sure the townsfolk are delighted
with their new freedom and I trust the pedestrian precinct, which
started as an experiment, still holds the traffic at bay.

Back on the coast at the mouth of the Blyth, Walberswick and
Southwold face each other rather distantly from opposite banks. Of
the two I much prefer Southwold. Walberswick has become the haunt
of the WORCers – Well-Off Retired Celebrities – and one critic has
likened it to a seaside Hampstead Garden Suburb. It has nice sands and

some splendid views, but its origins as a fishing village are difficult to trace, whereas Southwold is precisely what it has always been, an unspoilt seaside town where the atmosphere can hardly have changed since the Battle of Sole Bay, and where Victorian holidaymakers would still feel completely at home.

Walberswick anchorage, with Southwold on the sky-line across the river. That boat in the foreground has probably been sold by now.

The *Companion Guide* says simply, 'I cannot think of anything bad to say about Southwold,' and nor can I. Nor shall I say much about it at all, because the only way to keep it like this is to make sure it stays unfashionable. If the Blyth had not silted up and the little railway had been the right gauge, it is a sobering thought that shipping might have built up here instead of further south and Southwold could have become another Felixstowe. Even in 1987 the council attempted to develop a marina, which could have put it on a par with Shotley Bay.

Mercifully neither of these nightmares has materialised and Southwold continues to be the only small seaside town I know which can accommodate a brewery in its centre and still not lose its charm. The brewery helps to maintain the Victorian atmosphere by making its local deliveries by horse-drawn dray. Also in the town instead of on the cliff is the lighthouse, very handy for the Sole Bay Inn – it must have been Trinity House's most sought-after posting. The inn is a reminder of the bloody encounter between the Dutch and English fleets just off Southwold, which like so many bloody encounters was rendered quite pointless ten years later when William of Orange was invited to be King of England and the two countries decided to be mates after all.

I should mention the cannon on Gun Hill because two totally different histories are credited to them, and you may like to select the one you prefer. One version says they were captured from the English Army by the Scots during the '45 Rebellion, then recaptured

Southwold lighthouse
must have been Trinity
House's most popular posting, just round the corner
from the Sole Bay Inn. The
brewery is quite close too –
which is good news for the
horse.

at Culloden by the Duke of Cumberland. He presented them, for no
obvious reason, to Southwold – perhaps he had enjoyed a holiday there.
The other story, which I personally favour because it has a certain
dotty logic about it, is that George II presented the guns to Southwold
after the town had complained that 'this place is in a very dangerous
condition for want of guns and ammunition, being naked and exposed
to the insults of the Common Enemy'. Whichever is correct, the guns
have never been fired in anger, and they now provide a sort of antique
adventure playground for young visitors.

I must get you away from Southwold before you become too
enamoured of it. We pass Wolsey's Bridge, where the Cardinal is said
to have plodded behind his father's cattle as a boy (he lived in Ipswich
so it was quite a plod), on through Wangford and Uggeshall (neither of
which is as unprepossessing as its name) and so to Westhall. This is
an isolated hamlet on a tributary of the Blyth, and judging by the back
gardens I saw near the church the residents are mostly scrap dealers

or in the firewood business, but the church itself is the attraction. Its very isolation made it a useful rendezvous for smugglers, and it is said that while thatchers were at work on it, a gang pursued by the Revenue men hid their booty in the gully between the two roofs, and the thatchers promptly covered it with their reeds.

Even the beach chalets have a certain innocent charm, painted to look like children's toys.

According to the church guidebook the hiding place was a space above the rafters in the chancel, but I prefer to picture those workmen calmly 'thatching' the casks on the roof while the Revenue men chased about in the churchyard below. The double roof and the gully are still there and the nave is still thatched, but I could not spot the casks.

There is one more foray to the coast before reaching the environs of Lowestoft. The road through South Cove – a deceptive name since it is well inland – leads to Covehithe, where it stops abruptly on the cliff edge. It used to go much further but the sea washed it away. Even in this isolated dead-end there is the depressing sign, 'Motorists Beware of Thieves', so it must have its share of visitors, legitimate and otherwise. If they have not come to break into cars they are there to walk along the crumbling cliffs or to study the strange skeleton of Covehithe Church. For once it was not a victim of storm or neglect; the parishioners pulled much of it down themselves in the seventeenth century, having decided they could not maintain such a big building. They used the stone from the walls to build a smaller one inside the shell of the original, and there it sits like a chicken inside a cracked egg. No doubt other parishes saddled with maintaining enormous churches might feel tempted to do the same, but I have to say the result looks a mess. They might have done better to demolish all of it and start afresh.

The only way out of Covehithe is back on to the trunk road, but I can offer you respite before you face the rigours of Lowestoft. A tiny lane loops away towards the sea again. It never actually reaches it, but it leads you to Benacre, a little village marooned in the open country between the A12 and the coast. Tennyson quotes a Suffolk man who sums it up admirably: 'Thass a tittley little place, ony a church and a few ould cottages. Lor, that on't harm nobuddy that on't.' That was fifty years ago and it is just as inoffensive and retiring today.

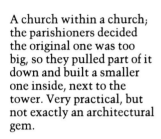

A church within a church; the parishioners decided the original one was too big, so they pulled part of it down and built a smaller one inside, next to the tower. Very practical, but not exactly an architectural gem.

Make the most of it, because next up the coast is Kessingland, and Tennyson had a word for that too: 'A dismal place, colourless and unattractively developed, a pimple on the fair face of the coast.' It does have the Suffolk Wildlife Park, featuring such typical Suffolk wildlife as parrots and macaws, but in effect Kessingland is a suburb of Lowestoft, devoted to holiday camps, campsites and caravans, and as such I am sure it is much appreciated by many thousands of happy holidaymakers.

Pakefield lies between Kessingland and Lowestoft but it does preserve a little individuality, though it fights a war on two fronts against the sea and the developers. Many of its original streets and houses are under the waves. The church, which was seven hundred feet from the cliff edge a hundred years ago, was only fifty feet from it in 1939. The gap does not seem to have narrowed since, so maybe Pakefield has won one of its battles, if not the other.

And so into Lowestoft itself, past a holiday camp on one side of the A12 and an enormous rubbish tip for industrial waste on the other, symbolic perhaps of the two faces of the town. It is essentially a fishing port, with the harbour still as busy as ever on the face of it, in spite of EEC reductions in cod quotas, but around the docks has grown a vast industrial estate, intermixed with holiday beaches and hotels. I find it difficult to be sure where the factories end and the fun begins. Perhaps it helps to have blinkers or tunnel vision to holiday in Lowestoft, because its industrial activity is all around you, but once you have climbed over the concrete seawall and down on to the sands it is just like any other holiday beach, with plenty of room for all.

I am doing my best to be fair to Lowestoft, but even a devoted Suffolkman like John Burke admits that its appeal is limited. 'I confess that I find Lowestoft drab and inhospitable, its back streets like those of a north-country slum without the northern vitality, its vauntedly picturesque "Scores" about as picturesque as the equally steep back alleys of a Welsh mining town, and its congested traffic quite appalling.' He wrote that nearly twenty years ago, and I can report it has changed since then. The traffic is far worse.

However not everybody takes this view of the town or its environs. Holiday camps thrive, from Kessingland to the county boundary at Corton. The American theme park, Pleasurewood Hills, welcomed its two-and-a-half millionth visitor in 1989. There are vast sandy beaches, and although they are often swept by that famous East Anglian 'lazy wind' – 'thass too lazy to go round yew, that go strairt through yew, boy' – there is a certain kudos in digging a sandcastle on the most easterly point in Britain.

Fishermen relax as best they can on Lowestoft Ness, the most easterly point in Britain and probably the windiest.

I hope many more thousands will be attracted to Lowestoft and Pleasurewood Hills and all the other holiday establishments in that far corner of Suffolk. It will leave more space in the hinterland, where camping is done in tens rather than thousands, where parks have trees and not themes, and where the woods and hills do not need trans-Atlantic help to provide pleasure.

Let's go.

8 The Hinterland
South and West Suffolk

I define the hinterland of Suffolk as that almost town-free area south of the A45 down to the Essex border, a maze of lanes and secluded villages tucked away in the wooded hills with only a couple of main roads cutting through them, and these so narrow and winding that they merge unobtrusively into the landscape. But hinterland implies unexplored territory, and this I am afraid no longer applies to the southern strip along the Stour valley, with its black-and-white timbered cottages and chocolate-box villages. This is now part of the Great Universal Charabanc Tour, where you can hardly move in the summer months for folk having a stare in Stoke-by-Clare or looking for the loos in Lavenham.

Out of season, however, it is still a pleasure to visit the old Suffolk wool towns, now period villages, and wander unimpeded round the streets. Among the picturesque frontages made so familiar by the tourist brochures there are still odd corners to be discovered, and if all else fails you can escape into the unknown hinterland, almost anywhere between Sudbury and Newmarket, where the locals still pause in their conversation if they see an unfamiliar face.

So I shall follow the route of the coach parties first, then strike off into the hills. And in the midst of the prettiest scenery in East Anglia I shall even venture into its most unalluring town. 'The streets speak of decay, and though few go back further than late Victorian days and most belong to recent decades they already reek with the dispiritedness of an industrial slum.' Don't miss it.

I have to start, I suppose, in Constable country. I say it with resignation, because there are other parts of East Anglia which are just as delightful but they lacked a Constable to immortalise them. Everyone has heard of Flatford Mill and Willy Lott's cottage and that high-profile haywain, but few people appreciate that there are dozens more which are just as attractive and a lot less crowded.

John Constable himself tried to create the impression that
his own patch was unique. He wrote, 'The gentle declivities, the
luxuriant meadow flats sprinkled with flocks and herds, and well
cultivated uplands, the woods and rivers, the numerous scattered
villages and churches with farms and picturesque cottages, all impart
to this particular spot an amenity and elegance hardly anywhere else
to be found.' What rubbish, Mr C. It can be found almost anywhere else
in the Suffolk hinterland. If he had been born in Hartest or Great Bradley
or Dunstall Green he would doubtless have said the same. And any one
of these villages presents a more attractive sight these days than his
famous birthplace East Bergholt. It has become a sprawling community
much influenced by its proximity to the A12, with Colchester a few
miles one way and Ipswich a few miles the other.

However in spite of its expansion he would still recognise the
area around the church and in particular the bellcage in the churchyard
containing the five heaviest bells in England. That is not why they were
left at ground level. They should have hung in the church tower but
it was never finished. This was another of Wolsey's projects, like the
college he planned in Ipswich, which he had to abandon when he fell
from grace. In Ipswich all he managed to build were the college gates;
in East Bergholt he only got as far as the bells. This must be a source
of continuing discomfort to generations of ringers, who have to operate
them at unusually close range and must risk the loss of their hearing
every Sunday. But the bellcage does make a very charming picture,
and in Constable country that is what counts.

The bellcage at East Bergholt. Cardinal Wolsey planned to build a tower for
them but never got around
to it, so they are still at
ground level.

Stratford St Mary used to be on the old trunk road and even in
Constable's day the traffic must have been quite heavy. It eventually
became quite appalling, but the new A12 bypasses the village and if
you can ignore both the distant hum from the dual carriageways and
the much closer presence of a water pumping station that not even

The Hinterland

Constable could have beautified, then you can share his enjoyment of the Weaver's House and the Tudor cottages in the main street in comparative safety. Only comparative, because Stratford St Mary lies on the recommended route for touring Constable country, and the lorries have been largely replaced by coaches.

You may already be tempted to escape into the hinterland that lies to the north-west, but we must first pay our respects to the other well-publicised villages on the route. Half of them lie on the other bank of the Stour in Essex and are thus out of our purview, but on the Suffolk side we still have Stoke-by-Nayland and Nayland itself.

'If there be such a thing as a perfect village, then Stoke-by-Nayland must come very near to it,' wrote Julian Tennyson with his usual impartiality. 'Even the council houses have a meek and pleasant look, as if to let you know that they will never intrude on the harmony of this old village.' Constable had to do without the council houses but included most of the rest of it in his famous painting of the parish church. He seems to have much preferred Stoke-by-Nayland to Nayland and so did Tennyson, who went on for a couple of pages about the delights of Stoke but dismissed Nayland in a paragraph. They seemed to think the mapmakers had got their priorities wrong and Nayland should be Nayland-by-Stoke. Personally I prefer the more discreet cluster of old timbered houses down by the Stour, with the watermill and the lock and the old bridge, to the 'perfect village' with its ostentatious and out-of-proportion church. But even in Nayland you cannot escape the Constable connection. One of his few sacred paintings, a portrayal of the Last Supper, was put behind the altar in the church.

This marks the limit of Constable country, which must be a great relief to the residents of Polstead and Boxford, a few miles further on. These villages in my view are just as near to perfect as Stoke-by-Nayland and it is remarkable that Constable did not take more notice of them. They escaped his publicity, but Polstead achieved its own notoriety thanks to the Murder in the Red Barn, and although the murder was 150 years ago and the barn has long since been burned down, the sightseers still come to view the thatched cottage where Maria Marten lived until she was murdered by William Corder, and to read the sign in the churchyard which marks her grave. The original tombstone was chipped to pieces by souvenir hunters.

I first saw an enactment of the murder long before I visited Polstead. In the nineteen-fifties a band of travelling players came to our Norfolk village and performed the whole story, with our village hall standing in for the Red Barn. It was high drama at its highest: they portrayed how Maria disappeared after having a child by Corder, how letters were received from him in Ipswich and later in Yarmouth saying they were happily married, how her stepmother dreamed for three nights running that Maria had been murdered and was buried in the barn, how her husband found the body just as she had dreamed it, and how Corder was tracked down, convicted and hanged at Bury St Edmunds.

far left Stoke-by-Nayland church and cottages, much favoured by John Constable, and *left* Polstead Pool, much favoured by witch-hunters. Suspects were 'swum' in a Catch-22 situation; if they floated they were witches and burned, if they sank they were innocent – but drowned.

It was a splendid performance with much weeping and shrieking and sinister snarling, and it only needed Sweeney Todd to appear in the interval with his collapsible barber's chair to complete the evening. I came away imagining Polstead to be a very creepy place indeed, peopled entirely by terrified young women, murderous ne'er-do-wells and elderly clairvoyants. It was almost a disappointment to find instead a peaceful village green flanked by thatched and pink-washed cottages, a lane leading down the hill to a pond surrounded by shady trees, and a pleasant Georgian hall. There are tales of hauntings, naturally, but an old friend who lives in the village assures me there are no supernatural presences. He was the BBC's religious affairs correspondent, so he should know.

There is one minor mystery of a less gruesome nature. The church has Norman arches which are made of brick, and experts say this is very odd because the Normans did not make bricks. The Romans did, and so did the Tudors, but theirs were different sizes. Could some Norman mason in Polstead have accidentally re-invented the brick, used it to build the arches, then was murdered by a stonemason competitor, taking the secret with him? It has the makings of another great evening at the theatre.

The thousand-year-old Polstead Oak, which like many others was claimed to be the oldest in East Anglia, grew in the churchyard, but there is about as much of it left as Maria Marten's tombstone. A new oak has been planted by the remnant of its stump to give the record books something to argue about in a thousand years' time.

Boxford is tucked away in a dip off the main road from Sudbury to Ipswich. Architectural historians, the ones who can tell a Roman

The Hinterland

brick from a Tudor one, go to Boxford to admire its extra north porch, probably the oldest wooden porch in the country. I go there partly to enjoy the hospitality of the BBC's former political editor (East Anglia produced a lot of BBC staff and most of them return), and partly to enjoy Boxford itself. This was a prosperous wool town in the seventeenth century, but now it is a quiet haven of thatch and timber, disturbed occasionally by people who have confused it with Boxted in Essex, one of the hapless villages on the Constable tour.

Boxford is outside Constable Country but just as picturesque. Its church has probably the oldest wooden porch in Britain, and there are fine timbered houses in Butcher's Lane.

Other Suffolk wool towns have not achieved such tranquillity. We are within range now of the most famous of them all. Every signpost in this area seems to point to Lavenham – and every coach driver has it on his itinerary.

It is difficult to picture Lavenham without tourists, but surprisingly its fame is comparatively recent. A traveller in the nineteen-sixties wrote of it: 'Fortunately it has not been "discovered" as a tourist attraction or as a fashionable place to live, and it is still an attractive and unaffected old town without the garish trappings of modern civilisation or alternatively the coy "olde-worldiness" of the professional tourist trap.'

It has been thoroughly discovered now, and I imagine the Swan Hotel in the heart of the town is one of Trust House Forte's most profitable investments. Lavenham looks a lot smarter now than it did a hundred years ago, when the ancient Guildhall was left derelict with all its windows smashed, and the whole place had 'a deserted and moribund air'. There was an attempt to introduce a sugar beet processing plant, and if it had succeeded we might today have a Cantley-size refinery on the edge of town, and the Tudor cottages cleared away for factory workers' terraces.

Lavenham avoided all that, as it earlier avoided the rebuilding that Sudbury underwent in Georgian times. Now the old cottages have been smartened up, the Guildhall, with its windows restored, is now in the safe hands of the National Trust, and even the old Wool Hall, which was due to be demolished, has been restored and incorporated in the Swan Hotel. The town is now one of Suffolk's main tourist attractions, and long may it remain so, to keep attention away from places like Chelsworth and Kersey, which are too small to cope with mass tourism and look crowded if just one coach party disembarks in the village street.

Kersey, I fear, faces a losing battle. It is such a picture-postcard village, with its old cottages running down to the watersplash in the centre of the village, that it is photographed almost as frequently as Lavenham. Even the ducks at the watersplash will pose in just the right spot at the sight of a camera. Weavers' cottages are there from the days when they wove Kersey cloth, and the White Horse Inn opposite them looks, as its name suggests, like a stage set for an olde-worlde operetta. Many people would say that Kersey in fact is the prettiest village in Suffolk. Julian Tennyson, as usual, has his own favourite.

Kersey *is* on the main tourist route and even the ducks know where to pose for photographs.

'I can't tell you why I think Chelsworth is perfect,' he wrote. 'Perhaps it is because it has been left to itself, because it is unmarred by discovery, because it epitomises in a dozen cottages what Kersey and Stoke-by-Nayland attempt with fifty.'

And certainly Chelsworth does seem to have escaped the coach parties and retains its privacy. The cottages are scattered along the bank of a stream, and when I last visited it the only bridge across it was closed for repairs, which was a further discouragement to visitors – perhaps it is 'closed for repairs' on purpose. It may be for the same reason that the house at the entrance to the village has been painted a most appalling mauve, which could well scare off any casual trippers before they disturbed the tranquillity of Chelsworth itself.

The Hinterland

Chelsworth was Julian Tennyson's favourite Suffolk village. 'It epitomises in a dozen cottages what Kersey and Stoke-by-Nayland attempt with fifty.'

Lindsey, like Kersey, gave its name to a cloth, but there the resemblance ends. It is a very ordinary village and no doubt the inhabitants are delighted to keep it that way. Bildeston, on the other hand, is attractive enough, but has the misfortune to be on a busy main road, which has brought it plenty of trade but no peace at all. The trade does not entirely come from tourism; Wattisham RAF station is only a few miles away.

I went in search of Wattisham village with some trepidation, remembering the sad mediocrity of the village which gives Lakenheath air base its name. Remarkably it turned out to be a very pleasant and secluded little community. Further round the perimeter, Ringshall was just as pleasant and even more secluded. It was only when I had nearly completed the circuit that I found where all the airmen were, in a mass of married quarters near the main gate. It seems strange the base was not named after Great Bricett, because that is the village nearest all the activity.

Great Bricett itself is fairly pleasant and fairly secluded, and the little square by the church is very secluded indeed. But not the church itself. Unexpectedly it has a private house built on to it, attached to the west wall. When I strolled through the churchyard a lady was washing up in the kitchen where the west door would normally be. This is the Manor House, and I gather the north door of the church opens into its garden, so for once I can understand why the church is kept locked. The house appears to be much later than the church, which was once part of a priory, and not even that great authority Professor M.R. James explains why they are connected. Perhaps the lady in the kitchen could have told me but I did not like to intrude on the washing-up.

The only town still big enough to merit the name in this area, once so rich in wool towns, is Hadleigh. It has a splendid assortment of architecture in its main street and has managed to keep its market town atmosphere in spite of the scattering of factories on the outskirts. As well as producing wool it also produced some remarkable clerics who have left their mark in various unlikely ways.

Overall House, for instance, is not an Army surplus store but the former home of Bishop John Overall, one of the learned scholars who translated the Authorised Version of the Bible for James I. On Aldham Common a memorial marks where Dr Rowland Taylor, a Protestant Rector who attempted to stop a Catholic Mass in the church during the reign of Queen Mary, was burned at the stake amidst the lamentations of his flock. And the astonishing Deanery Tower was the gatehouse erected by Archdeacon Pykenham in 1495 for his very un-archdeaconly residence, a palace fit for an archbishop. The palace has been pulled down, possibly by the embarrassed archdeacons who followed him, but the tower remains as a reminder of his extravagant tastes. It was in the tower incidentally that another Hadleigh cleric, Dean Rose – who confusingly was not a dean but the Rector – launched with some fellow intellectuals what became known as the Oxford Movement. By rights it should have been named after Hadleigh but I suppose Oxford sounds more important.

What did get named after Hadleigh was a television series about life in a grand country house. Some years later another series with a similar theme was named after nearby Chelsworth. These places obviously have an up-market ring about them, and create an image of stately homes, sweeping parkland and good living. In fact the closest Hadleigh comes to a stately home is Hintlesham Hall, which does indeed have a park and offers very good living, but at a price. The original Elizabethan house was altered drastically in the eighteenth century, and in the 1970s caught the eye of Robert Carrier, who turned it into a restaurant of international repute. It was sold again in the 1980s and developed as a country house hotel, with food and furnishings as luxurious as any television set designer could desire. A weekend stay for the Newmarket races runs into four figures and just one night's bed and breakfast can run into three. The next stately home soap-opera must surely be called 'Hintlesham'.

You will gather that Hintlesham is not synonymous with hinterland. This area of Suffolk does not have well-trodden paths but well-motored lanes, and while not many coaches find their way up the drive to Hintlesham Hall, they are almost everywhere else. For a glimpse of tripper-free Suffolk you must go north of the old wool towns to villages like Rattlesden and Poystreet Green, Thorpe Morieux and Battisford Tye, names that roll mellifluously off a Suffolk tongue. There are no stately homes or luxury restaurants here, no coach parks or ice-cream vans, and any picture postcards you may find are probably still in sepia. This is just rolling farmland and little hamlets, the occasional substantial farmhouse, village streets which have a dash of thatch and a touch of timber but are there to be lived in rather than looked at. Only one modest main road runs through this quiet corner of Central Suffolk, and on it lies Hitcham, home of about the only character in these parts to make a national impact.

Lavenham: turn any corner and there's another picture. . .

John Henslow was a Hitcham Rector who became professor
of minerals and botany at Cambridge and gave Charles Darwin
the ideas which led to *Origin of Species*. It was not the result he
might have desired; as a clergyman he must have found Darwin's
theory difficult to swallow. But if it is any consolation to him, it
would probably have been thought of sooner or later, even without
his help.

The boundary of this Central Suffolk hinterland is marked by
the main road from Bury St Edmunds to Sudbury, and near it are the
three Bradfields: St Clare, St George, and Combust. Bradfield Combust
is actually alongside the A134 and thus is rather busier than the rest.
It acquired its ominous name when the local manor house was burned
down in the fourteenth century by peasants rioting against the Abbot of
St Edmundsbury who owned it. Later Bradfield Combust was the home
of Arthur Young, secretary to the newly created Board of Agriculture in
the eighteenth century, who carried out a survey of the state of British
farming, county by county, and concluded to the surprise of nobody
that East Anglia was 'Backward'.

Now we are on the main Sudbury road we can plunge back
into tourist territory. It leads not only to Sudbury but first to another
Suffolk showplace, Long Melford. Indeed it goes through the middle
of it for close on two miles, the longest and widest village street in
the country. Melford's main treasures are on show as you enter it: a
magnificent church, a fine old timbered inn, and a double helping of
stately homes.

The church is in proportion to the village street, long and wide.
It is 810 feet from the west wall of the tower to the east wall of the
Lady Chapel, with nearly a hundred windows in between. This makes
it the longest church in Suffolk and probably the finest. It sits at the
top of the triangular green, broadside on like a cruise liner tied up at the
dock. Experts have tried to find fault with it: the tower which replaced
the original is out of proportion, the Lady Chapel is the wrong shape for
the rest of the church, the north wall away from the green has been
left much plainer than the south, and inside there is a monument to
Sir William Cordell which, like so many church monuments, is much
too big. There are also complaints that the hospital which Sir William
built on the green in 1573 has spoiled the view of the church ever since.
All this seems to be an exercise in nit-picking; it is a quite splendid
church.

Sir William lived in Melford Hall, on the opposite side of the green,
and created the fine buildings that stand there today, so I think we can
forgive him for the hospital – it must have spoilt his view too. For the
past two hundred years it has been occupied by the Parker family, one
of whom, the fourth baronet, whimsically christened his son Hyde. In
spite of sounding like a West End kerb-crawler, Hyde Parker became
an admiral, and so did his son, Hyde Parker the Second. The latter was

Curlicues on the roof, a
semi-circular window,
more curls on the lintel,
blue paintwork on a back-
ground of golden brick, and
assorted inscriptions all
over – an office oddity in
Long Melford. One
assumes it must be well
insured. . .

involved in a clash with another East Anglian during the American War of Independence, though he may not have realised it at the time. He led the British ships which forced their way up the Hudson River against a boom which had been stretched across it by one of the immigrant Townshends of Norfolk.

The Hall has another connection with the colonists. A window contains the arms of John Winthrop who emigrated from Groton, a few miles away, and became Governor of Massachusetts. The present occupant is Sir Richard Hyde Parker – yes, the name stuck – but it is now owned by the National Trust.

Kentwell Hall, Melford's second stately home and another redbrick Tudor mansion, is out of sight up a long drive leading off the green. The family who bought it in a dilapidated condition in 1971 have restored the house and gardens, and stage various attractions to help pay for it, ranging from open-air Shakespeare to a sheep-shearing Sunday. The house is inside a brick-lined moat with a mosaic maze in the courtyard, and there is a moathouse where schoolchildren sample Tudor life. On a grander scale there are 'Historical Re-Creations' with a cast of two hundred playing cowherds, shepherds, goosegirls, kitchen wenches and footmen. There are sawyers in the sawpit, potters in the pottery, smiths in the forge. It is all very jolly and hearty, and youngsters can learn a little history between giggles. If you find it a little overwhelming you can always escape to the Bull Inn just down the road, where you can still enjoy Tudor surroundings and have a quiet drink as well.

A more familiar façade in Long Melford: Kentwell Hall, one of its two stately homes.

The assortment of period buildings in the village culminates at the far end in a very recent development, the conversion of an old mill and its extensive outbuildings into luxury apartments. I remember the place in its original condition and the transformation is impressive. But it does make Long Melford just that little bit longer.

Acton is only a couple of miles away, a village as unremarkable on the face of it as its namesake in the West London suburbs, but enthusiasts make pilgrimages here to see the lifesize brass in the church of Sir Robert de Bures. Some say it is the oldest surviving brass in Suffolk and the third oldest in England, others say it is one of five chainmail effigies going back to 1302. They all seem to agree it is the most famous military brass in the country, and the best preserved. If you like 700-year-old effigies of cross-legged Crusaders in full armour with an ornamental baldric on the hip (so that is where Blackadder's servant got his name!) then Acton is the place for you.

There are two strange tales attached to this village which I find more fascinating than Sir Robert's baldric. It is said that on certain nights the park gates swing open 'withouten hands' and out comes a ghostly carriage drawn by four spectral horses with headless grooms and outriders, to rampage round the streets. It is also said that in a nearby pond there is a chest of money, and if you throw a stone you will hear it clang against the box and a voice will cry defiantly, 'That's mine!' I have not verified either coach or chest, but who is to say they are not there?

Just up the Piccadilly line from Acton in West London is Sudbury, one of the pleasanter corners of the London Borough of Brent. About the same distance from the Acton of baldric and bogeyman fame is another Sudbury, of quite a different ilk. The suburban Sudbury I used to cycle round for the *Wembley News* in search of church fêtes and funerals could hardly be mistaken for this ancient wool town on the banks of the Stour.

Even so, earlier writers have been unimpressed by it. Dickens rechristened it Eatanswill in the *Pickwick Papers*, and Defoe merely commented, 'I know nothing for which this town is remarkable except for being very populous and very poor.' The French traveller de la Rochefoucauld went a lot further. 'The town and the neighbourhood are inhabited only by people without any fortune, by smugglers, bankrupts and the like. It is a misfortune for which I cannot account, that there is not a decent man in the place.' Happily things have looked up a bit since then. Some of my best friends, I should say, live in Sudbury.

Certainly it suffered with the other wool and weaving towns when Lancashire took over the trade in the nineteenth century, and it must have gone through hard times. But it had the benefit of the river as a trading link; barges could reach it from Manningtree. So instead of fossilising or fading away like its neighbours, Sudbury built wharves and basins and warehouses and diversified into other fields. This meant that its eighteenth-century residents could afford to modernise their homes, and unfortunately modernisation in those days had much the same depressing result as it often has today. The old Tudor buildings were covered with grey Georgian frontages, and any exposed timber is a rarity.

The Hinterland

The Stour is no longer open to barges, and even when it was there were problems. The towpath switched from bank to bank about thirty times and there were no bridges, so the horses had to balance in a small boat each time to be rowed across. There were also stiles which the horses had to vault, though I suppose the tow-rope was detached while they did it. It sounds more like a circus than a quiet tow up the river, and the equine population of South Suffolk must have been greatly relieved when the Stour became too clogged for navigation.

A quiet stretch of the Stour at Sudbury. This is Gainsborough Country, and his statue stands outside the church, but he seemed to prefer posh portraits to local landscapes.

The streets of Sudbury became very clogged too, but a bypass was built in the 1980s and it is now easier to stand on Market Hill and admire the statue of Thomas Gainsborough, one of the town's two famous sons. If Gainsborough had spent more time on landscapes and less on portraits this part of the Stour could have become Gainsborough country, for better or worse. However the city fathers have done their best to preserve his name. There is not only the Gainsborough statue but a Gainsborough Street, a Gainsborough school, a Gainsborough Museum, and even a Gainsborough cinema, and café, and hotel. Unfortunately there is a shortage of actual Gainsboroughs, which come a little expensive for a small Suffolk town.

A less obvious reminder of the Gainsborough family is a Nonconformist chapel which was built by one of Thomas's sisters after she quarrelled with the minister of the existing one. I gather it was known locally as the Spite Chapel . . .

Sudbury's other famous son was the victim of much more violent spite. Simon Tybald, Bishop of Sudbury, became Archbishop of Canterbury, a post he managed to combine with the Chancellor of the Exchequer – not even the Thatcher government has thought of that. Mrs T. did, however, adopt one of his ideas, because in his capacity as Chancellor he introduced a poll tax, which in his case at any rate had disastrous results. It led to the Peasants' Rebellion of 1381, and the peasants managed to track down the Chancellor-Archbishop in the Tower of London. Although it was only the Chancellor they were after, the Archbishop had to go too, and their joint head was removed from its shoulders on Tower Green. It was eventually retrieved and brought back to St Gregory's, Sudbury, the church he built himself in happier times. The skull is still preserved in the vestry, and glares balefully if any rebellious peasants wander in.

Sudbury was once a thriving river port but the barges no longer ply along the Stour, and the quayside is now a theatre.

Above Sudbury and Long Melford the Stour escapes into open countryside for a while, but it returns to the charabanc circuit to pass through three of Suffolk's well-known showplaces, Cavendish, Clare and Stoke-by-Clare.

Cavendish seems unimpressive as you drive into it from Long Melford along a busy modern street, but it opens up into a sloping triangular green which is much frequented by amateur photographers, trying to decide which of its three sides makes the most attractive picture. Even a modern house which has been inserted among the thatched cottages manages to blend in without offence. So does Alfonso's Restaurant, though the name looks a little odd in such a traditionally English setting.

The village still has a Railway Arms as a reminder of the Stour Valley Railway, which ran alongside the river from Sudbury to Clare. Clare has managed to retain its railway station and goods depot, but the station is now a lifesize toy for the children and the depot is the country park's information centre – or 'Clare Ark Centre' as it was called when I was last there, perhaps anticipating a wet winter.

You can look down on them from the ruins of Clare Castle, since the railway was actually built across the castle bailey, to much local

opposition at the time. Only a fragment of the keep remains, but the climb up the spiral path to the top of the castle mound is worth the effort to be able to view the little town without being disturbed by the traffic. Nethergate Street in particular, which is full of fine old merchants' houses, is difficult to examine in comfort at ground level. You can even enjoy the pargeting on the houses near the church if you remember to take binoculars.

From this vantage point you can get an idea of how important this place must have been in medieval days, when it gave its name to the Earls of Clare, to County Clare in Ireland, to Clare College, Cambridge, to the dukedom of Clarence and to the Clarencieux King of Arms – not forgetting countless female babies.

The mound is not quite as peaceful as it used to be when Julian Tennyson 'laid me down, put a handkerchief over my face, and slept soundly throughout the summer afternoon'. If he tried that now he would be trampled underfoot by tourists. But on a fine day out of season it is a pleasant little haven, and an excellent viewing point for the countryside around. To the south you can see far into the flat farmland of Essex, and just across the river there is the priory established by the Augustinians in the thirteenth century and now occupied by them again. This was where a dishonest sacrist took half-burnt candles from the shrine and resold them to pilgrims, on the advice of a mysterious stranger who in return for his suggestion told him to set aside the first candle for him. When the stranger returned, however, he found the sacrist was so greedy he had sold that one too. Much irked, he smashed the sacrist's head on the steps – the stain, they say, is still there – and went off in a sulphurous huff.

To the north you can see beyond the rooftops of the town to the rolling hills of the Suffolk hinterland. It would be tempting to head that way, but Stoke-by-Clare still awaits, and a challenge. The church has reputedly the tiniest pulpit in the country, and unkind friends had suggested I would find it impossible to insert myself in it. I am glad to report I succeeded, though it felt as though I was wedged in an upturned barrel. It really is of very modest proportions, and might be thought to illustrate the economies practised by the family at the Big House next door.

The meanness of the Elwes clan has produced some remarkable stories. Sir Hervey Elwes never repaired a roof or replaced a window – neither his own, nor his tenants'. He never lit a fire except in the most bitter weather; indeed he rarely lit even a candle. He managed to live on £110 a year, and that included the wages of three house servants. His mother had been just as frugal; she starved herself to death and left a fortune. And when Sir Hervey died he left even more.

The nephew who succeeded him started off quite impressively, restoring the Hall and looking after the tenants, but he was affected by the same fixation and became the meanest of the lot. To save on

Patterns in plaster on an old house in Clare. There is more fine pargetry on Bishop Bonner's cottages in Dereham.

food bills John Elwes would eat a moorhen that had been killed by a rat, or a fish which had been partly digested by a pike. He would roam the hedgerows to gather his own firewood, and after harvest he would go gleaning for left-over grain in the fields. When he went riding he kept his horse off the road to save on horseshoes, and when he broke both legs he would only pay the doctor to put a splint on one then copied what he had done on the other. When he died in 1789 he left half-a-million pounds.

With all this record of parsimony it would be logical to assume that the church's tiny pulpit was the idea of John Elwes, to save on wood. Actually, it was built three centuries earlier in 1498.

The Big House is now in good order again and used as a private school. The church has not fared so well; in 1989 it had to launch an appeal for £50,000 and I picked my way to the pulpit through a maze of scaffolding and cables. What has remained unchanged through all this is the strange brick tower at the entrance to the Hall, just beside the church. It has the pattern of a portcullis and a mitre picked out on its walls, and it looks like a windowless gatehouse, or even a disguised water tower. It is in fact a Tudor dovecote, though I found it difficult to spot how the doves got in. At least the miserly Mr Elwes did not demolish it and sell off the bricks.

Beyond Stoke-by-Clare the road dips into Essex for a stretch, which seems a good excuse to answer the call of those beckoning Suffolk hills. But there is one other border town to visit in the far south-western corner of the county. Most people would advise you not to bother, but it would be improper to ignore a community which, even if it contributes nothing to Suffolk's scenic beauty, must contribute a great deal to the county's finances.

Julian Tennyson nevertheless ignored Haverhill. So did my other two favourite Suffolk writers, R.H. Mottram and Dr M.R. James. The *Companion Guide* merely observes that in Victorian times it was a sort of rural Leeds, then moved into the 'age of overspill' and was overwhelmed by factories and council houses. The nicest thing John Burke can say about it is that 'arriving in Haverhill, most people's first impulse will be to leave it as quickly as possible'. The nastiest thing he wrote about it I quoted at the start of this chapter. The place is so universally condemned I felt duty-bound to find some attractive feature that all the others had missed.

It was not easy. Haverhill is indeed an overspill town of the most unprepossessing kind, built with little regard for the traditions or characteristics of the countryside around it. The shopping centre has been pedestrianised so that visitors spend half their time looking for it and the other half trying to park. You approach it through dreary industrial estates. On the hills beyond the factories, that same range of hills which looks so delightful from Clare Castle, there is a solid mass of quite hideous houses.

The few Suffolk-born people who are left there tell wondrous tales of how the overspill came to Haverhill. One of them recalls how the industrial area was flooded regularly in the early stages, and a large sign saying 'Desirable Factory Sites for Sale' was often standing in five feet of water. Another recalls how a few months after the Londoners moved in there was a great rash of 'For Sale' signs on the estates, indicating how anxious they were to move out again. And there is the tale of the municipal dustcart, which had served the original town well for many years, but the development authority had plenty of government money and bought a new one for £2,500. They sold the old one to a farmer for thirty, and he used it around the farm on various duties for a couple of years with no trouble at all. Then the new one broke down and needed an extensive overhaul, so the authority asked the farmer if they could borrow the old one back. He charged them thirty pounds . . .

Yes, Haverhill has a lot to live down, but much to my relief, after a couple of involuntary circuits of the one-way system, I found a building which would not look out of place in Lavenham or Long Melford, a genuine Tudor mansion with all the requisite timbers and latticed windows. This is Anne of Cleves' House, now right on the pavement and flanked by undistinguished terraces and a nondescript Nonconformist church, but when Henry VIII presented it to Anne as part of the marriage settlement it presumably stood in its own extensive grounds.

The building was restored in 1986 as a private nursing home, and according to a plaque on the front wall in suitably Olde English lettering, it 'loudly echoes the tudor era of 400 years ago'. It seems unusual for a nursing home to wish to echo loudly, and why Tudor is not given the benefit of a capital letter only the carver can know, but this is Haverhill and we must be thankful that anything older than a hundred years still exists, however oddly it is labelled.

As for the town's other plus points, there is a large open green with a football pitch, an inoffensive parish church, and at least four roads that lead out of it. I made a mental excuse, and left.

The influence of Haverhill spreads into the nearby village of Kedington, which has a rash of new housing almost as unattractive as Haverhill itself, but the old part of the village near the church has been preserved, and the winding lane from the church down to the little bridge over the Stour seems unaltered since the days of the horse and cart. It is thus quite lethal when the Haverhill commuters come hurrying home.

Inside the church the old box pews and the memorials to the Barnardiston family have not changed either. It was the close-cropped head of Samuel Barnardiston, a notable Puritan, which prompted Queen Henrietta Maria to observe, 'What a handsome round head is there' – and the Puritans were known as Roundheads thenceforth. The squire's pew is divided in two, one for the menfolk and the other

for the ladies, and I did enquire discreetly if the practice still persisted. The last occupant that anyone could recall was a Miss Sainsbury from Great Wratting Hall back in the thirties, and as she was alone she could occupy whichever half she wished. It is now used to store vestments, so male chauvinism in Kedington would seem to be suppressed, if not extinct.

Beside the pulpit is an hourglass stand, which is not unusual in old churches, and a wig pole, which is. This has a large knob on which the parson hung his wig during the sermon, presumably to avoid embarrassment if his gestures became so dramatic that the wig flew off. Sitting in one of the box pews it is easy to picture the bareheaded parson racing against the trickling sand in the hourglass, with the wig perched on the knob before him his most devoted and attentive listener . . .

Kedington church pulpit has an hourglass stand, which is not unusual in old churches, and a wig pole, which is. The parson hung his wig on the pole, either for safety or for comfort. The flowers are a later addition.

Now we can head off to Great Wratting and Thurlow and into the real Suffolk hinterland. This is the western edge of it, and for once there is no river to define the county boundary. The line wanders inconsequentially through the lanes and fields in no particular direction, while the Stour sheds its responsibilities and meanders away into the hinterland on its own. It passes through Great Bradley, where the church looks nothing special until you walk round to the south side and find an imposing porch of Tudor brick which seems to have been tacked on to cheer the place up. It was put there by a rather special brickmaker, Henry VIII's personal appointee. What he was doing in this obscure Suffolk village is not clear; perhaps he was part of a sixteenth-century overspill plan which never got off the ground.

To make sure you do not stray inadvertently into Essex it is best to head eastward, where the heart of the Suffolk hinterland lies before you. It is such a confusion of little lanes I do not suggest any particular route. The best plan is just to explore where you will, with no destination in mind, and if a name on a signpost takes your fancy, then that is the road to pursue.

Moulton, Dalham and Ousden I have already mentioned, where the hinterland joins the commuter corridor alongside the A45. The proximity of Bury and Newmarket has brought them a scattering of new houses, but villages like the Bradleys and Cowlinge and Hargrave are far enough away to remain unspoilt. There is little of great note about any of these hinterland villages. They all have a church which is worth a look, and one or two have a manor house tucked away in the trees, but they are an unassuming lot and like to stay that way. Lidgate did once produce a Chaucerian-style poet, John Lydgate, whose much restored home still stands, but I suspect there are few people in Lidgate who have read his verses, and even fewer outside.

The further into the hinterland you go the quieter it becomes, and the villages scarcer. Hargrave, Hawstead, Hawkedon, Hartest – they share a common tranquillity as well as the same initial. Perhaps Hawkedon is the pick of them, the cottages perched on a hill looking across at the church where the figures on the screen are described tersely by Dr James as 'James, John, Dorothy (?) and another virgin'.

The Suffolk hinterland is rich in unspoilt villages and tranquil village greens. This is Hartest, but it could be Hargrave, Hawstead, Hawkedon. . .

The Hinterland

Boxted (the Suffolk one) is just as attractive but set down in a valley with the church on the hillside above. This is Poley-land; the Poleys have lived in the Big House for five centuries and the church is packed with them, so I am told, but the church was locked even though workmen were busy on the roof. I would have liked to see the statue of Sir John Poley with a frog hanging in its ear, because the story goes that this was the frog that would a-wooing go, 'Roley, Poley, Gammon and Spinach'. This baffling refrain is supposed to relate to four local families, the Poleys, the Rowleys, and would you believe, the Bacons and the Greenes. It may have been that workman on the roof but I think I heard a faint ho-ho . . .

Although I could not get inside, the view from the church car park made up for it. You can look across the village in the valley to the woods on the hills beyond, with a scattering of cottages among the trees and little lanes running down to the valley floor. Nothing dramatic, just a mellow, peaceful countryside. This is what the hinterland is all about.

The only place of any size in this area is Wickhambrook. It is also the only place where I saw a corrugated iron roof. Nonetheless it is still more attractive than Glemsford, which used to have a flax factory and still has the Victorian terraces to prove it. These days it seems popular with incomers, and it has the bungalows to prove that too. The combination is not common in this part of Suffolk, but it is right on the edge of the hinterland and one can easily escape northwards back to villages like Shimpling Street and Brockley Green. They are not quite unexplored; the education authorities discovered Chadacre Park and set up an agricultural college there, while Coldham Hall, it is confidently claimed, was discovered by the first Queen Elizabeth – and yes, she did sleep there. I am not sure that even a queen could obtain bed-and-breakfast in this area today.

If you keep heading north, before you hit the A45 corridor again, you come to Whepstead, which has the only church in the country dedicated to St Petronilla. Dr James does not consider this worth a mention, and indeed East Anglia does go in for one-off saints to such an extent that I suppose it is no longer a novelty. Bradfield St Clare, for instance, has nothing to do with the town or the Clare family but commemorates the St Clare who helped St Francis of Assisi; again it is unique in Britain. In Norfolk we have our local saints, St William of Norwich and St Walstan of Bawburgh, who are probably hardly known outside the county.

My favourite is St Wandregesilus, or Wandrede for short, who has a church dedicated to him at the minute village of Bixley, just outside Norwich, for reasons which remain obscure. He was a seventh-century courtier in what is now France, who decided to become a monk. The king was not amused and ordered him to return to court. On his way to the palace he came upon a carter trying to haul his horse out of the mud, and perhaps with sainthood in mind he helped to get it out. As a result he was very grubby indeed when he arrived. The king, instead of reprimanding him for being late and dropping mud on the carpet, praised him for his selfless action and sent him on his way.

Wandrede spent ten solitary years in the Jura Mountains – 'Wandrede lonely as a cloud?' – then founded a monastery near Rouen and died there. It all happened a very long way from Bixley, but the Bailiff of Norwich who built Bixley Church in 1272 decided to name it after this obscure French abbot. So far as I know he never explained why, but he obviously had some sort of affinity with him. Perhaps he was born under a Wandrede star. (Now you see why he is my favourite.)

All this talk of Norfolk saints has drawn me away from the Suffolk hinterland, and anyway I am due to return to my own territory. Suffolk is a fine county and its hinterland is mellow and restful and charming, while the corresponding area in Norfolk, the area where I live, is admittedly plainer and flatter and sometimes bleaker. The two counties have been said to represent the masculine and feminine aspects of East Anglia and I can understand why, so far as these areas are concerned: Suffolk with its gentle rolling hills and picturesque thatch and timbers, Norfolk with its workmanlike vistas of beet and barley, its sturdy flint and pantiled cottages, and its greater sense of isolation. It has hills and woods also, and streams and quiet valleys, as I hope to show you, but the overall effect is of a working landscape rather than a restful picture postcard. You need to find where the cultivation stops and the relaxation begins.

That is the Norfolk where I finished up, and where this book will finish too. Come and see it.

Not quite in character for an ancient wool town, but a bit of fun; a mock-Tudor mailbox outside the real thing in Kersey.

9 An Ever-decreasing Circle
A spiralling tour into High Norfolk

'High Norfolk' is a term that makes people outside Norfolk fall about. It is rarely higher than two hundred feet and most of it is much lower, but the geologists coined the phrase to describe the plateau of clay on top of the chalk, which does add slightly to ground level. This is the agricultural heart of the county, until recently oblivious to tourists and devoted to farming, hunting and shooting, not always in that order. Anywhere else it would be called Deep Norfolk, but Norfolkmen like to 'du different' even in geological terms, so they give it height instead of depth.

My own definition of High-Deep Norfolk does not quite tally with the geologists. We agree that it covers the Dereham area, and indeed Dereham proudly proclaims itself as the Heart of Norfolk, but in terms of remoteness I would add a much wider area around it, taking in Docking and Swaffham in the west and Reepham in the east. The geologists would say I am overlapping into Breckland, the sandy heathland which once covered South Norfolk. They would also say that the Docking region is technically called Good Sands, because unlike Breckland its soil was good for cultivation. But local government has already confused matters by creating a straggling new district called Breckland which encroaches on High Norfolk. As for Good Sands, the locals never use the term, and as Docking is actually higher than High Norfolk I don't feel too guilty about including it.

So there is this almost circular area of Mid-Norfolk, into which I disappeared, almost at its central point, when I left the BBC, and I have lived there ever since. One could explore it by zigzagging or taking it in sections, but my route will be in ever-decreasing circles, so that in due course I can disappear again . . .

To reach it from Norwich there is the A47 trunk road to Dereham or the less hazardous main road to Fakenham. Neither is very attractive in its early stages. The A47 carries all the heavy traffic from the Midlands and is permanently congested; during events at the Royal Norfolk showground, which is just beside it, everything comes to a standstill. On the other hand the suburban villages sprawl further out along the Fakenham road. It is hard to tell where Hellesdon ends and Drayton begins, and beyond Drayton there is hardly a blade of grass before you find yourself in Taverham. There was once a stretch of open country but they built a new 'village' called Thorpe Marriott which effectively blotted it out.

The only other expanse of green is the Royal Norwich Golf Club, which extends on both sides of the road. On a rainy day the tedium of this drive is relieved by the sight of sodden golfers huddled on the roadside, waiting to dash across to the next tee.

A development company bid millions of pounds to turn the golf course into a massive housing estate, and offered to provide a bigger, better course elsewhere. The planning authorities, showing rare good judgement, turned down the first application, and when the housing market slumped the company withdrew. However the golfers, no doubt dazzled by this glimpse of the Promised Land, announced early in 1990 that they were negotiating with other builders, so we could yet see bungalows in the bunkers, forecourts on the fairways and garages on the greens.

Between these two busy main roads out of Norwich there is another route which takes you almost immediately into the open country of the Wensum valley, and the Wensum leads into the heart of High Norfolk. It is not navigable by anything larger than a canoe, and the roads rarely run alongside it, but it is possible to rejoin it every couple of miles, and it winds through some of the pleasantest and quietest corners of the commuter country around the city. All this winding gave the Wensum its name – 'winds-some' – but 'winsome' would be almost as appropriate.

A spiralling tour into High Norfolk

Just beyond the Norwich suburbs the Wensum Valley reaches the open countryside at Ringland; *left* Ringland Hills and *right* on the river bank.

We can join it first at Old Costessey, a name to make newsreaders tremble – you pronounce it Cossey. There is a New Costessey which has grown up on the main road by the showground, but the old village is tucked away by the river. Very much a commuter village, of course, and so is Ringland upstream, but they have kept their character and Ringland is one of the few places on the Wensum which offers parking space on the riverbank. Children can paddle while their parents have a drink in the pub across the road. The best vantage point to see along the river valley is up in the Ringland Hills, but it is well wooded up there and all I could see was trees. I do not complain about that; trees are a delight to the eye compared with the view from the A47.

I like the view better from outside Taverham School, which overlooks the river and Taverham Bridge. There used to be mills here which provided the newsprint for *The Times*, long before it used up a copse of trees a day. Taverham has two faces, one on the main road and the other on the river; there are now nearly five thousand people in between.

Weston Longville, further up the valley, gives the impression it is devoted entirely to the memory of Parson James Woodforde, whose diaries, like the Paston Letters, the poems of William Cowper and the works of George Borrow, are something which everybody in Norfolk has heard of and is terribly proud of but has never actually read. The church is full of reminders of Parson Woodforde, the pub is named after him, and every guidebook gives him a respectful mention. However, what brought most people to Weston Longville in 1989 was not the diarist but the dinosaurs, a collection of plastic monsters installed on the Weston estate by the enterprising owner, along with a bygones museum, a maze and an adventure playground. The village has not seen such excitement since Parson Woodforde danced until two in the morning, buoyed up by the rum he acquired from Andrews the smuggler. (Yes, I have read a couple of pages . . .)

Life is a lot quieter at Reepham, where Parson Woodforde bought his non-contraband shopping, and has been for many a year. Indeed in the 1950s I wrote an article in the *Dereham & Fakenham Times* headed dramatically: 'Is Reepham Dying?' It was prompted by the retirement of the local chemist, who could find no one to replace him. 'Is the day of the small market town over?' he gloomily enquired.

Happily it was not. Reepham market place can still seem as sleepy as it was then, but it now has a lively sports centre, new houses have gone up, and although there is still no chemist the local doctor looks after his own prescriptions. What it lacks in chemists it makes up for in churches. Three parishes met in the town and each Lord of the Manor was determined to build his own church, preferably larger than the others. As a compromise they did agree to share the same churchyard. One was burned down 450 years ago but the other two still remain, and one contains a baffling memorial.

Why should Sir Roger de Kerdiston, a fourteenth-century knight, be lying on a bed of pebbles? His distant relative Sir Oliver de Ingham has the same uncomfortable resting place in Ingham Church. R.H. Mottram puts forward the ingenious theory that they may have been shipwrecked. Dr James, a great expert on such things, prefers the idea that they were 'bivouacking on the battlefield'. I think the sculptor just got bored with standard deathbeds and tried his hand at pebbles instead, working on the principle that some knights fell on stony ground.

A spiralling tour into High Norfolk

Two churches sharing the same churchyard at Reepham. There used to be three but the other one burned down.

The Reepham area is unusually rich in churches, even for Norfolk – not just in numbers but in architectural quality. The nearby villages of Cawston and Salle each claims to have the finest country church in the county. I would not choose between them, but Salle did gain slightly in prestige value by having the Prince of Wales at a church concert. He was invited by the Whites who live at the Big House, which was acquired by Timothy White in 1890 from the profits on aspirins and hot water bottles. Cawston could not compete with this; its Big House is now occupied by a school and lacks the necessary connections.

However Cawston Church does score on curiosities. The sixteenth-century rood screen shows St Matthew wearing an anachronistic pair of spectacles; the tower gallery contains a pub sign from the Old Plough Inn next door; and an inscription on the tower screen says it was paid for by a medieval 'church ale', perhaps the earliest evidence of a successful church fayre in the days when they really spelt it that way.

Not far away at Booton is a strange church which was rebuilt by a nineteenth-century Rector to his own design. He had no architectural training but he knew what he liked, and what he obviously liked most was pinnacles. He planted an assortment of them on the spindly twin towers and all round the roof.

His creation had a mixed reception. The villagers were very polite about it – he was Lord of the Manor as well as Rector – and they christened it, perhaps tongue in cheek, 'The Cathedral in the Fields'. Sir Edwin Lutyens, speaking as a friend of the family as well as an architect, said discreetly that it was 'very naughty, but built in the right spirit'. The final and crucial verdict came many years later, when the parishioners could no longer maintain it even if they wanted to, and the Redundant Churches Trust decided it was worth spending £20,000 on it to preserve it for posterity.

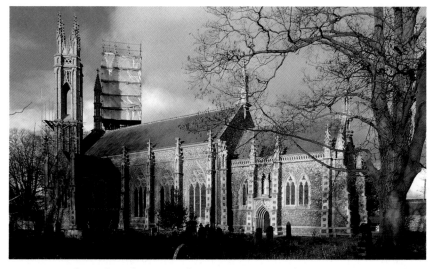

Two unorthodox Norfolk churches: Booton was built by a 19th-century rector with a passion for pinnacles, and his parishioners christened it, perhaps tongue in cheek, 'The Cathedral in the Fields'. . .

One other church is worth mentioning in this area, then I will leave off, though an entire book could be written about Norfolk's wealth of churches, and indeed many have been. But at Bawdeswell is a great rarity for these parts, a church built since the last war. The original was destroyed when a plane crashed on it in 1945. I remember reporting its completion ten years later, when people criticised it either for looking too modern or not modern enough. It is in classical colonial style, and one parishioner complained it would look better in Norfolk, Virginia. Someone else said the tower looked like 'a pathetic Gothic beehive'. These days the experts seem to approve of it and the locals seem reconciled to it; having seen some modern churches, they could have done far worse.

Bawdeswell has benefited greatly from the bypassing of the Norwich–Fakenham road and seems to be one of the few bypassed villages to remain free of traffic; one can admire or mock the church in comfort. On the other hand neighbouring Foxley was cut in two by the new road, and has compulsorily become Foxley East and Foxley West. Fortunately Foxley Wood, one of the most important areas of ancient woodland in Norfolk, remains unharmed. It covers about three hundred acres, and apart from an incongruous clump of postwar conifers slap in the middle, it is basically unaltered since the Domesday Book. The Norfolk Naturalists Trust now looks after it and will be replacing those conifers as soon as they can.

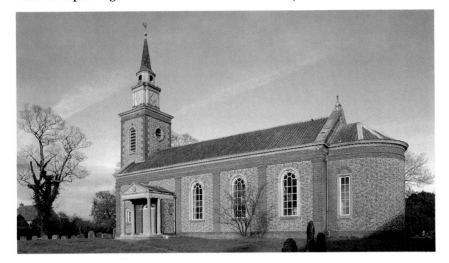

Bawdeswell was built by a 1950s architect who was keen on classic Colonial, and one critic complained it would look better in Norfolk, Virginia.

The area north of Foxley and the main road is typical High Norfolk. There is nothing much there except fields and a few woods and a scattering of villages. Themelthorpe, Wood Dalling, Guestwick – these are quiet little places with large churches and a Big House lurking out of sight. Hindolveston is rather a contrast; the main street goes on and on, getting longer all the time as another builder tacks on another couple of chalet-bungalows. But the real jolt for visitors is Melton Constable, which looks like a Victorian industrial village plucked out of the Midlands and planted in rural Norfolk.

That is just about what it is. Melton Constable was called the Crewe of North Norfolk. It was the main junction for the Midland and Great Northern Line – the 'Muddle and Get Nowhere' we called it, not entirely inaccurately, since it meandered around the county in a quite unpredictable fashion. Before it came there was just the tiny parish of Burgh Parva and Melton Constable Hall, built by the Astleys in 1670, their third home in the park they had owned since 1236. When the railway village was built to house the men who worked in the goods yards and engine sheds it took its name from the Hall. The only reminder of Burgh Parva is its ruined church.

Trains based at Melton Constable linked Norwich with Fakenham, King's Lynn and the Midlands, but very slowly and very unprofitably. In the 1950s the line was one of the first to go, and a community of eleven hundred people was deprived of its employment. Since then the population has halved, but the village looks much the same and has linked up with its neighbour Briston to provide a modest social and business centre for the tiny villages around.

An Ever-decreasing Circle

The ruined church tower behind its more recent successor is a reminder of what Burgh Parva was like before the railway created Melton Constable village.

Meanwhile changes have taken place at the Hall. A few years after the closure of the railway (though I doubt he ever used it) the 22nd Baron Hastings decided that Melton Constable was no longer the place for him, and sold the estate. He did after all have other homes to go to, not least a little place in Northumberland called Seaton Delaval. It was a complicated transaction, and as he embarked upon it he may well have repeated the prayer of his ancestor before the Battle of Edgehill: 'Oh Lord, Thou knowest how busy I must be this day. If I forget Thee, do not Thou forget me.'

Lord Hastings may not have been forgotten, but the Hall apparently was. It remained deserted for so long it was wryly dubbed the finest empty country house in England. It had occasional moments of glory as a film set – remember *The Go-Between*? – but nothing else happened until it was resold in the late 1980s to a development company, which restored it as a conference and entertainments centre. So a new chapter has opened in the contrasting histories of the two Melton Constables, the Victorian railway village and the Jacobean stately home.

A few miles away at Thursford another form of entertainment centre awaits. Across the fields you may hear the strains of 'Roll Out the Barrel' on a mighty Wurlitzer, coming from an outsize barn. It is not as incongruous as it seems. There is a process of development which makes a cinema organ seem very appropriate in deepest Norfolk. Melton Constable lived through steam trains for many years, but there is another steam engine which refreshes the parts the railways never reached, the steam generators which travelling showmen brought to rural communities to provide power for their mechanical rides and the lights and music that went with them. The steam organs provided the music for the bioscope shows, the earliest form of cinema, and they were succeeded by organs like the one at Thursford, which reached its Norfolk farmyard home via New York and the Paramount Cinema, Leeds.

The Thursford Collection of steam engines, organs and round-abouts is one of the most unlikely success stories of rural tourism. The high spot is its annual Christmas extravaganza, a schmaltzy combination of carols, dancing, trumpeters, marchers, community singing and of course the Wurlitzer holding it all together. It even finishes up with a candle-light procession, balloons falling from a ceiling and a flight of white doves. The locals go over and over again to see it, and the show is booked up a year ahead. Sugar beet was never as profitable as this.

Neighbouring villages have adjusted to the changing times too, though not so spectacularly. The old mill at Hindringham has been converted into a restaurant. The Hall at Thornage, once the home of Henry VIII's physician (who was probably too busy with his royal patients to spend much time there), is now a home for the handicapped run by the Camphill Trust. And the unusual schoolhouse at Gunthorpe, with its lofty chimney and a big round window, given to the village by the Sparkes family at the Big House, is now a holiday home. The Big House was sold some years ago, and the Sparkes flew.

But away from the sound of that Wurlitzer this is still a secluded area, handy for the sea but off the tourist track, and not surprisingly it is a popular hideaway for public figures. One well-known MP has a second home at Sharrington, another lives in Swanton Novers, both well concealed from casual trippers, and a former MP who was also a television newsreader told me he rather fancied living in the village that lies between. It is called Brinton.

There is a very different atmosphere at Little Walsingham, which is little no longer. It is invaded regularly by thousands of pilgrims and tourists, and the quaint old high street has been largely given over to postcard and souvenir shops – the souvenirs in this case being statuettes of Our Lady of Walsingham. The route from the Slipper Chapel to the two shrines, Anglican and Roman Catholic, has been trodden by pilgrims from all over the world, many of them barefooted, and you may wish to join their number, but when your devotions are over there are other corners of Little Walsingham which do not appear in the brochures but are well worth a look.

You may not associate this ancient place of pilgrimage with Methodism, but the village has the oldest Methodist chapel in Norfolk still in current use. The parish church, tucked away behind the Priory grounds, has the church bells which inspired a former Rector to write a catchy little carol called 'Ding-dong merrily on high'; the tower has been restored to ensure they can ding-dong merrily and still stay on high. And in another back street is a two-hundred-year-old jail, as gloomy now as when sixty felons were crammed into its eight cells, sentenced perhaps to a year's hard labour for stealing a sack of oats. It is the only privately-owned jail in Britain; the last I heard, it was being optimistically offered for sale as a holiday home.

You may be tempted to visit Great Snoring in the hope of meeting its best-known family the Gotobeds (honestly!), and you may want a glimpse of the much-photographed Tudor façade and fancy chimneys of East Barsham Hall, but then I suggest you leave these well-beaten paths and head for a higher High Norfolk, the vast empty spaces of the Good Sands around Docking. Here indeed you can see the effects of 'prairieisation', huge rolling fields with hardly a hedge or a tree to be seen. A subsidy was offered after the war for ripping out hedges and the farmers of the Good Sands made the most of it. Now tastes have changed, and some of them are putting the hedges back again, but they take a lot longer to grow than to demolish. At least it does allow you a sweeping panorama of Norfolk's finest farmland.

The lanes run straight and unwavering across this undulating emptiness, like a miniature version of Salisbury Plain. There is a certain grandeur about it, all this expanse of earth and sky, and if you follow it far enough you get a glimpse of blue sea in the distance as the land drops away to the coast. There are fewer villages here than anywhere else in East Anglia, and even Docking, where all the roads converge, has only a population of twelve hundred.

But in the midst of all this emptiness there are some unexpected corners. There are the tiny hamlets of Bagthorpe and Barmer, so tiny indeed that they can no longer support their churches and the Norfolk Churches Trust looks after them both. Barmer All Saints, with its round tower, is particularly attractive but sad as well, standing deserted among the trees in the park of a Big House which no longer exists.

There is Great Bircham Mill, which was derelict until 1976 but has now been restored with a new cap and fantail and a pair of sails. From the stone-floored gallery round it you can see even further across the Good Sands. Ringstead has a mill too, but it has been privately owned and occupied for over sixty years. You are better advised to visit Ringstead Downs, a grass-covered chalk valley where you can feel quite isolated from the vast acres of barley and beet all around.

Stanhoe is another island in this sea of gold and green, with a pond full of avaricious ducks, and North and South Creake have a stream flowing through the middle of them which gives them quite a Suffolk flavour. I once accused South Creake of having arguably the ugliest building in High Norfolk, an old razor blade factory which loomed forbiddingly over the centre of the village. I am glad to report that an enlightened developer – and there are just one or two – has converted this depressing building into an unorthodox but surprisingly attractive private house. It no longer looms, it just towers. You still can't miss it, but now there is no need to.

Bircham Mill, restored since 1976, very typical of the High Norfolk landscape. . .

Peddars Way, the ancient Roman route to the coast now restored as a public footpath, runs through the middle of the Good Sands. If you head south down it you pass the Houghton Estate, where it is a change to find the fields are full of white deer instead of wheat or barley. They are also frequently full of people, since Houghton Hall is one of Norfolk's star tourist attractions. It might have been more famous still if the Royal Family had decided to buy it, but they bought Sandringham instead and Houghton remains in the family of the man who built it, Sir Robert Walpole, the first Prime Minister. He decided the village spoilt the view across the park, so he knocked it all down and built New Houghton outside the gates, a double row of square white dwellings far enough apart to allow two carriages to pass, and thus totally different from any other Norfolk village.

. . . and very untypical, the square white cottages at New Houghton built by Sir Robert Walpole when he moved the whole village out of his park.

An Ever-decreasing Circle

Sir Robert's descendant, the dowager Marchioness of Cholmondeley, took a rather different approach. Instead of banishing the locals from the park she opened the house to the public and often sat at the entrance to welcome the visitors. It became the scene of spectacular musical displays by military bands, almost a Norfolk Tattoo. Many of the paintings on display in the Hall were put there by the Marchioness – her own family combined the talents of the Sassoons with the finances of the Rothschilds, which gave her quite an advantage as a collector. She died on Boxing Day 1989 at the age of 95.

South of the Houghton estate there is another great tract of open country, with hardly a village and only the occasional lane. Great Massingham is the largest and most photogenic, with five village ponds, thanks to the monks who used to live there and needed fishponds. East Walton has no ponds, but it does have a wheelwright's oven on the village green, a narrow brick building the height of a man which looks like a very small air raid shelter or a very large kennel. The metal tyre was heated in the oven to expand it, then fitted round the wheel and cooled with water to shrink tightly on to the wood. The tricky part was cooling the metal quick enough to stop it burning the wheel.

Two peaceful villages well away from any tourist route: Great Massingham has a series of ponds on its village green. . .

Gayton Thorpe has the remnants of a Roman villa which the experts say was paved with Italian marble, had well-hinged doors with fixed locks, a verandah for the summer and central heating for the winter. It must have been the Roman equivalent of Narford Hall, the nearest Big House and home of the remarkable Fountaine family. You will know you are in its environs when you meet one of the large signs which command all the surrounding lanes. 'Speak Up Now for Norfolk', they proclaim. 'Granary of Britain, or GLC Rubbish Dump?' And on the reverse: 'Enjoy the Countryside While You May. Government Plans Will Abolish It Tomorrow.'

Mr Fountaine, as you can see, holds strong convictions, and since he also holds most of the land hereabouts I suppose nobody has ventured to point out that the GLC no longer exists, and that nothing spoils the look of the countryside more than plastering it with noticeboards. It is not for nothing that the family coat of arms features three trumpeting elephants.

Hasten across the hazardous A47 and the former Roman road that forks off it to Downham Market and you are in among the woods and streams of Beachamwell Warren. Here is the delightfully named Cockley Cley, which used to remind me of Eliza Doolittle's 'Not Cockle-Likely' until I found it was pronounced rather differently. It has found itself on the tourist maps thanks to its reconstituted Iceni village, a wooden-walled enclave reminiscent of the stockade in *Treasure Island* except it is also equipped with a snakepit, complete with not-quite-genuine snake.

Nearby is St Mary's church, which started life somewhere around 700 AD with the Saxons, was converted into a cottage in Tudor times and has now been restored as a church. It is unlikely the Saxons would recognise it, but a few bits of the original are still incorporated in it. The other feature of Cockley Cley is the Twenty Churchwardens pub, formerly the village school. When they were searching for a name the Rector mentioned his group of ten parishes, each with two churchwardens, and it was dedicated to them all.

Beachamwell village is a little-known haven where I once borrowed a cottage before returning permanently to Norfolk, and it gave me a foretaste of the pleasures to come. The village is set around a broad green with the pub at one end and the round-towered church in the middle. It is well away from any main road and none of the lanes seem to go anywhere in particular. The Saxons had a devil's dyke outside the village to discourage visitors, and it still seems to work. If I had had any doubts about returning to Norfolk, Beachamwell would have dispelled them.

. . . the centrepiece of Beachamwell's village green is the walled church-yard and Saxon-towered church. The octagonal bit on top was added later.

An Ever-decreasing Circle

South of Beachamwell you will bump into the odd tourist again, this time heading for Oxburgh Hall, which likes to du different in its spelling from the village of Oxborough where it stands. This is another National Trust showpiece, said to be the most exciting medieval house in Norfolk. The Bedingfield family built it in 1482, and although they were Catholics they survived all the eccentricities of the Tudors and their successors, and still live there today. Their tombs in a chapel next to the parish church are nearly as grand in miniature as the hall itself. Like the Bedingfields the tombs have a reputation for survival: the church steeple fell down in 1948 and wrecked the nave, but the chapel next to it was undamaged.

Oxburgh Hall, built by the Catholic Bedingfields in 1482. It survived all the religious upheavals and the family still live there today, care of The National Trust. The village, confusingly, is Oxborough.

If you prefer less spectacular attractions there are the water gardens at nearby Gooderstone, the ingenious creation of Bill Knights, who used to keep cows on the watermeadows until torrential rain caused the river to overflow and flood them. He forthwith removed the cows and turned the meadows into a seven-acre water garden instead.

Foulden watermill, a few miles away, has a more chequered history as a tourist attraction. Graham Martin gave up his job to rebuild the mill but fell out with the district council over direction signs and rateable values. He threatened to dismantle the mill machinery and move it all to a district where he thought they would be better appreciated. His scheme to 'Have watermill, will travel' was still being pondered when I last checked. By now I hope the mill is working again, either in Foulden or elsewhere.

Village signs in Norfolk are usually imaginative creations illustrating events in local history, but the Foulden sign merely depicts a pheasant. Since the county is full of pheasants this may seem less than original, but the Amherst family used to live at nearby Didlington Hall, and Lord Amherst brought home a new variety of silvery-coloured pheasant from his travels overseas. His lordship is long since dead and the Hall has been demolished, but the Amherst pheasant is not forgotten in Foulden.

Plastic farming, a fairly recent addition to the East Anglian landscape. The view is rather more attractive when the plastic comes off.

Heading eastward there is much more open country, but not accessible to visitors. This is the Stanford battle area, the Army's sole preserve. But on the edge of it is Little Cresssingham and its unique mill. Most mills are powered either by wind or water; Little Cressingham Mill could run on both. Two pairs of stones on the first floor were driven by a water wheel and two on the third floor by the sails. A secondary water wheel worked a pump which supplied water to Clermont Lodge, over a mile away, and even worked the fountains in the garden.

That was all a long time ago. The mill stopped functioning in 1916, and later the sails were taken away and the cap was concreted over. Even if it were restored it could not function in the same way again – the path of the stream has been diverted and the millpond is just an overgrown pit. Nevertheless the Norfolk Windmills Trust has been repairing the floors and stairways and the outside balcony. Another tourist attraction is in the making, but they don't expect to finish the work until the turn of the century. Meanwhile the Norfolk Churches Trust (Norfolk is a very Trust-orientated county) is keeping a friendly eye on Little Cressingham Church, which at first sight looks in a state of collapse, but it is only the west tower that is ruined, the rest of the church is in regular use.

Watton, the little market town which serves these villages on the edge of the battle area, still has a market but no market place. Instead it has a very long main street, which is much congested at the best of times and on market day, when the stalls are strung along

An Ever-decreasing Circle

it, almost impassable. The only reason I brave it is to visit my two favourite Watton characters, the Poorbox Man at one end of town and the Owl Man at the other.

The Poorbox Man is on the wall inside the parish church, a carved wooden figure just a couple of feet high with the words 'Remember the Poore 1639' carved across his chest. For three centuries kindly parishioners placed their offerings in his upturned hand. The coins slid through a slot into his body and down into the box on which he stands. Then came the age of the church vandal, and the box was broken into so often that it is no longer used. If you do hand the Poorbox Man a coin, you are advised to retrieve it from the unlocked box and place it in a more secure receptacle nearby.

The Owl Man lives up a lane which has the warning sign: 'Slow Down – Owls About.' Mercifully it does not add: 'Please Hoot.' He rescues baby barn owls which have been deserted or thrown out of their nests, rears them in his kitchen on a diet of day-old chicks rejected by the local hatchery, and puts them out to foster-parent farmers with convenient barns until they can look after themselves. Over the years the operation has become, one might say, an owling success.

Barn owls are the soppy-looking ones with the big white saucers round their eyes. They may look cuddly but their table manners are unattractive. They eat the chick, then cough up the bones and fur in pellets. I have seen them do it and it is not a pretty sight. They also hiss and screech a lot – only the tawny owl goes tu-whit tu-woo. But the Owl Man seems quite happy having a kitchen full of saucer-eyed little screechers, chewing day-old chicks and having a good spit. The baby owls ought to be grateful, but of course they don't give a hoot.

Completing the circle back to the Wensum involves passing through some of my old reporting area around Dereham, where the fields are smaller, the villages are closer, and, as I recall, the pubs are busier. Most writers seem to find this part of Norfolk rather boring and hardly mention it. They may refer in passing to the handsome lead cupola on Shipdham church tower, or the monkey puzzle tree at Letton Hall, or the eighteenth-century barrel organ still in use at Mattishall Burgh, but not much more.

It is an unremarkable area, not helped by its proximity to Dereham and the trunk road to Norwich. The new estates keep expanding and the villages get closer all the time. Mattishall, for instance, used to be a fairly isolated village of under a thousand people, memorable mainly for the redoubtable Fred Juby, who was village correspondent for the *Dereham & Fakenham Times* for fifty years. He used to augment his funeral reports by adding a few names from the gravestones to his list of mourners. When taxed with this (we noticed the same names at every funeral), he explained simply, 'Weren't they at the church too, boy?' We never queried it again.

The lead cupola on Shipdham church, a landmark for miles around.

Fred would not need to add any names today. There are nearly 2,500 people in Mattishall, quite enough to pack the churchyard at any funeral, though I wonder how many of them know each other, or have ever heard of Mr Juby.

Nevertheless one can still find the old village spirit and a sprinkling of great characters in this area. Reymerston, for instance, can claim both. Although it has expanded like its neighbours, the residents are still proud of their village status, and when a local farmer proposed to convert some of his land into a golf course there was a united cry of protest. The village atmosphere would be lost, they said, the traffic would become intolerable, the place would be invaded by 'foreign' golfers. The villagers won this battle, but there is big money in golf courses, either creating them or selling them, and they may have yet to win the war.

Reymerston's Big House is a Georgian hall in rather splendid grounds. It has had an assorted selection of squires – in my day it was occupied by a Dereham draper – but its notable resident in recent years has been Wing Commander Ken Wallis, inventor, stuntman and autogyro fanatic. If you saw James Bond performing his amazing aerial feats in an autogyro in *You Only Live Twice*, that was Ken Wallis at the controls. He won every world record for autogyro aircraft, he took part in the search for the Loch Ness monster and, later, in the rather different search of Newhaven Downs for the missing Lord Lucan.

Autogyros, he has always maintained, are a lot safer than helicopters, and in his seventies he continued to fly them regularly. There is a hangar at the Hall packed with the little aircraft that he designed and built himself, and although the locals are allergic to golfers they seem quite reconciled to his little buzzers.

Shipdham, where the onion-shaped cupola on the church tower is a landmark for miles around, is a long straggling village with a busy road right down the middle, but the byways may still be secluded enough for ghosts to lurk. There are strange tales of a fiddler who had his throat cut by an unknown assailant and whose fiddle can still be heard wailing mournfully across the beansticks and the Brussels sprouts on the village allotments; and of a maid at the Big House three hundred years ago who was sent home in disgrace after being discovered in embarrassing circumstances with the son of the house, and drowned herself in the village pond rather than face her parents.

I did take the trouble to check the story of the errant maid. One winter's evening as dusk was falling I stood quietly beside the mist-covered pond until the light had gone completely, waiting for her spectral figure to appear. She never did, but my visit was not quite wasted. As I returned to my car on the main road, some distance away, I passed a couple of villagers who were discussing the figure of a tall man they had just seen by the haunted pond, standing motionless and expectant at the water's edge. Could it be the guilt-ridden son of the house, returned after all these years to seek out his paramour? Well, why not . . .

This little corner of mid-Norfolk was once served by a railway linking Dereham with Wymondham and Norwich. The railway line is still there and many locals hope that one day it will be put into service again. Wymondham station is all ready for it: an enterprising businessman has leased and restored the old station buildings and won an award in 1990 for his efforts, including his 'Brief Encounter Tearoom', where you can visualise Trevor Howard looking soulful behind a corned-beef sandwich. The road between Wymondham and Dereham twists and turns over the line, with a couple of vicious right-angle bridges which bear the scars of countless bumpers and mudguards. Jeremiah James Colman may have passed this way in more leisurely times, since a hostelry at Whinburgh immortalises his memory. It is perhaps the only one in the country called The Mustard Pot.

The countryside here has only modest undulations, but on the other side of the trunk road between Norwich and Dereham we are back in the Wensum valley, having completed the outer circuit of High Norfolk, and there are woods and hills again. The villages are still within easy range of Dereham but somehow they seem less affected by it. Elsing, for instance, still seems comparatively unspoilt, with its old mill by the river, the Mermaid Inn opposite the church (something of an oddity so far from the sea), and Elsing Hall, one of Norfolk's finest moated manor houses, just visible from the road. The Hall and its predecessors were in the same family from Domesday Book days until 1958; it is currently owned by a top broadcasting executive.

There are trout in the Wensum if you know where to find them. These boys fancy their chances at Elsing.

At nearby Bylaugh, which like the Belaugh near Wroxham is disconcertingly called Beela, the Big House has not fared so well. It had a battering by military action during the war – they were our chaps, not the Germans – then the lead roof was stripped and the interior plundered, and it has been a ruin since 1952. Its stark outline on the hill above the village looks uncommonly sinister at dusk on a winter's evening. It is even less attractive during the day when you can see the Nissen huts and workyards which adjoin it. Most of the original parkland has long since been ploughed up. There have been various plans to restore the Hall and build log cabins or retirement homes around it, but the district council has been unenthusiastic. I gather they rather like it as it is, a Grade I listed ruin.

This stretch of the Wensum is an odd mixture of the picturesque and the ugly. It has attractive mills and quaint old bridges, and I am told the fishing is good, but you can round a bend and suddenly come upon a vast area of mineral workings, because the gravel is good here too. The little riverside hamlet of Worthing is an example. At one end is the delightful Mill House, straight out of a picture postcard. At the other are the gravel pits, which constantly threaten to spread closer, though the villagers have fought gallantly against them.

Different facets of the Wensum at Worthing: *left* the picturesque Mill with its series of descending roofs, and *right* the gravel pits, looking more picturesque at sunset than they can be in daylight.

On the other side of the workings the river recaptures its tranquillity before reaching Swanton Morley, which has one of Norfolk's quieter RAF stations with not a Tornado in sight. It has also one of the few village pubs which in recent years started from scratch. Originally there were two, The Angel at one end of the village and The Papermakers Arms at the other. The brewers decided one was enough and closed The Papermakers, but its regulars were reluctant to change ends and a local farmer, John Carrick, decided to fill the gap. He converted two cottages opposite the closed pub, persuaded the magistrates to grant him a licence and called his pub Darby's, after the family who used to live there.

Meanwhile the brewers, hearing of his plans, re-opened The Papermakers, so Swanton Morley, instead of being reduced to one pub, found itself with three. It could have been a disaster, but happily there were enough thirsts to go round – no doubt the RAF helped to meet the challenge – and all three have so far survived.

In North Elmham the situation was reversed. When I lived there in the nineteen-fifties it had a population of about a thousand, served

by three pubs. Now the pubs are reduced to two but the population is up to 1,500. As you drive up the road from Worthing a grim army of redbrick boxes come marching towards you across the fields. There are now old people's bungalows behind my former home at Windfall Cottage (long since renamed Windfall House in acknowledgement of soaring house prices) and part of the park of the Big House where we used to walk the dog is now a vineyard, which actually sells wine to a chain-store in France. Norfolk may seem an inhospitable county for vines, but the monks made wine there in medieval times and the climate is much the same.

There have been other changes too. The George and Dragon is now a private house and the ruins of the old Saxon cathedral behind it, which preceded Thetford and Norwich as the centre of the diocese, have been smartened up. But some things stay the same. The church still has its clock painted in the traditional Elmham blue which was rediscovered during my time there. The Memorial Institute where I used to play whist extremely badly is still the focal point of Elmham's social life; and there is still a fair sprinkling of the original villagers who helped to educate me, as a raw young man from the London suburbs, in the mystical ways of rural Norfolk life.

A mile or so outside Elmham is an enclave on the summit of a wooded hill called County School. I knew it as a boarding school for Barnardo boys, with its own chapel and staff houses and playing fields. Now there are chicken houses where the school used to be, and the handful of people who live up there are not schoolmasters but chicken farmers or work elsewhere. The only reminder of its earlier days is the station at the foot of the hill, still known as County School. In 1956 I stopped there on the first diesel train to replace the old steam engines and rolling stock. There were high hopes that this new service meant the line would be saved, but it turned out to be only a temporary reprieve. For many years the station was left derelict and in 1986 the line was removed.

Just three years later there was a change of heart and they started putting it back again and restoring the station, not to provide a train service but to create a tourist attraction, as well as an activity for Fakenham and Dereham Railway Society. Half a mile of track was to be replaced, and a diesel loco was deposited on it to make it more realistic, though there is nowhere for it to go. They also planted a traditional K6 telephone kiosk beside it – but without a telephone. It is all something of a museum piece, but even if it is largely make-believe it is still an improvement on leaving the place to disintegrate.

There is no other village nearby, and indeed they are much sparser now. This is the edge of the magical triangle formed by Dereham, Fakenham and Swaffham, the heart of High Norfolk and the area I patrolled for the *Dereham & Fakenham Times*. So I am reasonably familiar with the little villages between Elmham and Fakenham.

A corner of the Saxon Cathedral at North Elmham, which was there long before the Normans built its present successor in Norwich.

An Ever-decreasing Circle

Brisley has its vast common and the warnings about wandering sheep which predate electric fences. Guist's concrete council houses, built just after the war, contrast sharply with Sir Thomas Cook's neatly-gabled estate cottages, built only a couple of decades before. Instead of Philippo's second-hand junkyard where we furnished our cottage at five bob a table and a shilling a chair, Guist now has an elegant restaurant by the river, one of the many oases in what used to be considered Norfolk's gastronomic desert, though I doubt many of the villagers take advantage of it.

Further down the river is Bintree mill, its riverside garden not quite the picture it used to be but still attractive enough to be favoured by film-makers. Gateley is so tiny you can easily miss it, but in the middle of nowhere you come upon the imposing gateway to Gateley Hall.

left Bintree Mill sees more filming than milling these days – producers like its period flavour. *right* Fred the Ploughman at Stibbard has a period flavour too – he was created from old farm implements.

Stibbard has a unique village sign, a ploughman built out of old farm tools and scrap metal and known affectionately as Fred. Fred fits comfortably into the village scene; the Thai restaurant at the village pub is rather less indigenous. My own preference is for the steak and kidney pie at the Boar in Great Ryburgh. This is a workaday village dominated by a maltings. What a shame that such a useful substance has to be produced in such unlovely buildings. The Boar, however, retains its beams and its open fire, and it also offers a facility unmatched, so far as I know, by any other rural hostelry. The outside lavatory has been converted into a unisex hairdressing salon. If it has survived the new small business rating, which apparently did it no good at all, you may combine a clip with a sip – but mind the clippings don't drop into your beer . . .

The Wensum links Ryburgh with Fakenham, and in between is Pensthorpe Wildfowl Reserve, which offers the only argument I can think of in favour of gravel pits, unless you are a gravel merchant. The wildlife lakes alongside the river were all created from worked-out pits; the sides are sloped so the birds can enter the water, little islands have been left in the middle, the surroundings are landscaped with trees and shrubs, and an asphalt path allows chairbound visitors to make the complete tour. In 1986, the year it was opened, Pensthorpe had 35,000 visitors; the year after there were over 50,000. This is a Slimbridge-standard nature reserve in the heart of intensively cultivated farmland, a peaceful haven for people as well as birds. There is even a 'seashore' complete with artificial waves where you can sit in comfort and watch avocets and black-legged stilts just a few feet away instead of waiting for hours in a draughty hide. This is my kind of birdwatching.

Pensthorpe Wildfowl Reserve, in the heart of intensively farmed countryside, was created from worked-out gravel pits and has achieved Slimbridge standards.

And Fakenham is my kind of town. Its size has doubled since the war but it still has fewer than six thousand people. The market place has hardly changed since my earlier Norfolk days except that one of the pubs is now a tourist office and the cinema has switched to bingo. There are a couple of supermarkets but they are well tucked away. The *Dereham & Fakenham Times* office still has photographs of garden fêtes in the windows and piles of dusty newspapers on the shelves. Only the computer link with the Norwich office is new; they no longer have to send news copy and advertisements on the bus.

The old gasworks is still there but now it is a museum, the only one of its kind in the country. They say it is a sign of getting old when the policemen start looking younger. It is another sign when a gasworks which you remember as a going concern becomes a museum piece. It closed in the 1960s when natural gas became available – though not to villages like mine, even though we are within half a mile of the main pipeline from the Bacton terminal. I did suggest to a British Gas official, albeit facetiously, that I might bore a hole in it to extract a personal supply. 'Make a hole in that pipe,' he warned solemnly, 'and you'll be the first person to fly across the North Sea just by flapping your arms.'

Another successful conversion: Fakenham Mill has been turned into up-market apartments without spoiling the façade.

Further up the Wensum from Fakenham is Sculthorpe, best known for its American air base, though its size these days is much reduced. One of my more memorable reporting assignments was to cover the visit to the base of Jayne Mansfield, the sex symbol of the fifties, who managed to kick off a game of American football wearing a very tight-fitting dress and high heels. As I recall, it was not the high heels which caught the eye of our cameraman. The *Dereham & Fakenham Times* has never been in such demand.

Unexpectedly, within a mile or two of the base, there is one of the most secluded pubs in High Norfolk. Sculthorpe Mill is set astride the Wensum down a long narrow lane. Guests who use the pub's free minibus – a great boon for non-teetotallers – find themselves taking a shortcut through the ford below the millpond, where a wrong turn in mid-stream can land you in four or five feet of water. I recommend the longer route if you are driving yourself; I would not attempt the ford, sober or otherwise.

The next substantial building by the river, some miles away, is very substantial indeed. Raynham Hall looks down its drive to the lake through which the river flows. Some of the fine old trees lining the drive have been lost, but it is still an impressive vista. The Hall was built in the seventeenth century by the Townshends, who still live there. They included 'Turnip Townshend', the second viscount, who perceived the merits of this unlovely but useful vegetable and rotated it with cereal crops to clear the weeds and provide a winter feed. The present Marquess has been more involved in television than turnips

– he was chairman of Anglia TV – but British farming still benefits from the acumen of his ancestor.

On the edge of the estate is West Raynham RAF station, one of many operational RAF bases scattered around Norfolk during the last war, but while others in High Norfolk like Beeston and Little Snoring are now just a few crumbling runways and derelict huts, Raynham is still on active service as a Bloodhound anti-aircraft missile base. It is quite disconcerting to drive along the tiny country lanes and suddenly come upon rows of these sinister projectiles pointing skywards, only a few yards beyond the perimeter fence. When I first moved back into the area, unaware that Raynham had switched from planes to missiles, I asked a neighbour if he was troubled by much noise from the base. 'Du yew hear a noise from there, boy,' he said darkly, 'thass the last thing you ever will hear, yew can be sure o'that.'

An unexpected 'crop' to find down a peaceful country lane. Bloodhound missiles lurk behind the wire fence at West Raynham.

There are rather more attractive surprises to come upon in the wooded country around Raynham, including two contrasting relics of earlier periods. One is the ruin of Coxford Priory, which was used as a convenient stone quarry by the builders of Raynham Hall. The other is Raynham Halt, the tiny railway station on the old line between Fakenham and King's Lynn which must have been mainly to benefit the Big House, since there is no village of any size nearby. It is hidden in a wood on a little back lane and blends very discreetly into its surroundings. The tracks have long since gone but the owner has preserved the platforms, the signal-box and much of the old equipment, both for his own enjoyment and for anyone else who cares to stop by. In its way I find it more appealing than that commercialised station museum at Wolferton.

Similarly I prefer the hidden delights of South Acre and West Acre to the very obvious attractions of Castle Acre, which are clearly visible from the main road.

But on the way we should divert to Rougham, a compact little village in the middle of nowhere in particular, which can offer a modest

An Ever-decreasing Circle

Raynham Halt, one of the remote little stations left behind by the Midland & Great Northern Railway. It is privately occupied and carefully preserved.

surprise of its own. In the churchyard is a gravestone on which is carved an accurate reproduction of the Vickers Vimy bi-plane used by Alcock and Brown for the first non-stop flight across the Atlantic in 1919.

Here lies neither Mr Alcock nor Mr Brown, nor indeed their aeroplane, but Thomas Keppel North, one of the Norths who have lived at Rougham Hall for three centuries. His schoolteacher would have found it difficult to see the connection; he described young Thomas as 'hopelessly backward', always bottom of the form even though he was two years older than his classmates. His only interest, it seems, was in collecting pistols, perhaps to the alarm of his teacher, but his parents made the best of it and sent him off to the Colt revolver factory in America. The next thing they knew, he was designing aeroplanes at Vickers Armstrong. When Alcock and Brown planned their transatlantic flight it was Thomas Keppel North they consulted. He designed the Vickers Vimy and made the instruments for it.

Unhappily he did not live to see them fly it. He died of influenza aged 43, a few months before they flew non-stop from Newfoundland to County Galway in just over sixteen hours. Alcock and Brown got a *Daily Mail* prize of £10,000; North got an aeroplane on his tombstone.

I can delay you no longer from your inevitable visit to Castle Acre. By all means drive through the ancient gateway into the village, once the entrance to the castle, clamber over the site of the castle itself and marvel at the ruins of the Clunian priory on the banks of the Nar, but also spare the time to follow the Nar downstream. It had such a wealth of religious establishments that the valley used to be known as the Holy Land, and there are still some remains about, though the valley is attractive enough in its own right.

Few tourists find Raynham Halt, but nearly all of them find Castle Acre Priory, the best known ruins in Norfolk.

At West Acre, for instance, the Augustinian canons had an establishment even larger than Castle Acre, though only the gateway

remains. They built a school on the other side of the river, perhaps to keep the boys at a reasonable distance from their living quarters, and its remains can still be seen. Between West Acre and South Acre there are more ruins, this time of a chapel, in a vanished village called Calthorpe which even two hundred years ago no longer appeared on the maps. It is difficult to picture the Nar valley in medieval times, but it was a lot busier than it is now.

Swaffham on the other hand is quite the opposite. Much of it was built after Calthorpe had disappeared. Like Hingham it was a winter resort for the Georgian gentry. All that remains of any note from earlier times are the church and the legend of the Swaffham Pedlar, who went to London to find a fortune and met a stranger on London Bridge who said he had a better chance of finding one in his own back yard. Sure enough, he dug up bags of gold in his back garden, and built the north aisle of the church as a thanksgiving. Or rather, a man called John Chapman built it, whose name could mean 'pedlar', so why not give him the credit for the legend as well.

Swaffham was one of the busiest road junctions in mid-Norfolk until a bypass was built for the A47. The respite was only temporary. The traffic seems to have built up again, as it so often does, and the cry has gone up for a north-south bypass as well. It is best to visit Swaffham on a Sunday, when you get a better idea of what attracted the gentry from their country estates. One of them, the Earl of Orford, erected the butter cross in the market place, which is not a cross at all but a domed rotunda rather like an open-sided bandstand. The Goddess of Plenty perches on top, gazing down in astonishment at the queues of traffic below.

The Butter Cross in Swaffham market place might be mistaken for a bandstand, except for the Goddess of Plenty on top.

The town has one other claim to fame. Traditionally the townsfolk were so simple 'they du three days' thrarshin' for narthin'.' I recently learned the correct riposte if a local propounds this theory. 'Well, hent that sarthin'.' In other words, 'Gracious me, that is certainly something quite remarkable.'

Swaffham is the second corner of my magic triangle. The third side, the A47 to Dereham, is not magical at all, just noisy, congested and quite often lethal. Fortunately some safer stretches have been built which bypass villages like Wendling and Scarning, but it is not a road on which to linger, and you will be relieved to turn off it into Dereham, which has also been bypassed though there is so much traffic you would hardly guess it.

This is not the Dereham of the nineteen-fifties. Then I could walk across the market place and nearly every face would be familiar. Today it takes an iron nerve to walk across it at all, and many of the shops as well as the faces are quite new. The town has grown and altered almost beyond recognition. I remember when The King's Arms, a fine old coaching inn which was the hub of the town's social life, was demolished to make way for a Woolworth's. We shook our heads gloomily and said it was the beginning of the end of the old Dereham, and I am afraid we were right.

On the other hand the town has become an industrial and business centre providing homes and jobs for a great many more people. It may have been a jolt to return to such a transformation, but my friends who have lived through the changes seem to have emerged unscathed, and I must become reconciled too. Happily there is still the magnificent church in which my elder son, the only genuine Norfolkman in the family, was christened, and next to it Bishop Bonner's cottages, thatched and pargeted and certainly the most attractive legacy he left. He lived here as Rector in 1502, then went off to send people to the stake at Smithfield. He is renowned more for persecuting Protestants than pretty plasterwork.

Dereham's other famous names are George Borrow, who was born here, and William Cowper, who died here in a house on the market place where the Cowper Congregational Church now stands. 'England's sweetest and most pious bard', as Borrow called him, would not have found it quite so conducive to meditation today. As for Borrow, who wrote of Dereham as 'pretty quiet D—, thou pattern of an English market town, with thy clean but narrow streets branching out from thy modest market place, with thine oldfashioned houses, with here and there a roof of venerable thatch . . . ' – well, good luck to him too.

Dereham's origins have not been quite forgotten. The town sign that spans the High Street is one of the more dramatic carvings by the Swaffham schoolteacher Harry Carter, who helped parish councils and Women's Institutes all over Norfolk to commemorate the

An Ever-decreasing Circle

Queen's Coronation by producing imaginative village signs. It depicts St Withburga, who founded a convent in Dereham, with the deer from which she obtained milk during a time of hardship and which gave the town its name. She is being chased by some baddies across the High Street, but safely out of range of the traffic.

St Withburga and her deer being pursued by a baddie across Dereham High Street, well clear of the traffic below.

A reminder of the more recent past has been restored on the outskirts of the town. Dereham's 150-year-old cornmill is the only one in the country to be restored by the Manpower Services Commission under its community programme. It took them three years to rebuild the floors and stairs, fit new sails and cap, and restore the cast-iron shaft. It was opened to the public in 1989, just fifty years after it closed down. But there are few other buildings to commend, and I would say that Dereham's greatest attraction for the discerning visitor is its proximity to High Norfolk; in particular to the magical triangle, seventy square miles of peaceful unspoilt countryside where George Borrow and William Cowper and even the infamous Bishop Bonner could find room to relax.

There is only one secondary road through the triangle. The others are just narrow lanes, which may be hazardous in the sugar beet season when the lorries can be wider than the roadway, but normally one only meets the odd tractor. The countryside is not spectacular, but it is not boring either. There are enough woods and coppices to break up the even pattern of the fields, enough hills to vary the skyline, enough different colours – blue linseed, yellow rape and, in spite of the chemicals, red poppies – to contrast with the gold and green of the barley and beet. Dotted about in all this are the flint-walled, pantiled cottages, the half-hidden Big Houses, and all those splendid Norfolk churches.

It is best to wander in this area as you wish, but I can offer a few pointers. The largest village is Litcham, with all of six hundred people. It has a miniature market place, a reminder of its more important days, and some pleasant old houses around it, but its unexpected attraction is the nature walk which has been mapped out on the common, just beside the village. It covers only sixty acres but it leads you through woodland with deep pools and purple moorgrass, plantations of birch and oak, then across the lane into quite different heathland where the bracken is being driven back to make room for rowan and hornbeam. It is a reminder, in the heart of beet and barley country, of how rural Norfolk used to look before the tractors and the combines moved in. And if you need any sustenance after your stroll, the Bull Inn offers the best value in cod and chips in Norfolk.

East and West Lexham are tiny villages set in the parkland around the two Big Houses. The last Great Bustard was killed here in 1838 and not a lot has happened since, except that you can now hire horse-drawn caravans at West Lexham Hall. It is a measure of the remoteness and peacefulness of this area that you can take these round the lanes at walking pace without causing too much blood pressure among other road-users, though it is as well to follow the suggested route lest you finish up on the A47. You can also take a supply of wine from East Lexham, where Neal Foster has a vineyard. He lives in the larger of the two Big Houses, East Lexham Hall, which makes a fine sight from the lane that meanders past its park and artificial lake.

East Anglia might seem a little chilly for grapes, but the Romans had vineyards in Norfolk and wine is being produced again. These vineyards are at Lexham.

Gressenhall offers the only large-scale tourist attraction in the triangle, the Rural Life Museum, formerly a workhouse which in my reporting days had been converted, not very successfully, into an old people's home. It still looked like a workhouse, and when I accompanied the council chairman on his Christmas morning visit I quite expected to meet Mr Bumble in the corridor. It is a little more cheerful these days but there are parts of the building, like the punishment cell, which are still straight out of Dickens.

The village is overshadowed in more than one sense by its gloomy 'Big House'. Mention Gressenhall in Norfolk and that is what people first think of. But it also has one of the pleasantest village greens in High Norfolk, winner of the county's best-kept green competition, and there is an attractive mill house on the river at one end of the village and a twelfth-century church at the other. The epitaph on John Halcot's floorstone said: 'Him have we for a time lost, who bilt this gallery at his own cost.' Alas, the gallery is lost as well; it was demolished two hundred years after he bilt it. But there is still the Hastings chapel with its coloured roof, and a reminder of the Revd Dennis Hill, who was reputed to drink a bottle of port a day but survived as Rector here for sixty-five years.

Hoe must win any contest for the shortest village name in Norfolk, but it has other distinctions too. At one extreme there is the highly mechanised fruit farm at Gorgate Hall, one of the first to introduce mechanical blackcurrant-pickers into Britain. If you are a Ribena addict, you may well be drinking blackcurrant juice from Gorgate. In contrast there is Hoe Rough, untouched heathland and wet grassland owned by the Norfolk Naturalists Trust. David Bellamy opened it in 1989 with much arm-waving and leaping about, as a site of scientific interest.

Hoe village has also been designated a conservation area, which aroused unexpected protests from the villagers. They argued that the Keith family at the Big House, who own most of Hoe, looked after it quite adequately without any interference from those folk in the council offices. In my magical triangle, old habits and loyalties die hard.

The Dunhams are unremarkable these days except for a small museum in an old railway yard and a large restaurant in an old granary, but Great Dunham has two strange stories to tell. One was uncovered when a bundle of parish records, labelled, 'These documents are of no interest whatsoever,' turned out to be connected with a mass emigration to Canada in 1836. More than fifty men, women and children who had probably never ventured ten miles from Dunham, left this remote little village to set sail from Yarmouth in search of a new life across the Atlantic. They were all destitute, and the voyage was arranged by the Poor Law Commissioners, who paid their passages, provided food for the journey and gave each adult a sovereign to spend when they got there. The accounts even included the item: 'Tinware for paupers for use on board ship: £4.0s.4d.' It is a fascinating record of local history and I am glad the documents are now relabelled: 'The 1836 Emigration: *Very Important Papers*.'

The other story from Dunham's past is recorded by R.H. Mottram. His grandfather once met an aged inhabitant of the village who assured him Noah's Ark went aground on Dunham Common. 'Stand to reason,' he explained. 'Thass the highest land anywhere about, hent it?' I have heard less logical theories . . .

The highest land in the triangle is probably at Colkirk, which sits on top of a hill and looks down on Fakenham and the Wensum valley. Colkirk has an unexpected rural industry, an angora rabbit farm. The fur from these little woolly jumpers is made into large woolly jumpers at about a hundred pounds a time. There are also a lot of poplars around Colkirk. At one time farmers were urged to plant them to produce wood for matchsticks, then somebody invented the cigarette lighter.

Coke of Norfolk's family lived inside the triangle before Holkham Hall was built. Their home at Godwick is now reduced to fragments and Godwick church is just a ruined tower, but their memorials help to hold up the walls of Tittleshall church. Among them are those of the Lord Chief Justice, Sir Edward Coke, and Coke of Norfolk himself, the first Earl of Leicester.

Tittleshall these days would be much too sleepy for these grand folk, but the village street does come alive on Palm Sunday when there is the traditional procession to the church led by April the donkey. April is lent to the Church of England each year by her Roman Catholic owners, but the ecumenical spirit does not flow too strongly within her. The pilgrim who leads her has to valiant be, 'gainst all disaster. She can lean very heavily, glare very balefully and stamp very painfully. If you walk just behind her, as I have done, there are other natural hazards too. But we all get to the church eventually, even if it takes three repeats of 'All glory, laud and honour to thee, Redeemer King'.

Only a hundred yards from a busy main road, but few travellers pause to enjoy the tranquillity of Weasenham Green, one of many undiscovered delights of High Norfolk.

Weasenham used to lie on the main road from Swaffham to Fakenham but it has been bypassed for many years, and passing motorists who see the village name still displayed on the roadside must think it consists only of a church and a couple of pubs. Few of them turn off and find themselves on the unspoilt village green, with

245

flint cottages and mellow old houses spaced out around it and a heavily populated duck pond as the centrepiece. Weasenham is typical of the undiscovered gems which lie just off the main roads of East Anglia, if only one has time to pause and look.

Finally there is the tiny village of Wellingham and its mystery saint. The medieval rood screen has a painting of a figure in medieval armour, carrying a sword and lance and trampling on a small bearded king in crown and ermine tippet. It appears on the screen between St Sebastian covered in arrow-wounds and St George killing his dragon, but seems to have no connection with either. For years the church guidebook called him St Oswald, but he is linked with Oswestry and would be a long way from home. Sure enough, when the pulpit was moved in 1988 part of the name beneath the painting was revealed, and although only two or three letters are recognisable it clearly begins with 'M'. Speculation has ranged from St Maurice, who was a military man but generally portrayed as black, to St Martin, a Roman soldier who was converted and became Bishop of Tours. Neither has any track record for trampling on small kings. St Maximus was another guess, and his name has the right number of letters, but nothing else fits – he was a man of peace.

The most fascinating theory is that the saint was not a man at all, but St Margaret of Antioch, who is often represented in male clothing and is said to have provided the 'voices' that inspired Joan of Arc. Margaret was very popular among medieval artists because she promised that those who preserved her memory would have her prayers. And in Norfolk she was popular as a patron saint as well; nearly sixty churches are dedicated to her. But there are two snags. Margaret is generally depicted vanquishing the dragon which attempted to eat her; the prostrate figure underneath is definitely not a dragon. And unfortunately for the theory, Wellingham Church is dedicated to St Andrew. The mystery remains.

Very close to Wellingham are two enchanted hideaways at the heart of my magical triangle. They are both on private land so I cannot lead you there, but I have visited them both, and each has a special significance for me.

One is an isolated little lake, completely concealed by trees inside a fold in the rolling farmland. This is the source of the River Nar, which flows as a tiny stream past Litcham Common and through the parkland of the Lexhams to Castle Acre and the medieval 'Holy Land', then broadens out and heads westward to join the Great Ouse at King's Lynn. So the Nar links that silent, secluded lake with the noise and bustle of an industrial estate. It flows, not just through the Norfolk countryside, but through the centuries, and the closer you get to its source, the further back in time you travel.

On the same farm is another feature which is both an acknowledgement of the past and a gesture to the future. To put a round peg into a square hole is difficult enough, but to put a round wood in a square field of sugar beet is almost unheard-of, even in these conservation-minded days. My farming neighbour is creating a traditional round wood of oak and wild cherry and sweet chestnut, with a sprinkling of crab-apple and maple and holly, slap in the middle of a 67-acre field.

The field rises to a hill. It is only a Norfolk hill, all of two hundred feet above sea level, but it is visible for miles. I walked with him through the growing beet to the crest of the hill and stood there in the circle of tiny saplings. The brown and green fields of High Norfolk, and a surprising proportion of woodland and hedges, stretched to the horizon in every direction. By the turn of the century the saplings will be too tall to see over – they will be a new landmark to remind us how Norfolk used to be.

The project has had its problems. The idea came to him long before any set-aside schemes made it easier to plant trees on arable land. He had already planted many copses in out-of-the-way corners, but when it came to the round wood he found there was an ancient barrow on the hilltop, which the experts wanted untouched, so he planted a *hollow* round wood, and sowed the centre with wild flowers. Even that is trickier than it sounds. It takes very few seeds to produce an acre of daisies and white campion and sorrel, so to sprinkle them evenly he mixed them with sand in a cement mixer, then used a mechanical spreader. His men were disconcerted to find him apparently sowing sand.

But now it is done. The first shoots have appeared in what will surely be a magical circle in the heart of my magical triangle. Around them, thirteen hundred saplings have safely taken root, and around the saplings there will be a hedge of blackthorn and hazel and broom. My farming friend has wryly christened the round wood 'Robin's Folly'; I prefer to think of it as 'Robin's Legacy' . . .

Our explorations are over. You may not think this part of Norfolk is magical at all, and if so then I urge you not to linger. But if you find yourself drawn, as I was, by the empty lanes and sleepy villages, the honest working countryside under the great sweep of sky, and the down-to-earth, civilised way of life, then having followed me in this ever-decreasing circle you may decide to disappear in it too.

Further Reading

Brander, Michael. *Soho for East Anglia*,
    Country Book Club, 1963

Burke, John. *Suffolk*, London, Batsford, 1971

Dymond, David. *The Norfolk Landscape*,
    London, Hodder & Stoughton, 1985

Harris, John Ryden. 'East Anglia and America',
    Ipswich *East Anglian Magazine* Ltd, 1973

Harrod, Wilhelmine. *The Norfolk Guide*,
    Bury St Edmunds, Alastair Press, 1988

James, Dr M.R. *Suffolk and Norfolk*,
    London, J.M. Dent & Sons, 1930

Mee, Arthur. *Norfolk*,
    London, Hodder & Stoughton, 1951

Mottram, R.H. *East Anglia*,
    London, Chapman & Hall, 1933

Seymour, John. *Companion Guide to East Anglia*,
    London, Collins, 1988

Tennyson, Julian. *Suffolk Scene*,
    Glasgow, Blackie & Son, 1939

West, H. Mills. *Ghosts of East Anglia*,
    Norwich, Hopkinson Books, 1984

West, H. Mills. *Colourful Characters of East Anglia*,
    Norwich, Hopkinson Books, 1986

Index

Bold page numbers refer to illustrations.

253